THE POLITICAL ROAD TO WAR
WITH IRAQ

Was the 2003 war with Iraq inevitable? *The Political Road to War with Iraq* explores in close detail the events and factors leading up to the second Gulf War and considers whether the conflict was unavoidable.

This volume begins by setting the story of Iraq, Bush and 9/11 within the broader context of the importance of the Persian Gulf to US national security interests. It then examines US policy toward Iraq at the end of the Clinton administration, the growing opposition of conservative think-tanks to Clinton's strategy of containment and the evolution of Iraq policy during the first eight months of the Bush presidency. In the second part of the book, the authors explore the immediate focus on Iraq after the attacks of September 11, which marked a watershed in US national security policy, and chart the construction of the case against Iraq through 2002 and the Bush administration's determination to end Saddam Hussein's regime at all costs. The volume concludes with a step back to look at the impact of neo-conservatism on the Bush administration's Iraq policy and the decision to go to war, and questions the fact that 'neo-cons' are said to have hijacked the administration's policy.

This book will be of great interest to all students and scholars of US foreign policy, war and peace studies and international relations.

Nick Ritchie has worked for the Oxford Research Group researching and publishing on global security issues since 1999. He currently works in the Department of Peace Studies, University of Bradford, UK.

Paul Rogers is Professor of Peace Studies at the University of Bradford and international security consultant to the Oxford Research Group. He has published 20 books and over 200 papers. He is President of the British International Studies Association and a member of the International Academic Council of the United Nations University for Peace.

CONTEMPORARY SECURITY STUDIES

INTERNATIONAL CONFLICT PREVENTION AND PEACE-BUILDING: SUSTAINING THE PEACE IN POST CONFLICT SOCIETIES
T. David Mason and James D. Meernik (eds)

CONTROLLING THE WEAPONS OF WAR: POLITICS, PERSUASION, AND THE PROHIBITION OF INHUMANITY
Brian Rappert

CHANGING TRANSATLANTIC SECURITY RELATIONS: DO THE US, THE EU AND RUSSIA FORM A NEW STRATEGIC TRIANGLE?
Jan Hallenberg and Håkan Karlsson (eds)

THEORETICAL ROOTS OF US FOREIGN POLICY: MACHIAVELLI AND AMERICAN UNILATERALISM
Thomas M. Kane

CORPORATE SOLDIERS AND INTERNATIONAL SECURITY: THE RISE OF PRIVATE MILITARY COMPANIES
Christopher Kinsey

TRANSFORMING EUROPEAN MILITARIES: COALITION OPERATIONS AND THE TECHNOLOGY GAP
Gordon Adams and Guy Ben-Ari

GLOBALISATION, CONFLICT AND THE SECURITY STATE: NATIONAL SECURITY IN A 'NEW' STRATEGIC ERA
Robert G. Patman (ed)

THE POLITICAL ROAD TO WAR WITH IRAQ: BUSH, 9/11 AND THE DRIVE TO OVERTHROW SADDAM
Nick Ritchie and Paul Rogers

BOSNIAN SECURITY AFTER DAYTON: NEW PERSPECTIVES
Michael A. Innes (ed)

KENNEDY, JOHNSON AND NATO: BRITAIN, AMERICA AND THE DYNAMICS OF ALLIANCE
Andrew Priest

SMALL ARMS AND SECURITY; NEW EMERGING INTERNATIONAL NORMS
Denise Garcia

THE POLITICAL ROAD TO WAR WITH IRAQ

Bush, 9/11 and the drive to overthrow Saddam

Nick Ritchie and Paul Rogers

Routledge
Taylor & Francis Group

LONDON AND NEW YORK

First published 2007
by Routledge
2 Park Square, Milton Park, Abingdon, Oxon, OX14 4RN

Simultaneously published in the USA and Canada
by Routledge
270 Madison Ave, New York NY 10016

Routledge is an imprint of the Taylor & Francis Group, an informa business

Transferred to Digital Printing 2007

© 2007 Nick Ritchie and Paul Rogers

Typeset in Times by Keyword Group Ltd, Wallington

British Library Cataloguing in Publication Data

A catalogue record for this book is available from the British Library

Library of Congress Cataloging-in-Publication Data

Ritchie, Nick, 1975–
The political road to war with Iraq. Bush, 9/11, and the drive to
overthrow Saddam / Nick Ritchie and Paul Rogers.
p.cm. – (Contemporary security studies)
Includes bibliographical references and index.
1. United States–Foreign relations–Iraq. 2. Iraq–Foreign relations–United States.
3. United States–Foreign relations–2001. 4. United States–Foreign relations–1993–2001.
5. Iraq War, 2003– –Causes. 6. Bush, George W. (George Walker), 1946– –Political and social views.
7. September 11 Terrorist Attacks, 2001–Influence. 8. War on Terrorism, 2001– –Political aspects.
9. Intervention (International law). I. Rogers, Paul, 1943– II. Title. III. Series.
E183.8.I57R48   2006
327.730567–dc22
2006005511

ISBN10: 0-415-39732-4 (hbk)
ISBN10: 0-415-45950-8 (pbk)
ISBN10: 0-203-96454-3 (ebk)

ISBN13: 978-0-415-39732-2 (hbk)
ISBN13: 978-0-415-45950-1 (pbk)
ISBN13: 978-0-203-96454-5 (ebk)

NICK RITCHIE WOULD LIKE TO DEDICATE
THIS BOOK TO HIS WIFE, SALLY

CONTENTS

ACKNOWLEDGEMENTS

The authors would like to thank Stuart Fitzpatrick for the opportunity to initiate this research, Andrew Humphrys at Taylor and Francis, and the extraordinary wealth of knowledge, ideas and support at the Department of Peace Studies at the University of Bradford.

ABBREVIATIONS

ABM	Anti-Ballistic Missile (Treaty)
AEI	American Enterprise Institute
ANO	Abu Nidal Organization
CBW	chemical and biological weapons
CENTCOM	US Central Command
CIA	Central Intelligence Agency
CINC	Commander in Chief
CSP	Center for Security Policy
CTEG	Counter Terrorism Evaluation Group
CW	chemical weapons
DIA	Defense Intelligence Agency
DPG	Defense Planning Guidance
FBI	Federal Bureau of Investigation
IAEA	International Atomic Energy Agency
ILA	Iraq Liberation Act
INC	Iraqi National Congress
JINSA	Jewish Institute for National Security Affairs
JRDTF	Joint Rapid Deployment Task Force
NATO	North Atlantic Treaty Organization
NESA	Near East and South Asia
NIE	National Intelligence Estimate
NRO	National Reconnaissance Officer
NSA	National Security Agency
NSC	National Security Council
NSS	National Security Strategy
OAPEC	Organisation of Arab Petroleum Exporting Countries
OPEC	Organisation of Petroleum Exporting Countries
OSP	Office of Special Plans
PLF	Palestine Liberation Front
PNAC	Project for a New American Century
PUK	Patriotic Union of Kurdistan
UNICEF	United Nations Children's (Emergency) Fund

UNMOVIC	United Nations Monitoring, Verification and Inspection Commission
UNSC	United Nations Security Council
UNSCOM	United Nations Special Commission
WHIG	White House Iraq Group
WINEP	Washington Institute for Near East Policy
WMD	weapons of mass destruction

INTRODUCTION

After the attacks of 11 September 2001 ('9/11'), the Bush administration deliberated over its response. The immediate reaction was to focus on the organisation that was presumed to be directly responsible for the attacks, the al-Qaida movement, as well as the Taliban regime in Afghanistan that was seen as the guardian if not the sponsor of that movement.

By early 2002, the Taliban regime had been terminated and the paramilitaries in Afghanistan that had owed allegiance to Osama bin Laden and the al-Qaida movement had been largely dispersed, and the Bush administration moved on. In January 2002, President Bush delivered his State of the Union Address which introduced the concept of an 'axis of evil' of 'rogue' states. These were defined as those that sponsored terrorism, with the greatest danger being seen to come from those that were developing weapons of mass destruction (WMD), the three key members of the axis being North Korea, Iran and Iraq.

Shortly after the State of the Union Address, Mr Bush gave his West Point speech which developed the theme of pre-empting future threats to US security. This came at a time of much discussion in Washington concerning the need to deal with the Saddam Hussein regime in Iraq. While the views of most independent security analysts and political commentators during 2002 was that a full-scale war with Iraq was unlikely, there was already abundant evidence that a considerable weight of political opinion had moved in the direction of war.

This book is concerned with that phenomenon and its role in the political road to war. It argues, in particular, that a detailed examination of the political record demonstrates that war with Iraq was all but inevitable after the 9/11 attacks, exploring this in relation to a number of trends.

First, towards the end of the Clinton administration, over the period 1998–2000, Congressional leaders, future members of the Bush administration and the Clinton administration's conservative critics all insisted that the existing policy of containment of Iraq was failing, and that regime change was the only realistic solution to the problem of the Saddam Hussein regime and its ambition to develop and deploy WMD.

Second, following the presidential election of November 2000, but before the 9/11 attacks, the Bush administration had already begun to review Iraq policy as

1

a priority. Given the calls from senior members of the administration and supporters in Congress and think-tanks for regime change, the administration was likely to adopt a far more aggressive and confrontational policy towards Iraq. This would include, at the very least, full implementation of the Iraq Liberation Act of 1998, and might possibly extend to even more forceful action.

Third, shortly after the 9/11 attacks, regime change in Iraq became a strategic priority for the administration, following the destruction of the al-Qaida infrastructure in Afghanistan and the elimination of its Taliban host. Moreover, this led on to the construction of a post-9/11 security paradigm that placed Iraq at the centre of the global war on terror. This rapidly evolved into the dominant view in key parts of the administration that Iraq had extensive WMD programmes and a concrete relationship with al-Qaida. Experience had shown that it could not otherwise be contained and a pre-emptive attack aimed at regime termination was now the necessary policy.

Finally, the administration's determination to confront the Saddam Hussein regime was enhanced by strong support in Congress and by the near certainty that the regime would not offer responses sufficient to avert war.

It is relatively easy with hindsight and the benefit of the historical record to construct a linear argument to somehow prove that a government's intentions at time A would inevitably lead to actions at time B, based on the selective presentation of government statements and other evidence. This analysis does not intend to prove that war was inevitable or that the entire course of events that led to the war in Iraq and the wider prosecution of the war on terrorism was predictable.

What it seeks to do is to set out the case that the paradigm constructed by the Bush administration shortly after 9/11 was highly likely to lead to a limited range of outcomes regarding Iraq, with military-led regime change the most probable, if not inevitable, given the administration's vehement criticism of Clinton's containment strategy and the fact that it was already determined to take a more aggressive stand against the regime before the 9/11 attacks. 'Inevitability' here is a subjective judgement, rather than a suggestion of an objectively preordained sequence of events. The extent to which this paradigm was constructed with the *deliberate and unequivocal intention* of forcibly removing the Saddam Hussein regime is a different question and open to debate.

More generally, one can make a robust case, not least from the evidence analysed here, that the broad parameters of the post-9/11 paradigm, with its emphasis on military force, the Middle East in general and Iraq in particular, and countering the spread of weapons of mass destruction, were foreseeable. They were based on the central elements of the neo-conservative and assertive nationalist worldviews that characterised the Bush administration, particularly the experiences and views of some of its most senior and influential members and those of its supporters in Congress and in Washington's conservative national security think-tanks.

Looking back on the development of this paradigm some three years after the start of the Iraq War, two aspects of its longer-term significance are apparent.

One is that it was sufficiently robust for there to be little doubt that the Saddam Hussein regime would not survive, but second, and perhaps more significantly, it has been sufficiently robust for there to have been little or no further development of the paradigm since the start of the Iraq War in 2003. This is in spite of the manifest problems facing the United States, not just in Iraq where the insurgency is about to enter its fourth year, but in Afghanistan and quite possibly Iran too. In seeking to explore in some depth the political road to war with Iraq we therefore hope that this book might help illuminate the foundations of this paradigm and explain its resilience in the face of adversity.

Finally, this analysis is based in large part on an exhaustive review of statements made by senior members of the administration and Congress and other key figures. The nature of a book such as this necessitates a degree of selectivity; we are, after all, presenting a case. But the analysis quotes many of these statements, sometimes at length and referenced with direct URLs to enable the reader to have access to the full source.

Nick Ritchie and Paul Rogers
February 2006

Part I

CONTAINING SADDAM

1

OIL AND PERSIAN GULF SECURITY – THE CONTEXT OF REGIME TERMINATION

Introduction

In August 1990, Iraqi forces invaded and occupied Kuwait, leading to immediate international condemnation and the rapid formation of an international coalition. This was sufficient to be capable of taking military action to evict the Iraqi forces from Kuwait should diplomatic negotiations fail. Some forces were moved into Saudi Arabia and other western Gulf states almost at once, partly to forestall any Iraqi moves into Saudi Arabia, and US naval forces began to gather in force in the Persian Gulf and the Arabian Sea within a month. Between early September and late December 1990, a force of nearly 600,000 troops and over 1,000 aircraft was amassed, mostly in Saudi Arabia but also on ships at sea.

The force was drawn primarily from the US armed forces, with major contingents from the UK, France, Saudi Arabia, Syria and Egypt, but the US forces made up about two-thirds of the total. In any other circumstance it would not have been possible to assemble such a force, and have it ready to take major military action, over 6,000 miles from the continental United States, within four months. Ordinarily, temporary air bases would have had to be established, port facilities upgraded and massive storage depots erected, yet virtually none of this proved necessary in 1990.

The primary reason for this was that facilities were already in place to handle such a crisis. In Saudi Arabia itself, air bases had been constructed for the Royal Saudi Air Force, which had facilities far larger than were needed, and these were able to cope when deployments reached at least four times the peacetime complement. Port facilities were similarly capable of handling the huge logistical problems occasioned by the rapid movement of personnel, munitions and supplies, and a major forward operating base had been constructed over the previous decade on the Indian Ocean territory of Diego Garcia. This had previously been leased by Britain to the United States, the Illois inhabitants of Diego Garcia and other islands in the group having been summarily removed to Mauritius.

The ability of the United States to mount the Desert Storm operation was a direct result of a military posture that had evolved over the previous 40 years, having its origins in the early 1940s but being boosted by the Cold War confrontation, primarily in relation to control of the region's oil reserves. This included the creation of the Rapid Deployment Force at the end of the 1970s, and its expansion into US Central Command (CENTCOM) in the early 1980s. CENTCOM was responsible for the conduct of Desert Storm in 1991 and has been responsible for regime termination in Afghanistan in 2001 and Iraq in 2003.

The increasing significance of Persian Gulf oil is a key aspect of the underlying context of the Iraq War that started in March 2003, and this chapter outlines its origins and development. It also examines two specific aspects of the 1991 war that have a particular relevance to the drive for regime termination in Iraq before and after the 9/11 attacks. These are the effects of the Iraqi use of medium-range ballistic missiles during the 1991 war and the Iraqi programmes to develop chemical and biological weapons together with delivery systems. While this book is primarily a detailed account of the political road to war in 2003, an appreciation of these factors – oil security and regional weapons proliferation – provide essential insights into the reasons for going to war.

They are essentially long-term issues that may be seen as being above and beyond the impact of the 9/11 attacks and the specific ideology of the Bush administration. Oil security, and its specific link to the Persian Gulf, was an aspect of the US military posture for 30 years before 2003, and Iraq was of concern to the US foreign policy elite well before the Bush election of 2000 and the attacks of 9/11.

Recognising the relevance of Gulf oil

While the world oil industry has its origins in the United States and the Caucasus in the latter part of the nineteenth century, by the early twentieth century the Dutch East Indies and Venezuela were also becoming significant.[1] Demand for oil was relatively limited until the First World War, and there was little in the way of a surge during the recession years of the 1920s and early 1930s. By the late 1930s, though, with the industrial recovery under way in Europe and North America, and the rapid economic growth of Japan, demand for oil surged just as reserves began to be discovered in the Persian Gulf.

The United States was, at this time, very well endowed with oil reserves, the early fields in Pennsylvania and Ohio having been greatly overshadowed by the new developments in Oklahoma, Texas, California and later Louisiana. Even so, the sheer demand for oil resulting from the massive war economy of the early 1940s was sufficient reason for the Roosevelt administration to have concerns over long-term sources of supply. At the time the United States had some 20 billion barrels of oil in proved reserves, by far the largest of any country, but such was the wartime demand that this would be exhausted within 13 years.[2] There was some confidence that more reserves would be discovered, but this was not sufficient to assuage concerns. As a consequence, it was seen as desirable to encourage US commercial oversight of new reserves, and the Persian Gulf region of the Middle East was recognised as the zone of greatest potential. By the late 1940s and early 1950s it was evident that countries such as Iran, Iraq and Saudi Arabia had substantial reserves and that these countries were either under the influence of the UK and France or, in the case of Saudi Arabia, had close commercial links with major US oil companies.

During the course of the 1950s, the United States consolidated commercial links with the ruling House of Saud in Saudi Arabia and, just as important, established very close political and military links with the Shah of Iran. US influence increased still further following the Suez debacle of 1956, which did much to damage British and French influence across the region. This was also the period when Israel became a close ally of the United States, not least as some Arab regimes such as Egypt and Syria developed close links with the Soviet Union in the wake of the rise of Arab nationalism.

By the end of the 1960s, Persian Gulf oil was established as the world's major cluster of reserves, far outstripping the reserves of the United States or the Soviet Union. Meanwhile, the United States itself had become a modest oil importer in the 1950s, not so much because of declining domestic reserves but because of the ready availability of cheap supplies from Latin America. There were concerns over possible competition with the Soviet Union during the heightened tensions of the Cold War, but these were not central to the US security outlook; the really major oil producers of the Gulf region such as Saudi Arabia, Kuwait, Iran and the Emirates were virtually client states.

OPEC, the Yom Kippur/Ramadan War and the oil weapon

By the early 1970s, US domestic oil reserves were beginning to run down so that the United States was becoming a substantial net oil importer, with every prospect that this would become steadily more significant in decades to come. Although new technologies were becoming available to exploit undersea reserves in the Gulf of Mexico and Arctic reserves in Alaska, these were not going to be sufficient to prevent a growing import dependency. This was still not of great concern, given the low price of oil before 1973, and it was the shock of a series of actions by oil producers towards the end of 1973 that changed the view from Washington substantially.

The Organisation of Petroleum Exporting Countries (OPEC) had been established in 1960, following an earlier failed attempt prompted by Venezuela in 1949.[3] It operated throughout the 1960s as a relatively weak producer organisation, comprising initially Iraq, Iran, Saudi Arabia, Kuwait and Venezuela, but acquired an increasing significance by the end of the 1960s. This was in part due to an increased membership as Nigeria, the Emirates, Algeria and Indonesia joined the organisation, but it was also due to the discovery of major additional oil fields within the boundaries of OPEC member states, in contrast to the slowing down of discoveries in 'older' oil-producing states such as the United States. Neither Alaska nor the new North Sea reserves were as significant as the countries concerned believed. Alaska had less than 2 per cent of world oil reserves and the North Sea perhaps 3.5 per cent. Most of the oil was located in OPEC states.

Even by 1973, there were few concerns in North America or Western Europe – the price of oil was low, supplies were plentiful and Iran was an appropriate buffer to any Soviet ambitions in the Persian Gulf. The change was sudden and wholly unexpected. Following Israel's successful prosecution of the Six Day War in 1967, taking control of the West Bank, the Golan Heights, the Gaza Strip and Sinai, Egypt and Syria regrouped and staged a surprise attack into the Israeli-occupied territories of Sinai and the Golan Heights six years later in October 1973. Despite early successes, within ten days of the start of the war both countries were at the limits of their military advances and Egypt was facing a major Israeli counter-offensive, Israel being much aided by a massive airlift of supplies by the United States.

Before the war, key members of OPEC such as Iran and Venezuela had been pushing the organisation to be more aggressive in its pricing policies, but with little success. Now, the prospect of a defeat for Egypt was sufficient to encourage the members of an inner OPEC group, the Organisation of Arab Petroleum Exporting Countries (OAPEC) to use oil as a political weapon in order to pressurise Israel's allies to gain an early ceasefire. On 17 October 1973, OAPEC announced cuts in production of around 15 per cent, a price increase averaging over 70 per cent and an embargo of oil exports to the United States and South Africa because of their support for Israel and the Netherlands from where oil was shipped to Israel.

The action caused a general rise in oil prices, combining open market speculation with further price rises agreed by the whole OPEC membership, including a 140 per cent rise in December.[4] Over an eight-month period from October 1973 to May 1974, world oil prices rose by an average of over 400 per cent, holding much of that value for the following two years. Although the major effects of the OAPEC/OPEC actions were economic, causing a profound impact on the world economy and ushering in a period of inflation coupled with economic stagnation, there was also a major impact on the US security outlook. In spite of close links with Middle East oil producers, it was clear that these countries would, when necessary, act in their own interests and were capable of acting in a united manner that had simply not been anticipated.

There was a particular concern in Washington that a more serious crisis might have resulted in a temporary shut-down of oil supplies from key Persian Gulf producers, an action that would have had a far greater impact even than the damaging price increases of 1973/4. As a result of these concerns, studies were initiated into the possibility of engaging in military responses to serious interruptions in oil supplies. While most were classified, one of the most substantial was undertaken by the Congressional Research Service for the Special Subcommittee on Investigations of the House Committee on International Relations and published in August 1975.[5] Entitled *Oil Fields as Military Objectives: A Feasibility Study*, it analysed the requirements for the US military to take over oil fields in a range of countries, principally in the Middle East and North Africa. Its conclusions were that the United States did not have the means to do so, especially if installations were sabotaged and there was a risk of Soviet intervention:

> military operations to rescue the United States (much less its key allies) from an airtight oil embargo would combine high costs with high risks. U.S. strategic reserves would be stripped. Prospects would be poor, and plights of far-reaching political, economic, social, psychological, and perhaps military consequences the penalty for failure.[6]

The Rapid Deployment Force and CENTCOM

A consequence of this and other assessments was the decision of the Carter administration to issue Presidential Directive 18 in 1977 ordering the Department of Defense to identify existing forces that might be tasked for operations in remote areas.[7] There followed a period of inter-service in-fighting, but the Joint Chiefs of Staff responded with a plan to pool forces from the four branches of the armed forces. They would be based in the United States but trained, equipped and provided with transport for action worldwide. Popularly known as the Rapid Deployment Force, the Joint Rapid Deployment Task Force (JRDTF) was established at the end of the Carter period in 1980, almost at the same time as the Iranian Revolution, the hostage crisis, the Soviet intervention in Afghanistan, a new hike in oil prices and the election of Ronald Reagan.

The Reagan administration came to power on a policy of re-arming America and facing down the 'evil empire' of the Soviet Union, and most of the subsequent attention of defence analysts was focused on the build-up of strategic and tactical nuclear forces. In practice, though, the new administration had a particular concern with oil security, with some of its supporters advocating an immediate scaling up of the JRDTF into a unified military command devoted directly to maintaining security in the Persian Gulf.

While most of the emphasis was on the perceived Soviet threat, there was also a concern for potential regional crises. One remarkably prescient analysis by Jeffrey Record,[8] published in February 1981 just after Ronald Reagan had taken office, pointed to the risk of aggression by a regional power, with Iraq being cited as the most likely threat:

> The prospect of an Iraqi attack on Kuwait or Saudi Arabia merits particular attention because (1) even before the Iraqi–Iranian war such a contingency exerted a major influence on U.S. force planning for non-NATO contingencies; (2) Iraq's Soviet-supplied armed forces are the largest of any in the Gulf region; and (3) the principal oil fields of Kuwait and Saudi Arabia are within comparatively easy reach from Iraq's southern border.

The first of the Military Posture Statements from the Organization of the Joint Chiefs of Staff for the incoming Reagan presidency was the Statement for Fiscal Year 1982, published in March 1981. It focused to a remarkable extent on the vulnerability of US and allied oil supplies, especially from the Persian Gulf. According to the report, 'Petroleum has become of major strategic importance for virtually every nation of the world' and it went on to say that 'Geopolitically, the energy problem for the United States and its allies centers on the Persian Gulf. The countries of the Gulf littoral, many of them strife-prone and politically unstable, supply about 65 per cent of total world imports, and hold about 55 per cent of projected world oil reserves.' If there were to be major problems, the report stated baldly that 'Were Persian Gulf oil cut off altogether, estimates are that the Western economic and military capabilities, even with oil rationing, could be gravely weakened within months.'[9]

Because of these and other assessments, and in the wake of the Iranian Revolution, the Reagan administration took the decision to expand the JRDTF into an entirely new military command, Central Command (CENTCOM) with responsibility for US security interests in an arc of 19 countries stretching from Kenya across north-east Africa and the Middle East to Pakistan. Established in 1983, the forces available to CENTCOM within a year included four army divisions and a brigade, and a marine division and a brigade, together with comprehensive air and sea support. A key aspect of its development was mobility combined with readiness, much of this centred on the army's 82nd Airborne Division. Within the division, an army brigade of 4,000 troops with air-mobile artillery and air defences was to be available for air transport at 20 hours' notice.[10]

By the late 1980s, CENTCOM had been further expanded with some 300,000 personnel from the four branches of the armed forces assigned to it, including three carrier battle groups, the Ninth Air Force, elements of Strategic Air Command and substantial intelligence, reconnaissance and special forces units. Under its commander, General Norman Schwarzkopf, it led the 1991 operation, Desert Storm, to evict Iraqi forces from Kuwait.

Oil and US security

Although much of the development of the JRDTF and CENTCOM had originated in the era of the Cold War, and from fears of Soviet intervention in the Persian Gulf, it arose in the context of long-term trends in the location of oil reserves and the decreasing significance of the United States.

Table 1.1 shows the share of world oil reserves by the ten leading holders in 1990 at the time of the Iraqi occupation of Kuwait. By that move alone, Iraq took control of almost one-fifth of world oil reserves, compared with 3.4 per cent for the United States. Given the size of the US reserves in Texas, Louisiana, the Gulf of Mexico and California, this may seem surprising, but the key factor is that the rate of domestic consumption of oil and oil products within the United States in

Table 1.1 World oil reserves, 1990 (percentage of total)

Saudi Arabia	25.5
Iraq	10.0
Kuwait	9.4
Iran	9.3
Emirates	9.2
Venezuela	5.8
Soviet Union	5.8
Mexico	5.6
United States	3.4
China	2.4

Source: Adapted from *Middle East and North Africa Yearbook*, Europa Press, London, 1991.

the postwar period was such that the days of massive domestic oil reserve holdings were largely over.

Within 14 years, as Table 1.2 shows, the situation had moved even further against US domestic oil security. By 2004, the United States had slipped to twelfth in terms of oil reserves, and China, with its rapidly increasing domestic demand and import requirements, was not even in the top 14.

It is important to recognise that the issue here is essentially a matter of long-term strategy. Many arguments have been raised that regime termination in Iraq was motivated in part by the requirement to take control of Iraqi oil fields and to open them up for exploitation by US-based trans-national oil corporations (TNOCs). Other arguments concern the possibility of the Saddam Hussein regime trading oil in euros rather than dollars, thereby undermining the international financial status of the dollar. Whatever the truth of such claims, the concern here is with the steadily increasing significance of the Persian Gulf as the source, by the end of the 1980s, of over 60 per cent of the world's oil reserves.

Table 1.2 World oil reserves, 2004 (percentage of total)

Saudi Arabia	22.1
Iran	11.1
Iraq	9.7
Kuwait	8.3
Emirates	8.2
Venezuela	6.5
Russia	6.1
Kazakhstan	3.3
Libya	3.3
Nigeria	3.0
United States	2.5
Canada	1.4
Mexico	1.2

Source: British Petroleum, 2005.

Current trends suggest that intensive efforts will be made to develop oil fields in parts of Africa, South America and the Caspian Basin, but that they will not substantially affect the status of the Persian Gulf fields. Moreover, China and India are joining the United States, Japan and Western Europe as industrialised regions increasingly dependent on the Gulf supplies. This is a trend that seems likely to continue for several decades and means that security oversight of the Persian Gulf region is a matter of underlying concern in Washington, given the widespread view in neo-conservative circles that China will ultimately present the greatest challenge to the United States.

By 2000, the situation for US interests in the Persian Gulf was problematic for three reasons. One was that Iran continued its independent path of some hostility to the United States and successive US administrations were deeply suspicious of Iran. A second was that there were increasing doubts over Saudi reliability. Substantial US forces had been based in the Kingdom in the years following the 1991 war, but this had resulted in internal hostility to the foreign presence in the Kingdom of the Two Holy Places, extending to violence such as the 1996 bombing of the Khobar Towers barracks block at the Dhahran air base. In 1998, the United States and the UK embarked on the four-day Desert Fox operation against Iraq but Saudi Arabia refused to allow its bases to be used to support the operation. Furthermore, it even refused to allow the US Air Force to relocate key strike aircraft normally based in Saudi Arabia to bases in other countries in the region.

If Saudi Arabia was causing problems, then the Iraq issue was even more difficult. A regime that might once have been a close ally in the 1980s was now entirely unacceptable to the United States. The Washington view was increasingly that it was not in US security interests to have a situation in which Saudi Arabia was of somewhat dubious reliability, Iran was clearly set on a path divergent from that of the United States and Iraq was under the control of a repressive regime that had previously occupied a neighbouring state. Moreover, Iraq was assumed to be developing nuclear, chemical and biological weapons and had a proven ability to develop and produce medium-range ballistic missiles. All of this was within a region that had by far the greatest geopolitical significance of any part of the world.

Scuds and their impact

If long-term issues of oil resources are hugely significant in relation to US security policy in the Persian Gulf, then two more immediate aspects of the 1991 Iraq War are also relevant – missiles and chemical and biological weapons. The political context of the war will be discussed in the next chapter, whereas the aim here is to look at the impact of the Iraqi use of medium-range Scud-type missiles during the war, and Iraq's ability to develop a range of chemical and biological weapons in the years before the war. Both phenomena formed part of a process of asymmetric conflict. Although Iraq had amassed a very large army before and during its eight-year conflict with Iran up to 1988, its forces were far less well equipped than those of the United States and its coalition partners, and the expulsion of Iraqi forces from Kuwait was accomplished in barely six weeks. At the same time, both the Scud problem and the Iraqi possession of chemical and biological weapons were to have a considerable effect on US military thinking, adding to concerns over the potential capabilities of the Saddam Hussein regime once it had survived the war itself.

The first night of the war involved a wide range of air strikes and cruise missile attacks. The latter included the world's longest ever air raid, when a flight of seven B-52G bombers took off from Barksdale Air Force Base in Louisiana and undertook a 35-hour 14,000-mile flight to launch 35 air-launched cruise missiles at eight targets in Iraq, including a power plant in Mosul and a telephone exchange in Basra.[11] The air and sea-launched cruise missiles used by the US Air Force and Navy represented very recent technology, most of the systems having been deployed during the 1980s, whereas the Scud missiles of the Iraqi armed forces were essentially based on 30-year-old 1950s technologies developed by the Soviet Union. Whereas the cruise missiles could operate with an accuracy of around 50 metres over a 2,400 km range, the Iraqi Scuds had an accuracy of perhaps 1,000 metres at a range of 500 km.

The political impact of these obsolete systems was therefore remarkable. After the first night of air strikes, the sheer intensity of the coalition capabilities made it seem possible that a week or so of air attacks followed by a substantial ground invasion would see the Iraqis evicted from Kuwait in barely a fortnight. This outlook changed abruptly during the second night of the war, when several Israeli cities came under attack from Scud missiles and their longer-range Iraqi variant, the Al-Hussein. The psychological and political impacts were considerable, partly because the Israelis feared that incoming missiles might have chemical or biological warheads but, more generally, because of a sense of vulnerability within Israeli society that had not been felt since the early days of the 1973 Yom Kippur/Ramadan War.

In practice, the human impact of the attacks on Israel was relatively small – four people were killed and 185 injured – but the political outcome was massive as the United States endeavoured to prevent Israel entering the war against Iraq. Having managed to develop a coalition against Iraq that included substantial Egyptian and Syrian forces, the United States could not afford to see Israel involved, as that would entirely change the orientation of the war. It was probable that several key Arab members of the coalition would withdraw, and that Saddam Hussein's regime could then represent the war as a Western crusade against the putative leader of the Arab world.

As a result of these fears, Patriot anti-aircraft missile batteries were rushed to Israel as they were claimed to have a limited anti-missile capability. More significantly, coalition air power and special forces were devoted to an intensive hunt for the Scud and Al-Hussein missile launch facilities. Given that these were mobile and typically had a 45-minute launch window, this proved a major prob-

lem, diverting coalition air forces from other targeting and substantially extending the air war that necessarily preceded the ground force invasion that finally
ended the war. It was therefore the case that in these defined political circumstances, Iraq's possession of a relatively small force of conventionally armed and
obsolete missiles had a substantial effect on the conduct of the war.

Iraqi ballistic missiles had another impact that was less evident at the time.
During the war, Iraqi forces also launched missiles at coalition targets in Saudi
Arabia. Forty-six missiles were fired but most of these fell in open country, doing
little damage, and a few may have been intercepted by Patriot missile batteries.
There were, however, two exceptions. On 25 February 1991, a missile hit a warehouse in the Saudi city of Dhahran that housed the 475th Quartermaster Group
(Provisional), destroying the warehouse, killing 27 US military personnel and
injuring 98 others. This was the largest single loss of life among the US armed
forces of the entire war and was an indicator that obsolete missiles could, in some
circumstances, have a direct military effect.[12]

Nine days earlier, on 16 February, another missile narrowly missed a large
pier complex at the Saudi port of Al Jubayl. At the time, the complex included a
large ammunition storage area and a petrol tanker parking area. At the wharves
around the pier were anchored a large amphibious warfare ship, the USS *Tarawa*,
and an aviation support ship, the USS *Wright*. The missile landed in the sea 100
metres from the *Wright* and did not cause any damage or injuries. If it had hit the
ammunition storage area, the results would have been catastrophic, potentially
causing massive damage to the port and many hundreds of casualties.[13]

The two Scud incidents, along with the diversionary 'Scud hunt', were to give
a substantial boost to US plans for missile defence, even though many of the programmes had been scaled back with the ending of the Cold War. In particular,
there was a recognition that relatively weak states could, with limited ballistic
missile technology, constrain US military operations in regional conflicts. This
was to result in intensive efforts to develop naval anti-ballistic missile systems.[14]
It also gave a boost to the development of directed energy systems that might be
particularly appropriate for theatre missile defence.[15]

Iraqi chemical and biological weapons

The second influential issue relating to the 1991 Iraq War was the manner in
which the Saddam Hussein regime had developed chemical and biological
weapons (CBW) and was seeking a nuclear capability. As later chapters will
show, this was repeatedly used by proponents of regime termination as a key
motivation, but these people rarely alluded to the manner in which the regime
had actually had CBW systems ready for use in the 1991 war.

After Israeli strike aircraft had destroyed the Osiraq nuclear reactor near
Baghdad in 1981, the Iraqis sought to develop multiple routes to nuclear
weapons, primarily through a dispersed system of uranium enrichment
processes. Programmes for developing chemical weapons (CW) were also accel-

erated and such systems were used during the Iraq–Iran War against Iranian troops and against Iraqi Kurds, most notably in the attack on the town of Halabja in March 1988. The regime also initiated the development of biological weapons in 1985, after an earlier programme had been curtailed. The biological weapons programme made rapid progress and included work on anthrax and botulinum toxin as well as the organism that causes gas gangrene. This latter programme was intended to produce cluster munitions impregnated with the organism, thereby greatly increasing the risk of gas gangrene as a result of anti-personnel shrapnel fragments delivered by the cluster munitions. Uniquely, the Iraqis also worked on another toxin, aflatoxin, a cancer-inducing mycotoxin produced by fungi.[16]

By 1988, the Iraqi biological weapons programme had developed into a full-scale agent production capability and a parallel programme was initiated to develop and produce weapons that could deliver the agents in the field. Trials commenced in 1988 and included work on 122 mm artillery rockets, and bombs and spray tanks for delivery from aircraft. They continued for two years until August 1990, when Iraq occupied Kuwait.

Following that invasion, it was almost immediately evident to the regime that there would be a massive military reaction led by the United States and that this would involve the eviction of Iraqi forces from Kuwait and possibly the destruction of the regime itself. One response was to embark on a crash programme of chemical and biological weaponisation using systems that could be employed as a crude deterrent against regime termination.

By January 1991, still barely six years after the start of the Iraqi biological weapons (BW) development programme, the regime had 176 bombs ready for use, 110 filled with botulinum toxin, 50 filled with anthrax spores and 16 filled with aflatoxin. Furthermore, an emergency programme to produce BW warheads for the Al-Hussein missile was initiated in August 1990. By January 1991, 25 missile warheads had been produced and these were fitted to missiles, 13 armed with botulinum toxin, 10 with anthrax and two with aflatoxin. In the period immediately before the outbreak of the war, on 16 January 1991, the missiles were moved to four isolated locations and remained there throughout the war.[17]

These missiles, and chemical warheads, were intended for use in the event of the destruction of Baghdad and presumed regime termination. Perhaps most significantly, authority to launch the missiles was pre-delegated from Baghdad to regional commanders, a remarkably risky move giving rise to the possibility of the unauthorised use of the systems during a chaotic and rapidly changing war.[18] Moreover, perhaps the most significant feature of the entire process was that elements of the US intelligence community were aware of the main features of the Iraqi BW programme, including an assessment that the Iraqis were likely to use chemical and biological weapons if the regime was terminated. This was the subject of a National Intelligence Estimate in November 1990, three months after the Iraqi invasion of Kuwait and two months before the outbreak of the war.[19]

Far more information on the entire Iraqi CBW programme, and on the wartime deployment of the weapons, came into the public domain with the publication of a key UNSCOM report to the UN Security Council in October 1995.[20] Although this did not establish that Iraq had weapons systems sufficient to be a major threat outside the region in 1991, it did confirm the assessment that there was a crude deterrent capability aimed at ensuring regime survival.

The two issues of the political and military impact of the Scud and Al-Hussein missiles and the Iraqi CBW capability were both to have a substantial impact on the outlook of the US military as well as the intelligence agencies. Although these rarely figured in the public pronouncements that will be discussed later in this book, they form an important part of the context to US military and security thinking in the late 1990s. The intelligence agencies, in particular, became more alert to the constraining impact on military freedom of manoeuvre that might result from middle-ranking powers developing crude weapons of mass destruction and appropriate delivery systems.

It is quite possible that the Iraqi missiles equipped with CBW warheads at the time of the 1991 war might not have worked if they had been fired – there is an absence of evidence to indicate, for example, whether the Iraqis had solved the difficult technical problems of dispersing chemical and biological agents from warheads undergoing the heat of atmospheric re-entry. This is not the point. There had to be an assumption that such systems might work, and this was what gave rise to the very real concerns that 'rogue' states might constrain US security interests. Clinton's first Director of Central Intelligence had made this point during confirmation proceedings in the Senate (February 1994), when he characterised the change for the United States of the passing of the Cold War and the onset of a less certain world, by saying that the United States had slain the dragon but was now faced with a jungle full of poisonous snakes. By the late 1990s, the regime of Saddam Hussein had survived the 1991 war, the no-fly zones and sanctions, and was now seen as one of the leading snakes in the jungle.

Conclusion

Two separate issues, one long term and one more recent, served as important parts of the context of the moves towards regime termination in Iraq during the latter part of the 1990s and the early years of the Bush administration. Oil security was an underlying issue in US defence policy, rising up the agenda in the 1970s as a result of the OAPEC/OPEC actions of 1973/4 and getting a further boost with the Iranian Revolution at the end of the decade. While most of the concerns related to Cold War tensions with the Soviet Union and the risk of Soviet interference with Gulf oil supplies in the event of an East–West confrontation, there was a secondary fear of regional destabilisation. The main response was the formation of CENTCOM and the development of forces that could be used to safeguard the security of the region from a US perspective.

With the United States increasingly dependent on imported oil, and with China also rapidly becoming a major oil importer, the Persian Gulf had, by 2000, become a region of intense significance for the United States. By the time of the election of President Bush, Iran was to be regarded as a 'rogue state', Saudi Arabia had severely constrained US military operations in the Kingdom and Iraq was not subject to external control in spite of a decade of sanctions. Moreover, two aspects of the 1991 war – Iraqi missiles and CBW systems – had had a notable impact on US military outlooks as they demonstrated instances of relatively weak states having the capacity to constrain the actions of a superpower. Coupled with political changes in the United States, especially the rise of the idea of a New American Century, they provide the context for the political road to war with Iraq in 2003.

Throughout the 1990s Iraq epitomised the seemingly intractable problem of a 'rogue' middle power armed with ballistic missiles and, potentially, weapons of mass destruction, thereby able to limit or even prevent US action in pursuit of its own security in a region of enormous geopolitical significance. With containment eroding at the end of the 1990s and increasingly regarded as an obsolete if not failed approach, the United States was faced with the long-term prospect of a hostile regime in Baghdad. That regime may well have been crippled by sanctions, yet, it could be argued, retained its long-term aim of dominating the region, including its vast oil reserves. Removing Saddam Hussein's regime was therefore an attractive option well before the attacks of 11 September 2001.

2

CONTAINMENT-PLUS: CLINTON AND IRAQ AT THE END OF THE 1990s

Introduction

After the 1991 Gulf War allied and Iraqi military leaders met on the battlefield and agreed the terms of a formal ceasefire in which Iraq agreed to abide by all UN Security Council resolutions that had been passed against it. This included demands that Iraq destroy all of its chemical and biological weapons and its ballistic missiles over a certain range, and dismantle its chemical, biological and nuclear weapons programmes (collectively referred to hereafter as weapons of mass destruction, or WMD). The United Nations Special Commission (UNSCOM) was established to inspect and monitor the elimination of the non-nuclear disarmament provisions of the resolutions and to assist the International Atomic Energy Agency (IAEA) in the nuclear areas.

US President George H. W. Bush hoped that Saddam Hussein's regime would collapse in the aftermath of the Gulf War. After it became clear that the Iraqi leader was going to retain his grip on power, the administration resorted to a policy of containment to keep the regime in check. This was achieved through ongoing UNSCOM inspections, economic sanctions and the establishment of safe havens for the Kurdish population in the north and the Shi'ite population in the south. These were protected by no-fly zones patrolled by US and UK warplanes.

In 1993 Bill Clinton was elected to the White House and continued his predecessor's containment strategy in Iraq. By the beginning of 1998 the Clinton administration still considered Iraq a significant threat to US vital interests and regional security in the Middle East. The threat stemmed primarily from the proscribed biological weapons, chemical weapons and ballistic missiles Iraq was suspected of possessing and ongoing clandestine biological, chemical and nuclear weapons programmes and ballistic missile programmes. The Clinton administration continued to implement a strategy of containment until it left office at the end of 2000. It considered this approach to be the most effective solution to the problems posed by Saddam Hussein and Iraq's WMD and, after two terms in office, judged containment a success.

Not everyone agreed with this conclusion, and the containment strategy came under severe pressure during the administration's last few years. Saddam

Hussein insisted that Iraq no longer possessed WMD or WMD programmes and after a series of crises in late 1997 and 1998 UNSCOM inspectors left Iraq. The United States and the UK responded in December 1998 with Operation Desert Fox, a four-day bombing campaign against suspected Iraqi WMD sites. After Desert Fox Saddam Hussein refused to submit to any further UN inspections. The United States now had to rely on economic sanctions and enforcement of the no-fly zones to contain the Iraqi regime. The sanctions regime steadily crumbled during Clinton's last few years. The sanctions were widely regarded as a major cause of the suffering borne by the Iraqi people and by 2000 Iraq was showing clear signs of a gradual reintegration into the region.

This led to strong criticism from prominent conservatives in Congress and Washington's network of conservative national security think-tanks. These critics argued that the administration's strategy was a failure. Containment was no longer sustainable and urgent action was required to decisively address the threat posed by Saddam Hussein. These critics lobbied the administration to take a much more aggressive stand against Saddam Hussein in order to remove him from power through an explicit policy of regime change. The views of these critics are explored in the next chapter. In response to this criticism the administration supplemented its containment policy with the long-term goal of regime change, the so-called 'containment-plus' strategy. The administration was extremely reluctant to adopt a more forceful posture against Iraq. By the time Clinton left office at the end of 2000 the containment strategy was unravelling. UN inspectors had not been allowed into Iraq since late 1998, the sanctions regime was buckling under international pressure and the administration refused to remove Saddam Hussein by force.

This chapter analyses the Clinton administration's policy towards Iraq during its last years in office. It explores the perceived threat from Iraq, the growing pressure on Clinton's containment strategy, the administration's reluctance to use force and its views on the concept of regime change. What becomes clear is that whoever replaced Clinton in the White House, be that Gore or Bush, would have to radically rethink US policy toward Iraq in terms of a much lower level of long-term unilateral containment or decisive action to terminate the regime in Baghdad.

UNSCOM

After the 1991 Gulf War, United Nations Security Council (UNSC) resolution 687 of 3 April 1991 set out the terms and conditions for the formal ceasefire between Iraq and the US-led coalition that had expelled Iraqi forces from Kuwait. The resolution established UNSCOM to work with the IAEA to verifiably eliminate all Iraqi WMD and ballistic missiles with a range greater than 150 km, all related items and production facilities, and to implement measures to ensure that the acquisition and production of prohibited WMD and ballistic missiles were not resumed. Iraq, however, systematically deceived and obstructed the UN weapons inspectors. Baghdad regularly denied having a biological weapons programme and successfully kept its biological weapons activities hidden from the UN until Saddam Hussein's son-in-law, Lt Gen. Hussein Kamal, Minister of Industry and Minerals and former Director of Iraq's Military Industrialization Corporation with responsibility for all of Iraq's weapons programmes, defected and provided detailed information about Iraq's comprehensive biological weapons programme in 1995. Throughout UNSCOM's existence Iraq provided five 'full, final and complete disclosures' on its biological weapons programme, three on its chemical weapons programme and three on its ballistic missile programme.[1] Each time Baghdad assured UNSCOM that its latest report was the final account of its activities.[2] Iraq's nuclear weapons programme was inspected by the IAEA, to whom Baghdad provided three final declarations.

The threat from Iraq

By 1998 UNSCOM had achieved a great deal, having supervised the destruction of long-range missiles and missile warheads, thousands of chemical munitions, tons of chemical agents, and Iraq's biological weapons production facilities.[3] But after seven years of inspections the Clinton administration remained convinced that Saddam Hussein posed a major threat to the United States, its allies and interests. This threat stemmed primarily from US intelligence analysis and UNSCOM reports that Iraq still possessed chemical and biological weapons and retained elements of its chemical and biological weapons programmes, its long-range ballistic missile programme and, most significantly, its nuclear weapons programme. Iraq vehemently denied this, but after years of deceit, concealment, obstruction and confrontation nobody in the administration believed Saddam Hussein.

During the last years of the administration senior officials continued to highlight the WMD threat from Iraq. In February 1998 Clinton insisted that the UN inspectors had much work still to do because 'Iraq continues to conceal chemical and biological weapons and missiles that can deliver them. And Iraq has the capacity to quickly restart production of these weapons.'[4] February also saw the release of the State Department's white paper *Iraq Weapons of Mass Destruction Programs*, which gave detailed information and analysis on Iraq's chemical, biological and nuclear weapons programmes, its ballistic missile programme and its refusal to cooperate with UNSCOM and IAEA inspectors.[5] In November 1999 CIA Director George Tenet remarked that Iraq had the technological expertise to produce biological weapons in a matter of weeks[6] and in December Secretary of Defense William Cohen stated that Iraq was still trying to acquire nuclear materials or nuclear weapons and insisted UN inspectors return to Iraq to prevent that occurring.[7] In March 2000 Tenet outlined the ongoing WMD threat posed by Saddam Hussein. He said Iraq could deploy long-range ballistic missiles capable of striking the US within a decade with foreign assistance, and that Iraq either still possessed or was actively pursuing offensive biological and chemical weapons and had 'not given up its nuclear ambitions despite a decade of sanctions and inspections'.[8] The administration assumed that in the absence of UN inspections Iraq was manufacturing chemical and biological weapons and actively pursuing a nuclear weapons programme.[9] Richard Butler, UNSCOM's Executive Chairman from 1997 to 1999, agreed: 'It would be foolish in the extreme', he wrote in 2000, 'to assume that he [Saddam Hussein] is not developing long-range missile capability, at work again on nuclear weapons, and adding to the chemical and biological warfare weapons he concealed during the UNSCOM inspection period.'[10]

There was no doubt in the administration's collective mind about the existence of Iraqi WMD and ongoing clandestine WMD programmes, and that this alone continued to pose a major threat to the United States. This assessment was supported by the UN. In 1999 the UNSC established a panel to assess Iraq's disarmament and current and future ongoing monitoring and verification issues in Iraq. The report of the panel, known as the Amorim Report after its chair, Brazilian Ambassador Celso Amorim, stated that Iraq could not be declared to have fully disarmed its WMD and ballistic missile programmes and was therefore not in compliance with its obligations under UNSC resolutions passed after the Gulf War. It listed a number of outstanding disarmament questions that needed to be resolved by the Iraqi regime.[11] Iraq's conduct was taken by UNSCOM and most governments as evidence that Iraq was hiding proscribed weapons and weapons programmes.[12]

Iraq was perceived to be a threat in other ways. The obstruction of UN inspections was portrayed by the administration as a threat of equal magnitude to the existence of the WMD and WMD programmes themselves. In December 1998 Clinton declared in a letter to Congressional leaders that the absence of inspectors in Iraq presented a 'clear and present danger to the stability of the Persian Gulf and the safety of people everywhere'.[13] Secretary of State Madeleine Albright insisted that Saddam's attempts to dictate the terms and conditions of UN inspections and deny access to important suspect sites were 'flagrant acts of obstruction' and 'a profound threat to the international security and peace'.[14]

Iraq's involvement in terrorist activity exacerbated the perceived threat. According to the US State Department's *Patterns of Global Terrorism 2000*, this activity primarily targeted internal opponents of the regime. But Iraq also supported regional terrorist organisations such as the Arab Liberation Front, the inactive 15 May Organization, the Palestine Liberation Front (PLF) and the Abu Nidal Organization (ANO).[15] However, the administration argued that Iraq's ability to cause trouble through international terrorism had been seriously undermined through years of containment.[16]

According to the Defense Department's 1998 *Annual Report to the President and Congress*, the administration's broad regional policy was to secure a peaceful Middle East with open access to 'strategic natural resources', such as Persian Gulf oil, at relatively stable prices.[17] This objective required stability above all else, and stability required a lasting and comprehensive peace between Arabs and

Israelis and full compliance by Iraq with all UNSC resolutions.[18] Iraq's WMD capabilities, its obstruction of UNSCOM, its terrorist activities and its wars with Iran and Kuwait clashed with this broad strategy and meant that Iraq constituted a much wider threat to regional security in the Middle East. The threat from Iraq was summed up by Edward Walker, Assistant Secretary of State at the Bureau of Near Eastern Affairs, in March 2000:

> Iraq under Saddam Hussein remains dangerous, unreconstructed and defiant. Saddam's record makes clear that he will remain a threat to regional peace and security as long as he remains in power. He will not relinquish what remains of his WMD arsenal. He will not live in peace with his neighbors. He will not cease the repression of the Iraqi people.[19]

Containment under pressure

This manifold threat from Saddam Hussein's regime was widely accepted and rarely contested in Washington towards the end of Clinton's presidency. The administration's primary objective of denying Iraq the capacity to use weapons of mass destruction, stated clearly in the President's 1998 State of the Union Address, was also uncontroversial.[20] There was widespread consensus, too, that Saddam Hussein himself and his obstructive and defiant behaviour was responsible for the enduring threat to US interests and Iraq's ongoing confrontation with the UN and the United States, rather than the entire Iraqi government, the Ba'ath Party, the social, political or military institutions, or the Iraqi population.

The Clinton administration's strategy for dealing with the threat from Iraq was the same as his predecessor's – containment until a suitable opportunity should arise at some point in the future to terminate Saddam Hussein's regime. Containment was designed to compel Iraq to change its behaviour, abide by international norms and comply with UNSC resolutions. But by the start of 1998 the containment policy was under sustained pressure from Baghdad, the UN Security Council and conservative critics in Washington, pressure that would eventually lead to the termination of Saddam Hussein's regime five years later in March 2003.

Pressure began to mount in mid-1997 when Iraq claimed that it had fully dismantled its WMD and WMD programmes and began to seriously hinder UNSCOM's activity and obstruct inspections. Iraq had periodically denied inspectors access to different facilities for years, but now began to demand specific conditions for continued inspections, such as the removal of US inspectors. The Security Council responded with resolution 1134, which threatened to impose travel restrictions on Iraqi officials for its 'flagrant breach' of previous UNSC resolutions.[21] Nevertheless Iraq continued to block UNSCOM activities to the extent that UNSCOM withdrew its inspectors in November 1997. Three things happened here that deeply affected US policy towards Iraq until the regime's demise in 2003. First, France, China and Russia abstained from resolution 1134, reflecting deep divisions within the Security Council. Second, in response to Iraq's continued defiance the United States and Britain amassed forces in the region but backed down from a punitive strike due to allies' unease. Third, Clinton allowed Russian Foreign Minister Yevgeny Primakov to strike a deal with Saddam Hussein that appeared to meet US demands for the return of UNSCOM and the resumption of unimpeded UN inspections.[22]

For many conservatives in Washington the divisions within the Security Council highlighted the inability of the UN to address the clear threat they saw in Saddam Hussein's regime. Furthermore, the decision not to punish Iraq for its defiance raised serious questions about the conditions under which the Clinton administration would ever use force against Iraq, force that many critics considered long overdue. Finally, the decision to allow a pro-Iraqi Russian minister to mediate on the United States' behalf appalled them. Actions at the start of 1998 confirmed that the late 1997 episode was not unique but rather a sign of things to come. In January 1998 Iraq once again obstructed UNSCOM activities and demanded that sanctions be lifted. Clinton threatened use of force, but in February accepted a deal agreed between Iraqi Foreign Minister Tariq Aziz and UN Secretary General Kofi Annan.[23] Conservatives were alarmed by Clinton's strategy, alarm that was compounded by Annan's declaration that Saddam Hussein was someone with whom he could 'do business'[24] and Albright's assertion that the agreement was not a compromise but a 'step back by Iraq' and a 'step forward' for the containment policy.[25]

Despite growing and sustained pressure the Clinton administration adhered to the containment policy for a number of reasons. Containment reflected the administration's liberal internationalist worldview with its emphasis on the authority of the United Nations, the international rule of law, 'assertive multilateralism' and action through coalitions of allies.[26] Containment was considered by far the most effective way of dealing with the Iraqi threat, even as it weakened in the late 1990s. The administration was averse to aggressive action beyond containment because this was not mandated by the UNSC resolutions the administration sought to enforce. It was not favoured by US allies and friends in the Middle East, and it could cause a host of problems that might embroil the US in a much more direct long-term commitment for years to come. Furthermore, Clinton's political freedom of action to reformulate or modify his long-term strategy on a difficult national security issue such as Iraq was constrained by impeachment proceedings initiated by a hostile Republican-controlled Congress over his relationship with White House intern Monica Lewinsky and by the historical inertia of a policy that had been operating since 1991. Containment would remain until the policy collapsed or Iraq capitulated.

Clinton's containment

Under Clinton containment continued to comprise the three core objectives established by Bush: UN inspections to disarm Iraq's WMD and dismantle its

WMD programmes; economic sanctions to prevent Iraq rebuilding its conventional military and WMD forces; and continued readiness to use military force to enforce the no-fly zones and to punish Iraqi intransigence if necessary.[27] Towards the end of the administration in 2000 these three objectives were supplemented with provision of humanitarian relief and a long-term strategy of regime change, and re-labelled 'containment-plus'.[28]

UN inspections

As pressure grew, the administration continued to insist that UN weapons inspections were crucial to prevent Iraq developing WMD; indeed they were the *best* way to achieve that goal, according to Clinton in February 1998.[29] 'Without a strong inspections system', he said in December 1998, 'Iraq would be free to retain and begin to rebuild its chemical, biological, and nuclear weapons programs in months, not years.'[30] Cohen forcefully agreed: 'it is absolutely necessary there be inspections in Iraq',[31] he said; 'the best solution for containing Saddam Hussein's weapons of mass destruction is to have the inspectors on the ground. There is no adequate substitute for that.'[32]

The administration was also clear about what it expected from Iraq to demonstrate the disarmament and dismantlement of its WMD and WMD programmes. Using language similar to that which would later be used by the Bush administration in 2002, Cohen made it clear in 1998 that not only did UN inspectors have to verify that Iraq no longer possessed WMD, but that Saddam Hussein had an 'affirmative obligation to produce evidence of the destruction of his chemical and biological weapons.... He has an obligation to show proof positive – of where, when, how and under what circumstances the materials were destroyed.'[33]

Throughout the second half of 1998 Iraq continued to obstruct UNSCOM and eventually decided to suspend cooperation with both UNSCOM and the IAEA. UNSCOM continued to state that it had not completed its work and could not declare that Iraq had fully disarmed its WMD and long-range ballistic missile programmes, despite pressure from Russia and France. As a result Iraq permanently ended the UNSCOM inspections in December 1998.[34] One year later the UNSC established the United Nations Monitoring, Verification and Inspection Commission (UNMOVIC) and in 2000 Hans Blix was named its head. Blix put together a team and began to prepare to go into Iraq at some point in the future.

Sanctions

The economic sanctions regime was imposed on Iraq when it annexed Kuwait in August 1990. Sanctions remained in place after Iraqi forces had been expelled in order to ensure Iraqi compliance with its postwar obligations established in successive UNSC resolutions. Towards the end of Clinton's presidency the leaking sanctions regime came under intense pressure from the humanitarian impact of sanctions, waning support in the UNSC, growing Iraqi oil exports and Iraq's regional reintegration.[35]

The sanctions regime had a devastating impact on the Iraqi population, catalogued in Geoff Simons's *The Scourging of Iraq*.[36] The United States and UNICEF (United Nations Children's (Emergency) Fund) asserted that Saddam Hussein's manipulation of sanctions was the cause of widespread humanitarian suffering in Iraq.[37] Following the establishment of the oil-for-food programme in 1996, which allowed Iraq to sell oil to finance the purchase of humanitarian goods, Baghdad had sufficient income to meet the basic needs of the Iraqi civilian population but did not do so.

Actions by UNSC members and other developments, particularly concerning the export of Iraqi oil, suggested that support for the sanctions regime and Iraq's international isolation were weakening. Both Russia and France seemed intent on engaging Baghdad and ending its decade of isolation. In October 2000, for instance, the Russian Foreign Ministry declared that it would seek to resolve the humanitarian impact of sanctions by suspending and then lifting the sanctions regime. This would occur in conjunction with a new process to monitor Iraqi WMD disarmament and a comprehensive review of all outstanding requirements.[38] A visit to Baghdad by Russian Foreign Minister Igor Ivanov followed in November 2000.[39] In March 2000 France also pressed the UNSC to lift economic sanctions, insisting that the humanitarian impact could no longer be ignored.[40] France promoted a more limited UN inspections system operation and a monitored lifting of sanctions.[41] France and Russia were not alone in suggesting an end to sanctions. In April 2000 *Voice of America* reported that a number of countries, as well as 70 US members of Congress, were urging Clinton to lift sanctions and a number of senior UN humanitarian officials resigned over the impact of the sanctions regime on the Iraqi population.[42] As UNSC support for maintaining sanctions faded, most observers considered the United States and Britain increasingly alone in seeking to ensure that Iraq fulfilled all its UN disarmament obligations.[43]

Other actions suggested that Iraq could soon return to the international community, an impression the Clinton administration tried to counter. Iraq had effectively rejoined the world oil market. By 2000 new oil agreements had been signed with Russian, Chinese and French consortia, Jordan and Turkey were preparing to reopen pipelines to Iraq, and the amount of oil Iraq could sell under the oil-for-food programme had rapidly escalated.[44] This occurred alongside rapid growth in Iraqi oil smuggling that netted Baghdad some $2–$3 billion per year in illegal oil sales.[45] Iraq's regional isolation showed clear signs of erosion when the country was invited to participate in a major Arab summit meeting in Cairo in October 2000. Its international isolation dissolved further when it reopened the international airport outside Baghdad in August 2000 and international flights resumed. In September Russia sent a flight to Baghdad followed by France, Jordan, Yemen, Syria and Morocco. In November 2000 Iraqi commercial flights began, further undermining the effectiveness of the no-fly zones.[46]

The deterioration of the sanctions regime and Iraq's international isolation became a rallying point for those opposed to US policy toward Iraq.[47] Nevertheless, Clinton insisted that economic sanctions would stay in place until Iraq fully complied with all UNSC resolutions.[48] 'There can be no relief and should be no relief from the sanctions' until UN inspectors were fully satisfied, Cohen said in December 1999.[49] Albright concurred in February 2000, insisting that 'lifting sanctions in the absence of compliance by Baghdad with its WMD obligations is not an option'.[50] Sanctions remained a critical element of the containment strategy because they prevented Saddam using Iraq's oil wealth to produce WMD and ballistic missiles.[51] Clinton was convinced that Saddam Hussein would undoubtedly have used the $120 billion denied him by sanctions to 'rebuild his weaponry' had it been available to him.[52] The administration was adamant that it would not accept any outcome that would give Saddam control of Iraq's oil revenues as long as he remained in defiance of UNSC resolutions.[53]

The administration recognised the humanitarian impact of the sanctions regime and hoped that relief could be delivered to the Iraqi people through the oil-for-food programme, but the blame for the suffering was placed firmly with Saddam.[54] Although the administration would work to alleviate the impact of sanctions, they would not be swayed from their chosen course. As Cohen declared in July 1999, 'We will continue to explore ways in which we can help the Iraqi people as we have done through our support for the Oil for Food program to be sure. But we are determined to preclude and prevent Saddam Hussein from rebuilding his military and thus the sanctions will remain in place.'[55]

Use of force

The administration was extremely reluctant to use force against Iraq beyond selective retaliation for Iraqi infringements of the no-fly zones. This reflected the administration's commitment to the authority of the United Nations that lay at the heart of its Iraq policy.

Any use of force by the United States was portrayed not as a US attack against Iraq to meet US objectives, but a UN attack against Iraq to meet UN objectives. For example, in August 1998 Albright argued that Iraq's obstruction of UN inspections was 'an Iraq–UN problem. . . . This, at this stage, is not a problem between Saddam Hussein and the United States.'[56] In December 1999 State Department Spokesman Jamie Rubin reiterated that 'The Iraqis would like to present their problem as a problem with the United States and we do not believe they have a problem with the United States; they have a problem with the United Nations.'[57] The use of force was only considered in the context of supporting the goals of containment and UNSC resolutions, not instead of containment or as a means of moving beyond containment. Clinton stated in December 1998 that 'The credible threat to use force, and when necessary, the actual use of force, is the surest way to *contain* Saddam's weapons of mass destruction program, curtail his aggression, and prevent another Gulf war [emphasis added].'[58] Echoing the George H. W. Bush administration's rationale for not removing Saddam Hussein in the 1991 Gulf War, Clinton argued against using military force to remove the regime in Baghdad because it was not a stated UN objective: 'Would the Iraqi people be better off if there were a change in leadership? I certainly think they would be. But that is not what the United Nations has authorized us to do; that is not what our immediate interest is about.'[59] Cohen agreed: 'It has never been the goal of the United Nations to remove him from power. Until such time as there is a change in the declaration of the UN policy, then it won't be ours either.'[60]

Given that force was only considered in the context of containment, the administration was mindful of the impact any use of force might have on the UN inspections process and the sanctions regime. 'If we take military action', Clinton said in November 1998, 'we can significantly degrade the capability of Saddam Hussein to develop weapons of mass destruction and to deliver them, but that would also mark the end of UNSCOM. So we would delay it, but we would then have no oversight, no insight, no involvement in what is going on within Iraq.'[61] Cohen echoed Clinton's view on the implications of using force. 'To the extent that there is a military option', he said, 'it is not an adequate substitute for inspectors being on the ground, having unfettered access.'[62] The use of force was clearly subordinate to the UN inspections process.

The Clinton administration was also unwilling to consider any use of force beyond air and missile strikes for domestic political reasons, and its reluctance to use ground troops and accept military casualties dominated military planning.[63] This stemmed from the disastrous engagement of US Rangers with Somali warlords in 1993, which resulted in pictures of the bodies of US soldiers being dragged through the streets of Mogadishu and beamed around the world on CNN. It was further reflected in the administration's strategy to repel Serbian forces from Kosovo in 2000 by bombing them from 15,000 feet. The administration also concluded that it would have little domestic support for a major military offensive to either punish or remove Saddam Hussein. Secretary Albright remarked in her memoirs that 'no serious consideration was given to actually invading Iraq...if President Clinton had proposed doing so in 1998, he would have been accused of being reckless and opposed by friends in the Gulf, our allies, most senior officers in our own military and leading Republicans.'[64]

These considerations led the administration to establish clear criteria for the use of force in Iraq. Force would only be used if Iraq tried to reconstitute its WMD or their delivery systems, threatened its neighbours, challenged allied aircraft patrolling the no-fly zones, or moved against its own Kurdish population.[65] These criteria were reflected in Operation Desert Fox, the administration's attack on Iraq in December 1998 after Baghdad's persistent refusal to allow unimpeded UN inspections. Clinton insisted that force would only be used to degrade Saddam's capacity to develop and deliver weapons of mass destruction and threaten the region.[66] Secretary Cohen made it clear that Saddam Hussein was not a target.[67] No one 'should be under the impression that this is going to be a mission which will accomplish the complete elimination of his weapons of mass destruction, or force him to say he surrenders, or remove him from power', he said. 'That would not be the goal of the United States and hopefully our allies in any sort of military operation.'[68] Cohen reportedly told troops that the mission to bomb Iraq was circumscribed in order to avoid any casualties.[69] The four-day Desert Fox campaign was conducted against 100 targets and considered a 'highly successful operation'.[70]

Given the administration's inclination to consider military action against Iraq only in the context of the authority of the UN, the explicit objectives of relevant UNSC resolutions and in support of its containment policy, it was accepted by the administration that there were 'no military solutions to many of the problems in dealing with Iraq and that military over-reaction would disserve our interests and needlessly endanger our personnel'.[71] The Clinton administration therefore remained convinced that playing the waiting game and containing Iraq as long as necessary was the best course of action and that military force should only be employed in support of that strategy.

Regime change under Clinton

Containment policy was always viewed by the administration as the most effective strategy for dealing with Saddam's Iraq until such a time as Saddam was no longer in power and a new regime emerged that would cooperate fully with both the United Nations and the United States. But after several failed and abortive assassination attempts in the early 1990s, the administration did not engage in any serious efforts to remove Saddam's regime. This changed in late 1998 following the passage of the Iraq Liberation Act (ILA) by Congress in October that year and a growing acceptance that the return of UN inspections was extremely unlikely after Operation Desert Fox. The ILA obliged the administration to make regime change a formal part of its Iraq policy by supporting Iraqi opposition groups and individuals within and outside Iraq and authorised $97 million to do so.

The year 1999 therefore saw the articulation of the containment-plus strategy based on three new developments. The United States would now not hesitate to strike Iraq's radar and anti-aircraft facilities when provoked in the no-fly zones as part of a low-intensity air war.[72] The administration planned to expand the oil-for-food programme and develop plans for 'smart sanctions' to target the regime and relieve the suffering of the Iraqi people as much as possible. Finally, the White House formally adopted a policy of regime change as an explicit goal of its Iraq policy.[73]

The administration began seriously to examine a realistic regime change policy in 1999 but US involvement in the Kosovo War and Clinton's personal quest to secure an Israel–Palestine peace agreement put an end to any serious consideration of a military-led regime change plan.[74] Consequently the administration's commitment to the regime change goals of the ILA remained largely declaratory.

The language of regime change was that of a long-term ambition rather than a strategic objective that the administration might prioritise above all else. Clinton warned that regime change would take time and effort: 'we must not harbor illusions, however, that change will come easily or quickly'.[75] He spoke of 'deepening our engagement with the forces for change in Iraq to help make the opposition a more effective voice for the aspirations of the Iraqi people'[76] and working towards some day when Iraq might have a government worthy of its people.[77] Cohen expressed his hope that change could be brought about and looked to a time when 'the administration, with our Kuwaiti friends, and others, [can] bring about a regime change at some point in the future'.[78]

The Clinton administration's position on regime change emphasised the role of the Iraqi opposition. Change must come from within Iraq, Assistant Secretary of State Edward Walker insisted, 'they alone must be the ones to determine the future of Iraq; we will assist them as we can, but we will not, indeed should not, be the ones to decide who will be the next leader of Iraq'.[79] 'If there is to be change', the State Department's 1999 *Saddam Hussein's Iraq* report stated, 'it must come from within Iraq, led by Iraqis. We do not seek to impose an American solution or a foreign opposition on the Iraqi people.'[80] The emphasis on the Iraqi opposition was undermined by in-fighting amongst the opposition groups under the umbrella of the Iraqi National Congress (INC).[81]

This compounded the administration's reluctance to engage in regime change through the INC for two reasons. The first was the view that the opposition did not fulfil the requirement of 'a credible, broad-based, Iraqi political umbrella movement, based on consensus'.[82] The second was the administration's concern that support for the opposition could divide Iraq, leading to a Balkanisation of the type that the United States had been heavily involved in ameliorating in south-east Europe throughout the 1990s. As Bruce Riedel, Special Assistant to the President and Senior Director, Near East and South Asian Affairs at the National Security Council, stated in April 1999, 'we want to see an Iraq that remains united, with its territorial integrity intact. We do not want to see another Afghanistan or Lebanon at the top of the Persian Gulf.'[83]

The administration was not prepared to commit to regime change in the manner envisaged in the ILA. Its rhetoric remained that of hope of regime change at an unspecified future time, rather than decisive action to change the regime in the short to medium term. It placed much responsibility for regime change with a divided Iraqi opposition of which it was wary. With containment under heavy pressure and regime change through a surrogate Iraqi opposition movement not considered a credible option, the question remained what was the administration's long-term strategy?

Long-term strategy

At the end of Clinton's presidency the administration's long-term approach remained indefinite continuation of the containment-plus strategy as long as

Saddam remained in power. The containment strategy would remain in place for a number of reasons. Moving beyond containment through aggressive use of force to displace Saddam Hussein was not considered a viable option, as explored above. Backing down was also not an option. As far as the administration was concerned, the threat from Saddam's WMD and WMD programmes remained potent and Saddam Hussein simply could not be trusted. Assistant Secretary Walker summed up this sentiment in March 2000: 'the regime of Saddam Hussein cannot be rehabilitated or reintegrated as a responsible member of the community of nations. Experience makes this conclusion manifest. That is why the United States is committed to containing Saddam Hussein as long as he remains in power.'[84] Backing down would also seriously undermine the credibility of the United States, as Clinton stated in December 1998:

> if we turn our backs on his defiance, the credibility of U.S. power as a check against Saddam will be destroyed ... if Saddam can cripple the weapons inspections system and get away with it, he would conclude that the international community, led by the United States, has simply lost its will. He will surmise that he has free rein to rebuild his arsenal of destruction. And some day, make no mistake, he will use it again, as he has in the past.[85]

Containment was the only credible option and it was regarded by the administration as a successful strategy, despite its shortcomings. In August 2000 Department of Defense Spokesperson Kenneth Bacon declared that Saddam Hussein was 'no longer a threat to his neighbors and is not seen as a threat to his neighbors. That's largely because of the containment that we have carried out.'[86] Secretary Albright regularly asserted that the United States was keeping Saddam Hussein successfully trapped 'in a strategic box' regardless of whether or not he readmitted UN inspectors.[87] CIA Director George Tenet concurred. His 2000 assessment maintained that Saddam Hussein was 'still on a downward path', with a deteriorating economic infrastructure, no control over the Kurdish area in the north of Iraq and very few sympathetic governments in the region or beyond.[88]

Nevertheless, the containment-plus strategy had lost one of its primary tools through the indefinite expulsion of UN weapons inspectors. This, however, had little effect on the administration's resolve. 'Our policy will continue as it is as one of containment, and I don't anticipate any change in that policy', Cohen insisted in April 2000, a few months before the November 2000 presidential election.[89] As a result considerable emphasis was placed on the sanctions regime, with the administration insisting that no consideration would be given to lifting sanctions until Baghdad complied with all UNSC resolutions.[90] In December 1999 the UNSC resolution that established UNMOVIC offered Baghdad some light at the end of the containment tunnel. It stated that if Iraq fulfilled a series of key disarmament tasks and cooperated with inspectors for 120 days, then a temporary suspension of sanctions, apart from those related to military imports, could be enacted with appropriate controls in place. The suspension would have to be renewed every 120 days.[91] After three successful 120-day periods sanctions could then be permanently removed.[92] This was, however, considered an implausible scenario: 'We are not fools,' ventured Francis Ricciardone, Special Coordinator for Transition in Iraq, when discussing whether sanctions might be lifted following full Iraqi compliance. 'We don't believe he ever will, which is why we think he ultimately has to go.'[93] In reality, without UNSCOM, sanctions were the key to containment and would only be lifted when Saddam had gone, regardless of his actions. In December 1998 Thomas Pickering, Under Secretary of State for Political Affairs, declared that if Iraq refused to re-admit UNSCOM, 'it has literally chosen for sanctions in perpetuity'.[94] Cohen had reinforced this view in November 1999, stating that sanctions could only be lifted and additional relief provided to the Iraqi population when there was a different regime in Iraq.[95]

Conclusion

On entering office in 1993 the Clinton administration continued the previous administration's policy of containing the threat posed by Saddam Hussein and his WMD programmes. As far as the new administration was concerned there was no question that Iraq was a major threat to regional security in the Middle East and US vital interests. The containment policy had three principal objectives: to locate and eliminate Iraq's WMD and WMD programmes through UN weapons inspections; to prevent Saddam rebuilding Iraq's conventional military forces and prevent Iraq accessing technology that might be used for clandestine WMD programmes through an economic sanctions regime; and to enforce the northern and southern no-fly zones through sporadic aerial bombardment. The wider use of military force was only considered in the context of supporting the first two containment objectives. This approach was consistent with the Clinton administration's liberal internationalist worldview, which placed considerable emphasis on multilateral diplomacy to address threats to international security, the legitimacy of the United Nations, and military action through broad coalitions of allies.

The Clinton administration successfully contained Saddam Hussein's regional power ambitions, reduced his sphere of influence within Iraq and for the most part thwarted his WMD and ballistic missile programmes. But as the Clinton era drew to a close at the end of 2000 Saddam Hussein's power base remained strong and containment was under severe pressure. Iraq was emerging from international isolation and beginning to reintegrate itself into the region. Saddam Hussein insisted that Iraq was free of WMD and had no residual WMD programmes, and prevented the UN weapons inspectors from continuing their work. At the same time the sanctions regime was beginning to crumble under pressure from France and Russia, both permanent members of the UNSC, massive illegal oil exports and extensive smuggling operations outside the oil-for-food programme, and popular opinion that laid the blame for the terrible humanitarian suffering of the Iraqi people squarely at the feet of the US administration's sanctions policy. Saddam remained as belligerent as ever. In September 2000 statements were made that Kuwait was stealing Iraqi oil.[96] Evidence emerged that Iraq was testing ballistic missiles and rebuilding facilities destroyed by Operation Desert Fox in 1998 presumably, the administration thought, for WMD purposes.[97] In December 2000 Saddam staged a huge show of military strength, partly to quash rumours of his ill health and partly as a show of force to the new US president.[98]

At the end of the Clinton administration the containment-plus strategy essentially comprised the porous sanctions regime and a low-intensity air war to degrade Iraq's military capabilities in response to no-fly zone violations. The other key aspects of the strategy were not functioning. UN inspections had ceased with no prospect of resumption. Despite agreement to form UNMOVIC to replace UNSCOM, the United States had few supporters in the UN for a tough new inspections process. In addition, the administration was wary of and had little faith in the ability of the Iraqi opposition to engender regime change and devoted minimal time and resources to that objective. Regime change remained a distant hope. By the end of the Clinton administration the US was increasingly isolated in its containment strategy. The countries that had joined or supported the 1991 coalition to expel Iraqi forces from Kuwait had little taste for further military action against Baghdad and wanted the sanctions regime changing, or even lifting altogether, to alleviate the suffering of the Iraqi people.

Despite the growing pressure on his containment strategy, Clinton insisted that it was still the best approach. He was not prepared to pursue an aggressive strategy either indirectly through a US-trained and -equipped Iraqi opposition force or directly through armed invasion. 'I don't believe we need to get into a direct war with Iraq over the leadership of the country,' Clinton said in February 1998, 'I don't believe we need to re-fight the Gulf war.'[99] Neither was he prepared to back down. Iraq was still a major threat for a number of reasons, but primarily because of its WMD programmes, US credibility was at stake and in the end Saddam Hussein simply could not be trusted to act in a manner considered responsible by the United States.

The administration's plan was to keep sanctions in place as best it could and otherwise 'enforce its red lines: no moves against the Kurds, no threats against its neighbors, no reconstitution of weapons of mass destruction, and we will rely on our intelligence to do that'.[100] The Clinton administration insisted that this state of affairs was acceptable and would successfully keep Saddam contained until he fully complied with all UNSC resolutions or indigenous forces brought down his regime. The administration would not consider lifting economic sanctions until Iraq had fully and verifiably complied with his commitments. These were detailed by the administration as a full declaration and destruction of its WMD programmes (UNSC resolutions 687, 707, 715 and 1051), the return of

Kuwaiti and third-country prisoners of war and missing persons (UNSC resolutions 686 and 687), the return of all Kuwait property stolen in the Gulf War (UNSC resolution 686), and an end to the repression of its civilian population (UNSC resolution 688).[101]

In the last year of the Clinton administration, foreign policy was focused on decisions about missile defence and negotiations with Russia on modifying the Anti-Ballistic Missile (ABM) Treaty, the decision to use military force against Serbia in defence of Kosovo, the Israel–Palestine peace initiative, and diplomatic engagement with the regime of Kim Jong-Il in North Korea. The development and robust implementation of actions to support the containment-plus strategy, such as tightening the sanctions regime and funnelling support to the Iraqi opposition in some form, would be left to the Gore administration if Clinton's vice president won the 2000 election.

During the 2000 presidential campaign Vice President Al Gore said that his policy would deviate little from Clinton's. He said he would continue to support the Iraqi opposition in its efforts to promote regime change while containing the threat posed by Saddam Hussein.[102] Nevertheless, there were doubts in the administration about the long-term viability of the containment strategy. In April 1999 Martin Indyk accepted that containment was not without its costs and that even a 'contained Iraq under the leadership of Saddam Hussein remains a threat both to the region and to the Iraqi people'.[103] Several years later Albright revealed in her memoirs that the key question she faced as Secretary of State was whether the United States could retain sufficient international support for containment 'despite passage of time, the economic and human costs of sanctions, and Saddam's propaganda'.[104]

For others in Congress and Washington's conservative think-tanks there were no doubts about the long-term viability of the Clinton administration's strategy. It was not viable and the state of affairs in 2000 was not acceptable. US policy toward Iraq under Clinton was, according to its critics, in urgent need of review. A number of issues became increasingly contentious in Washington, including the division in the Security Council over Iraq, particularly over the economic sanctions regime; the threat, extent and actual use of force against Iraq in response to the regime's repeated refusal to cooperate with UN inspectors; the nature of support for the Iraqi opposition; the effectiveness of the sanctions regime; and the degree to which the United States should unilaterally address the threat posed by Saddam Hussein. By the end of the Clinton administration, opinion on the future direction of US policy towards Iraq had become increasingly polarised between the liberal internationalists in the White House and hawkish conservatives in Congress and Washington's think-tanks who advocated a much more decisive approach to the threat from Iraq.

3

CONTAINMENT UNDER PRESSURE: OPPOSITION FROM CONGRESS AND CONSERVATIVE THINK-TANKS

Introduction

The Clinton administration's Iraq policy provoked considerable opposition from conservative critics within Congress and the wider national security establishment in Washington. These critics shared the Clinton administration's perception of the threat from Iraq and they agreed that Saddam Hussein was the root cause of this threat. Some argued that the threat was greater than that articulated by the White House. However, serious disagreement emerged on the viability of Clinton's containment strategy. Critics in Washington's conservative think-tanks denounced containment as a failure that was symptomatic of Clinton's 'feckless' foreign policy. They advocated a more aggressive approach to the threat posed by Baghdad centred on the removal of the regime, rather than indefinite containment. This was more than just a preferred policy option; it was portrayed as an imperative for US national security interests. Without regime change Iraq would emerge as a WMD-armed adversary in a region of enormous geopolitical importance. These critics insisted that military force should be used in conjunction with support for the Iraqi opposition to rid the world of Saddam Hussein. During the last two years of the Clinton administration, critics developed and advocated a coherent strategy for military-led regime change that, they argued, could be quickly and easily implemented.

The vehement opposition to Clinton's Iraq strategy was reflected in Congress, where the strategies for regime change developed and advocated by conservative think-tank experts found considerable support. Senior members of Congress also judged the administration's containment strategy a failure and insisted that it could not continue indefinitely. Congress compelled the White House to adopt a formal policy of regime change through the 1998 Iraq Liberation Act (ILA). The White House complied but did not implement the Act in the manner anticipated by its Congressional sponsors. Clinton viewed regime change as a long-term objective rather than an immediate military priority. Clinton's critics in Congress and conservative think-tanks wanted the containment policy jettisoned altogether and replaced by a robust policy of prompt regime change.

By the end of Clinton's presidency in 2000, support in Congress and from conservative think-tanks for a more combative approach to Iraq remained strong. Significantly, some of the most vociferous think-tank critics were appointed to senior positions within the George W. Bush administration at the beginning of 2001. This chapter examines the opposition from Congress and conservative think-tanks to the Clinton administration's approach, their views of containment and support for regime change.

Opposition from Congress

Congressional opposition to many of the Clinton administration's policies became increasingly widespread in the late 1990s. This began with the 1994 Congressional elections when the Republican Party took control of both the Senate and the House of Representatives with a strongly conservative manifesto. Opposition accelerated in 1998 when impeachment proceedings were brought against the President over the Monica Lewinsky affair. The administration's policy toward Iraq was no exception.

The administration and its critics in Congress shared a similar perception of the threat posed by Saddam Hussein's regime. Both argued that Iraq was still producing WMD and that Saddam Hussein remained an unreconstructed menace.[1] The administration also garnered considerable Congressional support for the use of force against Iraq in Operation Desert Fox. In August 1998 the Senate passed a resolution declaring Iraq to be in 'material breach' of its ceasefire agreement and urged Clinton to take whatever action necessary to bring Iraq back into compliance with UNSC resolutions.[2] In October 1998, 27 senators signed a letter encouraging the President to take military action against Iraq.[3]

However, the ongoing and increasingly serious obstruction of UNSCOM's activities and Clinton's reluctance to use force to punish Saddam Hussein's confrontational stance led to a growing chorus of opinion that the administration's Iraq policy was floundering. The criticism was directed by senior and influential Congressional figures. They considered Clinton's strategy a failure because Saddam was not being adequately contained, the containment strategy was unravelling and could not last, and the administration lacked a robust long-term strategy for dealing with the enduring threat from Baghdad. The solution, as they saw it, lay in getting rid of Saddam Hussein as soon as possible. Some critics saw this as a moral imperative, others saw it as the best of a poor set of options.

Concerted pressure in the Senate and the House led Congress to pass the Iraq Liberation Act in October 1998 to compel the administration to promote regime change to an explicit goal of its Iraq policy. Clinton signed the Act and announced his administration's full support for the objective of regime change in November 1998. Nevertheless, significant differences remained on how to implement the legislation. The administration favoured containment until the regime could be changed at some indefinite point in the future and prioritised the authority of the UN in dealing with Iraq. In contrast, critics in Congress advocated 'the Reagan doctrine of rollback, not the Truman doctrine of containment'.[4] They viewed the threat from Iraq as a problem for the United States to deal with, not the UN. The option of sending a massive occupation force into Iraq was not entertained by proponents of regime change at this stage. Instead the Iraqi opposition was considered the appropriate medium for regime change, and a number of strategies were developed and promulgated in support of that objective which found favour in Congress.

This is not to suggest that a more aggressive policy towards Iraq was uniformly advocated by Congress. There were many voices opposed to the idea of military-led regime change and in favour of lifting sanctions.[5] Nevertheless, statements from senior members of Congress (chairs of Senate or House committees, sub-committees or party policy committees) criticising different aspects of Clinton's Iraq policy and advocating regime change as an appropriate solution reflected the growing clamour for regime change in the late 1990s.

Clinton's Iraq policy considered a failure

A number of senior Congressional leaders strongly disagreed with the Clinton administration's assertion that the containment policy was a success. They argued instead that its policy towards Iraq was failing because of the administration's inability to act in the face of Iraqi defiance, the crumbling sanctions regime and the termination of UN inspections. They argued that this left the US constrained, rather than Saddam Hussein.

In March 1998 Senator John Kyl, then Chair of the Senate Judiciary Committee's Subcommittee on Terrorism and now (2005) Chair of the Senate Republican Policy Committee, argued that the administration had 'abdicated a significant part' of its responsibility for resolving the problem of Iraq.[6] A few months later he described the administration as 'frozen into inaction in dealing with Saddam Hussein'.[7] In October 1998 Representative Benjamin Gilman, Chair of the House Committee on International Relations, said the administration was 'paralyzed by indecision'. Iraq was in clear violation of UNSC resolutions, yet Clinton had 'never before been so obviously unwilling to do anything about it'.[8]

In February 1999 Senator Don Nickles, then Chair of the Republican Policy Committee, Republican Whip and later Chair of the National Republican Senatorial Committee, issued a damning indictment of the administration's Iraq policy.

> Saddam Hussein and the Iraqis and the Iraqi Government have really baffled the Clinton administration and, in my opinion, they have beaten the Clinton administration ... the administration's policy has been a total disaster ... Saddam Hussein is able to produce all the oil he wants. He is able to generate the moneys [*sic*] he needs, able to build the

38

weapons of mass destruction without anybody checking him whatsoever – not the United States, not the United Nations. As a result, the world is a much more dangerous place. The administration should be held accountable for their failed policies in Iraq.[9]

Senator Frank Murkowski, Chair of the Senate Energy and Natural Resources Committee, wholeheartedly agreed. 'Our Iraq policy is bankrupt', he asserted in October 1998. He accused the administration of relying on 'Kofi Annan and the Iraq appeasers to sign meaningless deals with Saddam Hussein regarding inspections that were useless from the moment they were signed. When we called back our aircraft at the last moment in October, despite the unanimous support of the Security Council for the attack, our Iraq policy suffered a near-fatal collapse.'[10]

In June 2000 Senator Sam Brownback chastised the government for presiding over 'the abolition of UNSCOM, the end of the sanctions review for a significant number of products imported into Iraq, and a staggering – a staggering erosion of international support for isolating the Saddam Hussein regime'.[11] Brownback was Chair of the Senate Foreign Relations Subcommittee on Near Eastern and South Asian Affairs and a consistent advocate of regime change.

Containment cannot last

With a strategy described as 'frozen', 'paralyzed', 'beaten' and 'bankrupt', Congressional critics of the administration's Iraq policy insisted that containment was unsustainable and that a new approach was required. Containment as it stood could not continue because the Gulf War coalition committed to containing Iraq had disintegrated and the international community had grown weary of the seemingly endless confrontation between the United States and Iraq. Without international support, near-unilateral containment was considered deeply problematic.

Senator Judd Gregg, now (2005) Chair of the Budget Committee, and Chair of the Appropriations Committee's Subcommittee on Homeland Security, highlighted the problem in February 1998. The United States' ability to deal with Iraq had been 'fundamentally undermined by [its] inability, one, to focus on the situation with an international alliance and, two, to have the capacity, because we do not have an international alliance, to take action which will end up being definitive'. Gregg's solution was to build a new alliance to remove Saddam Hussein from power.[12]

Senator John Kyl concurred with this assessment. He argued against playing a waiting game with Saddam because he thought that Saddam would win: 'He knows that if he defies us long enough, eventually our allies will desert us ... A, we don't have the capability anymore of keeping the coalition together and, B, the American people will get tired of the issue.' The solution again was to remove Saddam from power rather than attempt to contain him indefinitely.[13]

By November 1998, according to Representative Floyd Spence, then Chair of the House Committee on National Security and the House Armed Services

Committee, Clinton's containment policy had lost its way. Spence argued that 'the long-term resolve and ability of the United States to bring about the desired changes in Iraq' was being questioned. He warned that containment would not last because Iraq's repeated challenges to the UN and United States had left the coalition of states that ousted him from Kuwait in 1991 'frustrated, fatigued, and divided', with 'little political support among the countries of the original anti-Iraq coalition for unilateral U.S. military action'.[14] Representative Lee Hamilton, previously a supporter of containment, accepted this logic. He too declared containment unsustainable because it had not changed the defiant regime in Iraq, and 'seven years after the Gulf War, friends and allies have little enthusiasm for open-ended UN sanctions against Iraq'.[15]

The view that containment could not endure because of political fatigue and diminishing coalition support was reiterated in September 1999 by Senator Jesse Helms, then Chair of the Senate Committee on Foreign Relations. 'By a process of longevity, attrition, digging in', Helms argued, 'he [Saddam Hussein] has just decided that time is not a factor for him. And the world community in some respects has grown tired, tired of the continuation of the same problem, the recurrent Iraq syndrome.' The solution was by now a familiar one: '[if] the United States is serious about ensuring stability in that region by disarming Iraq', Helms concluded, 'Saddam is going to have to be ousted first.'[16]

Congressional criticism of the administration's containment strategy was compounded by the absence of a convincing long-term strategy for dealing with Saddam Hussein. As Senator Kyl implored in August 1998,

> Many of us in the Senate, through meetings with members of the administration, through correspondence, and through public hearings and statements, have tried to get the administration to focus on a long-term strategy that would have as its ultimate goal not containing Saddam Hussein but eliminating Saddam Hussein. No one believes that this is easy. It is a long-term project, and it takes a real commitment. This administration has not been willing to make that commitment.[17]

Not only was the administration unwilling to set out a strategy for regime change, but, according to its critics, it was also unable to present a credible long-term strategy of containment. As the administration geared up for air strikes in 1998 that eventually found form in Operation Desert Fox, Congressional critics expressed frustration at the absence of a long-term plan. 'It has become painfully clear', argued Senator Rod Grams in February 1998, 'that the Administration refuses or – perhaps more disturbingly – cannot consistently answer four basic questions: (1) What are the Administration's goals; (2) how will limited air strikes achieve those objectives; (3) what happens after the bombing stops; and (4) what is our endgame?'[18] As Operation Desert Fox drew to a close, Representative Spence protested that 'the administration has repeatedly failed to answer the 'what's next' question', adding that until the administration crafted a credible strategy for removing Saddam Hussein, future air strikes would reap diminishing returns until they had little or no effect.[19]

Congress and regime change

The solution to the failing Clinton policy and the absence of a credible long-term strategy for dealing with the enduring threat posed by Iraq was a new policy explicitly aimed at removing Saddam Hussein from power. Representative Christopher Cox, then Chair of the Republican Policy Committee, encapsulated this in February 1998: 'A thoughtful policy toward Iraq', he proposed, 'involves an active effort to deal with the root of the problem – not just weapons of mass murder, but the sadistic despot who has already used them against his own people.... Neither Iraq's people nor its neighbors can enjoy lasting security while Saddam Hussein remains in power.'[20]

Dismayed and alarmed at the administration's reluctance to embrace such a policy, Clinton's Congressional critics took matters into their own hands and passed the Iraq Liberation Act in October 1998. 'I would rather the administration develop a policy and a strategy and execute it with the cooperation of the Senate,' insisted Senator Kyl, 'but if the administration is unwilling to do that, then the Senate will have to get involved.'[21] The Act was introduced by Representative Ben Gilman in the House and then passed to the Senate. It explicitly called for the removal of Saddam Hussein's regime: 'It should be the policy of the United States to support efforts to remove the regime headed by Saddam Hussein from power in Iraq and to promote the emergence of a democratic government to replace that regime.'[22] The bill was passed in the House of Representatives by a vote of 360–38 and approved by unanimous consent in the Senate. Clinton signed the bill into law on 31 October 1998.[23] The unanimous passage in the Senate and small opposition in the House demonstrated unequivocal support for a change in policy.

Every Democrat Senator voted in favour of the legislation and accepted that regime change should be the main objective of the administration's Iraq policy, including two senior Democrat presidential hopefuls. Senator John Kerry, Democrat presidential candidate in 2004, said on *ABC News* in February 1998 that 'We have to be prepared to go the full distance, which is to do everything possible to disrupt [Saddam's] regime and to encourage the forces of democracy' and vowed that he was personally prepared to sanction use of ground troops if necessary.[24] In March 2000 Senator Joseph Biden, Democrat ranking member of the Senate Foreign Relations Committee, accepted this argument. 'Saddam is the problem. Saddam is in place. Saddam is not going anywhere unless we do something relatively drastic. It is clear our allies are not prepared to do anything drastic.' Biden was in fact ready to go further and declared his willingness to introduce a resolution with Republican Senator Sam Brownback 'calling for the use of force by the United States of America if we have to do it alone to go after Saddam Hussein' if Baghdad continued to refuse UN inspections.[25] Two years earlier in February 1998 Biden had argued that containment was the best approach.[26] Now he appeared to be advocating unilateral military action to remove Saddam Hussein from power.

The ILA placed considerable emphasis on the formation of a united Iraqi opposition centred on the Iraqi National Congress (INC) and allocated $97 million to assist the opposition to undermine Saddam Hussein's regime. The INC was established in June 1992 by the two main Kurdish militias – the Kurdistan Democratic Party (KDP) and the Patriotic Union of Kurdistan (PUK). In October 1992 the major Shi'ite groups came into the coalition and it evolved into an umbrella organisation for other Iraqi opposition groups such as the Iraqi National Accord, the Iraqi Communist Party and the Supreme Assembly of the Islamic Revolution in Iraq. The INC received substantial funding from Congress throughout the 1990s but it was plagued by in-fighting and was never in a position to mount a viable challenge to Saddam's regime.[27] From late 1998 until the end of the Clinton administration, however, the Iraqi opposition did become more united and received substantial support from members of Congress who favoured regime change.[28]

When Clinton signed the ILA into law the main supporters of the Act in Congress had a clear conception of what the government should do. They interpreted the legislation as a major shift in policy away from containment and towards regime change engineered by a US-trained and -equipped opposition force that would bring democracy to Iraq.[29] According to Senator Lott, the ILA was supposed to serve as a roadmap to removing Saddam Hussein in place of the unsustainable containment strategy.[30] Bob Kerrey, then a Democrat Senator and Vice Chair of the Senate Select Committee on Intelligence, articulated this view in March 2000: 'When he signed the Iraq Liberation Act into law on October 31, 1998, Clinton began the process of shifting away from the failed policy of using military force to contain Iraq to supporting military force to replace the military dictatorship of Saddam Hussein with a democratically elected government.'[31] In passing the ILA, Kerrey continued, 'Congress expressed its frustration with the status quo and provided resources with which the Administration could support the Iraqi opposition in their efforts to remove Saddam from power. In signing the Iraq Liberation Act, Clinton affirmed that U.S. policy was not merely to restrain Saddam but to see him replaced.'[32]

The Clinton administration had a different view. It saw the ILA as a means of facilitating regime change in the long term based on the activities of opposition groups inside and outside Iraq, aided by the US government though primarily non-military means. Before long the administration's Congressional critics were convinced that the White House was not prepared to fully support the INC or develop and prioritise a clear and robust strategy for regime change as required by the ILA. In November 1999 Senator Brownback berated the administration for its 'failure to match action to rhetoric in the case of Iraq' and for not 'moving nearly aggressively enough to remove Saddam Hussein'.[33] Brownback expressed his frustration again in June 2000: 'It is hard for me to figure out why administration officials, from President Clinton and Vice President Gore on down, keep insisting they are interested in ousting Saddam, and yet not one official of this administration has been willing to take even the most minimal steps toward that end.'[34] This exasperation culminated in a letter to Clinton in August 1999 from the 'principal proponents' of the ILA, Senators and Representatives Trent Lott, Joseph Lieberman, Jesse Helms, Robert Kerrey, Richard Shelby, Sam Brownback, Benjamin Gilman and Howard Berman. They wrote to express their dismay 'over the continued drift in U.S. Policy toward Iraq'. 'The Administration is not giving the Iraqi opposition the political support it needs to seriously challenge Saddam,' the letter stated. 'While Administration spokesmen sometimes have expressed support for the Iraq Liberation Act, all too often they distanced themselves from, if not ridiculed, the policy you endorsed last November 15.' The letter accused the administration of failing to use the money released by Congress to support Iraqi opposition activities. It claimed that the White House had spent less than $500,000 of the $8 million released in 1998 and that 'the opposition has received no assistance whatsoever from the $97 million in military assistance made available under the Iraq Liberation Act'.[35]

The frustration in Congress at the administration's inability to present a coherent long-term strategy and its reluctance to fully commit to the ILA was fuelled by fervent opposition from Washington's network of conservative think-tanks.

Opposition from Conservative think-tanks

Washington is home to a plethora of think-tanks that analyse and advocate policy on a host of issues. A number of them have strongly conservative views and focus on issues of national security. They include organisations such as the Project for a New American Century (PNAC), the Heritage Foundation, the American Enterprise Institute and the Center for Security Policy as well as more moderate conservative organisations such as the Washington Institute for Near East Policy (WINEP). A number of influential experts in the wider national security community were deeply critical of the administration's Iraq policy and fiercely advocated a strategy of regime change. Many were resident in these conservative think-tanks and had served in previous governments. These critics have been categorised as a cohesive group and often labelled 'neo-conservatives' in mainstream political discourse. They are considered to exert a significant amount of influence. Neo-conservatism and its influence on Iraq policy are explored in Chapter 10.

Many of these conservative national security experts first entered government during the administrations of Ronald Reagan and George H. W. Bush. When Clinton came to office in 1993, many took up positions as fellows, advisers or directors at conservative think-tanks that supported their views. The links between many of these people are substantial. Many have worked together in government, have sat on the same boards of advisers of conservative think-tanks or worked in the same institutes. As a result this network often shares a particular view on issues of US national security, views that are regularly published in the mainstream US press.[36] This section explores the consensus opinion on Clinton's Iraq policy at the end of his presidency.

Prominent individuals at these think-tanks and other organisations argued vigorously against containment throughout Clinton's final years. They viewed the administration's approach as weak and failing, and argued that this stemmed from Clinton's liberal internationalist foreign policy. The result of Clinton's failing containment, they argued, would be a WMD-armed Saddam Hussein able to dominate the Persian Gulf, and they concluded that an aggressive policy of regime change was the only effective solution. These criticisms reflected and supported those made in Congress.

These conservative experts developed a number of different strategies for achieving regime change and they presented them in testimony before Congressional committee hearings on Iraq policy, where they received considerable support. Their ideas were summed up in three important letters to the White House and Congress in 1998 that were signed by a host of influential conservative national security experts. A number of these went on to serve in the George W. Bush administration and had a major influence on the administration's decision to take the war on terrorism to Iraq. The criticisms of Clinton's containment strategy explored here reflect a view that became widespread within the George W. Bush administration.

A weak and failing strategy

Clinton's Iraq policy was regularly characterised as weak and failing, and was vociferously denounced by a number of conservative commentators. In February 1998 Kim Holmes and James Phillips of the Heritage Foundation argued that the Clinton administration had 'conveyed an image of weakness and indecision over the past five years in defense and foreign policy matters, particularly with regard to Iraq'.[37] In September 1998, John Bolton, later Under Secretary of State for Arms Control and International Security for George W. Bush, condemned the administration's Iraq policy as 'worse than incompetent', declaring containment unsustainable.[38] The following December he argued in the *Weekly Standard* that 'seven years of incompetence' had left the administration 'precious few options to reverse the downward drift of our Iraq policy', describing Clinton's foreign policy as 'inattentive' and 'feckless'.[39] The *Weekly Standard* is a leading conservative political journal edited by William Kristol, Chair of PNAC.

Beyond general indictments, conservative think-tanks levelled two fundamental criticisms at Clinton's policy that mirrored those made in Congress: containment was unsustainable and the White House lacked a credible long-term strategy for dealing with Saddam Hussein. In February 1998 Robert Kagan and William Kristol, co-founders of PNAC, challenged the administration's prognosis on Iraq. They argued that containment of Saddam Hussein was an illusion:

The notion that we can sustain a policy of deterring Saddam for another 10 or 20 years is ludicrous. The administration couldn't hold the international coalition together; it couldn't control the U.N. secretary general; it couldn't get Arab states to allow U.S. aircraft to launch attacks.... Who honestly believes this administration will be capable of sustaining a containment policy for another six months, much less into the next century?[40]

In testimony before the House International Relations Committee in October 1998, Senior Vice President of the American Enterprise Institute (AEI), John Bolton, tore down the administration's containment policy, claiming it had '(1) presided over the disintegration of the international coalition forged in the immediate aftermath of the Iraqi invasion of Kuwait, losing the bulk of both our European and Arab allies; (2) frustrated, restrained and undercut UNSCOM in a way that leaves its credibility shattered; and (3) lost any real opportunity to retain effective economic sanctions against Iraq'.[41]

The following January Robert Kagan accused Clinton of being 'bereft of a policy toward Iraq' and condemned Clinton's reluctance to pursue regime change. 'Clinton's national security team', he said, 'utters vague promises about containment, about keeping Saddam "in his box", but they cannot begin to explain how they intend to accomplish this.'[42] WINEP's Patrick Clawson berated the administration before the Senate for 'presenting regime change as a long-term aim ... with the implication that in the short term, little will be done to promote it'.[43] Richard Perle, resident scholar at AEI and later chair of the Defense Policy Board under George W. Bush, denounced Clinton's Iraq policy as a failure. 'The evidence', he said in June 2000, 'is overwhelming that during the lifetime of this administration Saddam's regime has become stronger and not weaker.'[44]

Liberal internationalism at fault

Clinton's weakness in respect of Iraq was often blamed on his administration's liberal internationalist worldview. This view in part explained Clinton's reluctance to use force against Iraq and his deferment to the UN in dealing with Saddam. It was a view abhorred by hard-line conservatives. In December 1998 Bolton summed this up in the *Weekly Standard*:

[Clinton's] embarrassing failure in November to punish Iraq militarily illuminates two broad and profoundly disturbing themes of his foreign policy. The first is his near-compulsive unwillingness to use decisive military force to achieve critical American objectives, even when conditions are nearly ideal. The second is his addictive adherence to multilateralism, reflected here in his continued preference for U.N. weapons inspections over the elimination of Saddam Hussein's regime.[45]

45

Bolton was joined by Reuel Marc Gerecht, Director of PNAC's Middle East Initiative, who accused the administration of camouflaging its indifference, weakness and 'small-power policy' toward Iraq 'in a loud internationalism characterized by half-hearted military action'.[46] He was joined by Robert Kagan, who attacked the administration's 'visceral commitment to multilateralism and international consensus' in its policy towards Iraq.[47] Holmes and Phillips of the Heritage Foundation argued that Clinton was sacrificing American national interests on Iraq 'on the altar of U.N. multilateralism'.[48] Meanwhile the Center for Security Policy deplored the administration's assertion that US and UN interests over Iraq were the same, insisting US interests were 'not identical to the lowest-common-denominator product of UN deliberations'.[49]

A WMD-armed Saddam

Conservative critics were convinced that Clinton's weak and failing Iraq policy would inevitably lead to the political accommodation of Saddam Hussein and a resurgent Iraq armed with WMD able to control the Persian Gulf and wider Middle East at will. As PNAC's Gary Schmitt argued in June 1998, Clinton's containment would 'inevitably lead to policies of accommodation by both the U.S. and its allies', and a WMD-armed Saddam Hussein able to deter the United States and dominate the Persian Gulf.[50] WINEP's Patrick Clawson concurred that the leaking sanctions regime would not stop Baghdad developing WMD. Instead it would inexorably transform Saddam Hussein 'from a tinhorn dictator into a world-class threat'.[51] Robert Kagan and William Kristol argued that containment would soon lead to 'détente' that would eventually become 'appeasement'. In the end, they claimed, 'ever more Kofi Annan-style concessions' would lead to the 'full emancipation of Saddam'.[52] With French and Russian proposals to lift sanctions and establish a diluted UN inspections process gathering momentum in 1999, Kagan was sure that the administration would soon buckle and accept their proposals.[53]

Conservative pressure for regime change

The solution to Clinton's weakness, the collapse of containment and the resurgence of Saddam was clear to the administration's critics: the regime had to be removed sooner rather than later and US military firepower was the key. 'By now it should be beyond debate', Bolton argued in December 1999, 'that only Saddam's removal can realistically forestall Iraq's ability to produce weapons of mass destruction.'[54] 'Saddam must go', championed Kagan and Kristol in January 1998,[55] and the administration should be 'willing to use U.S. air power and ground troops to get rid of him'.[56] Time was of the essence, and unless Saddam was removed soon he was sure to wield his WMD.[57]

The Heritage Foundation's James Anderson counselled that 'the evil lies in the person of Saddam, not in the weapons at his disposal'. Regime change was the way forward.[58] Robert Satloff, WINEP's Executive Director, warned that every day Saddam remained power was a setback for US interests, prestige and credibility,[59] while PNAC's Mark Lagon declared that 'the only solution for the threat Iraq poses is to remove Saddam'.[60] In testimony before the Senate Committee on Armed Services in September 2000 Richard Perle stated that 'the only solution to the danger posed by Saddam Hussein is a sustained, determined plan to remove him from power'.[61]

Strategies for regime change

With regime change the favoured solution to the perceived error of Clinton's ways on Iraq, a number of conservative critics advocated a range of plans for regime change from broad principles to well-formed strategies. The key to regime change did not lie in 'in marching U.S. soldiers to Baghdad, but in helping the Iraqi people to liberate themselves from Saddam'.[62] An 'enormous latent opposition' to Saddam existed, it was argued, but it required US military support to galvanise it into bringing down the regime in Baghdad. The Iraqi opposition could only effect this if it was backed by American military power from both the air and on the ground. 'Support for the opposition should be only a part of a broader political–military strategy', Mark Lagon argued, 'one which must include a willingness to send U.S. ground forces into Iraq to complete the unfinished business of the Gulf War.'[63]

The most clearly formulated plan came from Paul Wolfowitz, then Dean and Professor of International Relations at the Paul H. Nitze School of Advanced International Studies at Johns Hopkins University, and later Deputy Secretary of Defense under George W. Bush. He argued that a new 'liberated zone' should be established in southern Iraq where the Iraqi opposition and disaffected Iraqi army units could safely rally and organise a credible alternative to Saddam Hussein's regime. This zone would require US air protection, and ground troops if necessary. From there a provisional government could be established and gain international recognition and support. To facilitate this, the provisional government would take control of the largest oil field in Iraq and use that oil wealth for political, humanitarian and eventually military purposes under appropriate international supervision. This would enable the safe area to be expanded, leading to the liberation of larger and larger areas of Iraq and the unravelling of the regime.[64] Wolfowitz set out this strategy in a number of fora, including testimony before Congress in 1998 and a letter with former Republican Representative Stephen Solarz to the respected journal *Foreign Affairs* in March 1999. The letter argued that 'overthrowing Saddam would be a formidable undertaking, not one without problems and perils. But the risks of the gradual collapse of current U.S. policy are worse. The United States should be prepared to commit ground forces to protect a sanctuary in southern Iraq where the opposition could safely mobilize.'[65]

Richard Perle consistently argued for the use of military force to remove Saddam Hussein from power. In 1996 Perle and Douglas Feith, later Under

Secretary of Defense for Policy for George W. Bush, produced a report for the incoming Israeli government of Benjamin Netanyahu. The report, *A Clean Break: A New Strategy for Securing the Realm*, advocated forcibly removing Saddam Hussein from power.[66] In September 2000 Perle lent full support to the regime change plan developed by Wolfowitz. In testimony before Congress he contended that 'The United States, alone if necessary, with our friends if possible, should aggressively support the nascent opposition to Saddam's regime. We should organize, finance, equip, train and protect an Iraqi opposition broadly representative of all the people of Iraq.'[67]

In December 1998 James Phillips of the Heritage Foundation urged the administration to unite the INC and establish a provisional government in the area protected by the northern no-fly zone. The US should establish 'no-drive zones' for the Iraqi army in the north and south of the country and join the two no-fly zones to cover all of Iraq. To increase incentives for defections to the opposition, the United States should insist that the UN lift economic sanctions on territory controlled by the opposition. The opposition should then develop 'a strong guerrilla warfare infrastructure' to take control of Iraq's northern and southern oil fields with US assistance.[68]

In March 1998 Douglas Feith outlined a similar plan in the *Jerusalem Post* based on establishing 'no-drive zones', protecting the northern and southern no-fly zones for Iraqi opposition forces, giving the opposition control of Iraq's oil revenue, lifting sanctions from these areas, encouraging defections through a Radio Free Iraq and using US military power to repel any action by Saddam Hussein to disrupt such an operation.[69] A more moderate approach was espoused by the Washington Institute for Near East Policy. In late 2000 Executive Director Robert Satloff suggested that with sufficient provocation the US should 'mount debilitating air strikes on the pillars of the regime: the secret police, Saddam's personal guard units, and the Iraqi command-and-control system'. The hope here was that an opportunity to attack Saddam would arise if he stymied the efforts of a new UN inspections regime. In the meantime the US administration was urged to 'mount an aggressive public information campaign aimed at the Iraqi people, the Arab world, our allies, and the American polity' in preparation for a 'dramatic ratcheting-up of U.S. policy' to oust Saddam Hussein.[70]

Guaranteed success

The feasibility of these strategies was challenged by some, but those who advocated them were convinced they could work. Paul Wolfowitz argued in his statement before the House of Representatives in 1998 that 'The situation today is easier in many respects: Iraq is far weaker; American strength is much more evident to everyone.' All the administration had to do was 'muster the necessary strength of purpose' and then it could 'liberate ourselves, our friends and allies in the region, and the Iraqi people themselves, from the menace of Saddam Hussein'.[71] Similarly William Kristol insisted in March 1998 that 'Iraq has a regime that can easily be toppled with an assertive, proactive political and military strategy.'[72] In February 1998 the Center for Security Policy envisaged that the Iraqi people would rise up in support of US action and overthrow Saddam's regime.[73] In 2000, leading members of the Iraqi opposition met with the INC's supporters in Congress. They claimed they were ready to bring down Saddam's regime; all they needed was 'a stronger mandate from the United States'.[74] The administration's conservative critics demanded that Clinton grant such a mandate.

Many members of Congress and conservative national security experts argued that the Iraq Liberation Act gave the President full power to implement their plans. Under the Act Clinton could legitimately provide full economic, political and military support to the INC, establish a provisional Iraqi government in either the southern or northern areas of Iraq beyond Baghdad's control and use US military force to protect and expand the occupied area.[75]

Clinton's response

Whilst the administration firmly believed that the Iraqi people and regional security would be greatly enhanced if Saddam Hussein was no longer in power, it did not have much faith in the ability of opposition groups to mount a credible challenge to Saddam Hussein. In response to the regime change plans formulated by conservative think-tank critics, Secretary of State Madeleine Albright argued that

> some have suggested that the solution is to arm and encourage the Iraqi opposition to initiate a civil war. That option sounds – but is not – simple. We have worked with Iraqi opponents of Saddam Hussein in the past, and we are ready to work with them more effectively in the future. But the opposition is currently divided, and it would be wrong to create false or unsustainable expectations.[76]

In March 1999 there was still much work to be done before even considering arming the Iraqi opposition, as Assistant Secretary of State Martin Indyk explained: 'There are a host of issues that must be resolved before such equipment and training could be provided with confidence that it would advance our objectives of promoting a change of regime and not just lead to more Iraqis being killed unnecessarily.'[77] General Anthony Zinni, Head of US Central Command, openly opposed implementing the sort of insurgency plan in support of the Iraqi opposition advocated by members of Congress and hard-line conservative critics in Washington's think-tanks.[78]

A number of other knowledgeable commentators, such as James Noyes, Deputy Assistant Secretary of Defense for Near Eastern, Africa and South Asia Affairs from 1970 to 1976, poured scorn on the regime change plans. Noyes argued that 'the proposition that the United States can lead in the overthrow of Saddam and the engineering of a new political structure in Iraq is a pretense'.[79]

A damning 1999 *Foreign Affairs* article by Daniel Byman, Kenneth Pollack and Gideon Rose systematically debunked 'the rollback fantasy'. They argued that any form of US military support to an armed INC would fail because the Iraqi opposition fundamentally lacked unity, sufficient manpower, heavy weaponry or support from any of Iraq's neighbours for such a venture. Such an initiative would soon be crushed by Saddam's military forces and the US could quickly find itself sucked into a major long-term military commitment.[80]

Three letters

The hard-line position advocated against Iraq by influential experts and former policy-makers in Washington's conservative think-tanks was set out in three important letters, important because of their content and the signatories. Two were sent to Clinton and one to Republican Congressional leaders. The first letter to Clinton in January 1998 argued that

> current American policy toward Iraq is not succeeding ... we may soon face a threat in the Middle East more serious than any we have known since the end of the Cold War ... We urge you to seize that opportunity, and to enunciate a new strategy that would secure the interests of the U.S. and our friends and allies around the world. That strategy should aim, above all, at the removal of Saddam Hussein's regime from power.[81]

The second letter to Clinton was sent from the Committee for Peace and Security in the Gulf in October 1998. It insisted that 'only a determined program to change the regime in Baghdad will bring the Iraqi crisis to a satisfactory conclusion ... What is needed now is a comprehensive political and military strategy for bringing down Saddam and his regime ... ' The letter advocated establishing a provisional government in areas beyond Saddam Hussein's current control, protecting anti-Saddam forces in northern and southern parts of Iraq and launching 'a systematic air campaign against the pillars of his power – the Republican Guard divisions which prop him up and the military infrastructure that sustains him'.[82]

The third letter was sent to Newt Gingrich, Speaker of the House of Representatives, and Trent Lott, Senate Majority Leader (both Republicans) in May 1998. It declared that

> the administration has failed to provide sound leadership, we believe it is imperative that Congress take what steps it can to correct U.S. policy toward Iraq. That responsibility is especially pressing when presidential leadership is lacking or when the administration is pursuing a policy fundamentally at odds with vital American security interests ... U.S. policy should have as its explicit goal removing Saddam Hussein's

regime from power and establishing a peaceful and democratic Iraq in its place. We recognize that this goal will not be achieved easily. But the alternative is to leave the initiative to Saddam, who will continue to strengthen his position at home and in the region.[83]

The letter detailed a strategy based on three elements: the indictment of Saddam Hussein as a war criminal; the establishment of a provisional, representative government of Iraq in areas of Iraq not under Saddam's control; and the use of military force to protect these areas and, if necessary, to help remove Saddam Hussein from power.[84] Signatories of these letters, who went on to serve in the George W. Bush administration, are discussed in the next chapter.

Conclusion

During the Clinton administration's last few years its containment strategy foundered. There was little prospect of renewed inspections, the economic sanctions regime was crumbling and Clinton had no desire to use military force to resolve the problems posed by Saddam Hussein. The United States, it seemed, would have to sit tight and do what it could to keep Saddam contained unilaterally and hope that the Iraqi opposition might be capable of seizing power with US support at some point in the future.

This state of affairs was deemed unacceptable by influential national security intellectuals and former policy-makers resident at or involved with conservative think-tanks in Washington. Broad criticisms of Clinton's foreign policy found full force in strong opposition to the administration's Iraq policy. These criticisms judged that policy a failure. The sanctions regime, it was argued, was unravelling as the rot of 'sanctions fatigue' set in. The limited punitive use of force in Desert Fox achieved little and the unwillingness of the administration to go further was lamentable. UN weapons inspections had ceased and had failed to disarm Iraq of the WMD that it almost certainly still possessed. The Gulf War coalition had disintegrated because of the administration's refusal to deal decisively with Saddam Hussein's intransigence. In sum, containment was no longer viable and had ceased to be viable since 1998.

Senior members of Congress, primarily conservative Republicans, also articulated profound dissatisfaction with the administration's Iraq policy. They too considered the administration's policy a failure. They questioned the viability of containment as practised by the administration and were alarmed by the absence of a credible long-term strategy for dealing with Saddam Hussein. They condemned the administration's reluctance to use force beyond a few days of punitive air strikes in December 1998 and were troubled by the administration's apparent willingness to 'contract out US foreign policy' to the UN.[85] Congress and the network of conservative think-tanks represented two powerful centres of influence. Together they reinforced each other's views and lambasted the administration on Iraq.

51

Both sets of critics argued that only two options remained. The first was to do nothing and gradually release Baghdad from the obligations imposed immediately before and after the Gulf War while implementing a diluted and largely unilateral containment strategy. This would involve reverting to a deterrent relationship with Iraq while hoping that a more progressive government would replace Saddam's brutal regime. Clinton's critics rejected this because the end result, they argued, would be a nuclear-armed Saddam Hussein seizing Kuwaiti and Saudi oil fields. This scenario was not one that they wished to entertain. The belief that Saddam had been within six to twelve months of developing a nuclear weapon before the Gulf War unbeknownst to the IAEA, and the fact that he had invaded Kuwait and amassed forces on the Saudi border soon after, lent credence to this scenario.

The other option was to pro-actively work to replace the regime by uniting, training and arming the Iraqi opposition and supporting an opposition insurgency with US firepower. This required a shift in policy toward an explicit goal of regime change through a united Iraqi opposition. To encourage such a shift, a group of senior Senators and Representatives sponsored the Iraq Liberation Act to realise this goal. The legislation received overwhelming bipartisan support in both Houses of Congress. However, the administration neither interpreted the objective of regime change nor implemented strategies to depose Saddam Hussein in the manner intended by the ILA's sponsors. As James Noyes observed, Clinton had 'dawdled with a non-starter "regime change" policy for Iraq' in order to acquiesce 'in the latter's promotion by Congress to soothe political frustrations over Saddam's continued defiance'.[86]

The Congressional critics became increasingly exasperated with Clinton's Iraq policy and deeply concerned about the long-term threat posed by Saddam Hussein's WMD and his history of defiance and aggression. With the election of George W. Bush in November 2000, many of Clinton's conservative critics in Congress and Washington's conservative think-tanks hoped that a strategy of regime change would be swiftly adopted and implemented. When a number of hard-line conservative national security intellectuals who strongly advocated regime change were appointed to the Bush administration it seemed highly probable that a renewed confrontation with Iraq would occur during the new president's first term. The only questions were how and when. Nevertheless, an armed invasion to destroy the regime and then occupy the country until a transitional and then democratically elected representative government could be installed was not, at this stage, considered a viable option.

4

RETHINKING IRAQ: A NEW PRESIDENT AND NEW FOREIGN POLICY

Introduction

On 21 January 2001 George W. Bush was inaugurated as President of the United States. It soon became clear that the new administration was going to take a tough stand on two foreign policy issues: missile defence and 'rogue' states. It was also obvious that the Clinton administration's Iraq policy was going to be reviewed. Many in the Bush administration considered containment a failure. The regular and consistent criticism of Clinton's Iraq policy from residents of conservative think-tanks that were appointed to the new administration suggested that the Bush administration would replace Clinton's Iraq policy with a much more overt and forceful strategy of regime change.

When the administration entered office it did not have a fully fledged strategy for Iraq. Instead Iraq policy underwent a lengthy and comprehensive inter-departmental review, along with policy on other 'rogue' states such as North Korea. Iraq was one of a handful of national security priority issues for Bush, even though the new administration did not intend to take any decisive action in its first six to twelve months. In the second week of the new administration the president took part in a 75-minute meeting with the Joint Chiefs of Staff on conflict areas where the United States might need to send troops. Half of the meeting was devoted to Iraq and the Persian Gulf.[1] However, the most pressing national security issue was the development and deployment of ballistic missile defence systems and withdrawal from the constraints imposed by the 1972 Anti-Ballistic Missile (ABM) Treaty.

Until the policy review was completed, the containment-plus strategy would be followed and in the first six months of the Bush administration Iraq policy focused on shoring up and tightening the sanctions regime. In the absence of UN inspections this remained the vital heart of containment. This effort was led by Secretary of State Colin Powell until the terrorist attacks of 11 September 2001 that caused a broad revision of the administration's national security strategy. Powell made it clear from the outset that the new administration's policy towards Iraq had two distinct dimensions: the multilateral UN dimension involving other members of the international community that Powell was pursuing on behalf of the President; and the unilateral US dimension – the administration's own policy – that was currently under review and might prove to be incompatible with the UN Security Council's strategy for dealing with Iraq. The division of Iraq policy into separate UN and US components signalled a marked divergence from Clinton's view that US interests and UN interests over Iraq were essentially the same.

Bush supported Powell's efforts to agree a new smart sanctions package in the UNSC and to install UNMOVIC inspectors in Iraq while the administration's review continued. However, indefinite containment was not what the President had in mind. The threat from Iraq's WMD was considered real and growing, and senior members of the new administration strongly supported a regime change strategy, particularly those in the Defense Department. Advocates of regime change continued to receive considerable support from Congress and conservative think-tanks urged the administration to take decisive action against Baghdad. The complicating factor here was that Powell favoured a long-term policy of tough containment rather than an aggressive policy of regime change. This factor had a significant impact on the administration's Iraq policy after 9/11.

The Vulcans

During the presidential campaign Bush's foreign policy was informed and coordinated by a group of experts that came to be known as the 'Vulcans'. The Vulcans, led by Condoleezza Rice, comprised Richard Perle, Richard Armitage, Dov Zackheim, Paul Wolfowitz, Stephen Hadley, Robert Blackwill and Robert Zoellick. Dick Cheney was centrally involved in the campaign, Donald Rumsfeld to a lesser extent.[2] Powell was largely peripheral to the campaign. The group included a number of experts from the conservative think-tanks that had consistently advocated the removal of Saddam Hussein, and others who had signed the three letters to Clinton and to Gingrich and Lott, referred to in the previous chapter, fiercely criticising containment and supporting regime change plans developed by people such as Paul Wolfowitz.

All of the above people were appointed to the administration, several to senior positions within the defence and foreign policy bureaucracies: Perle as Chair of the Pentagon's Defense Policy Board, Armitage as Deputy Secretary of State, Zackheim as US Trade Representative, Blackwill as US Ambassador to India, Hadley as Deputy National Security Advisor, Rice as National Security Advisor, Rumsfeld as Secretary of Defense, and Wolfowitz as Deputy Secretary of Defense. Cheney was elected Vice President.

The January 1998 letter to Clinton was signed by Wolfowitz, Zoellick, Rumsfeld and Perle. The May 1998 letter to Gingrich and Lott was signed by Armitage, Wolfowitz, Zoellick, Rumsfeld and Perle. The October 1998 letter to Clinton from the Committee for Peace and Security in the Gulf was signed by Wolfowitz, Perle, Zackheim, Armitage and Rumsfeld. A number of other signatories who did not number among the Vulcans but signed all three letters and were appointed to the administration included: John Bolton, appointed Under Secretary of State for Arms Control and International Security; Paula Dobriansky, Under Secretary of State for Global Affairs; Peter Rodman, Assistant Secretary of Defense for International Security Affairs; Zalmay Khalilzad, Senior Director for Gulf, Southwest Asia and Other Regional Issues in the National Security Council and later appointed Ambassador to Afghanistan and the Special Presidential Envoy to Free Iraqis; and Elliot Abrams, Senior Director for Democracy, Human Rights, and International Operations in the National Security Council and later Senior Director for Near East and North African Affairs. Two other signatories of the third letter who were appointed to the administration were Douglas Feith, Under Secretary of Defense for Policy and David Wurmser, Special Adviser to John Bolton and later Dick Cheney's Middle East Advisor. The lists of signatories for all three letters were peppered with advocates of regime change from conservative think-tanks, including William Kristol and Gary Schmitt of PNAC, Robert Kagan and Frank Gaffney of CSP, and Joshua Muravchik, Michael Ledeen and Jeffrey Gedmin of AEI.

It is important to highlight the extent to which these like-minded individuals formed a coherent group centred on a small number of think-tanks that developed and advocated hard-line nationalist and neo-conservative positions on US national security policy throughout Clinton's second term. Cheney, for example, was a signatory of PNAC's founding principles in 1997, a senior fellow at AEI from 1993 to 1995 and a member of the Jewish Institute for National Security Affairs (JINSA) advisory board in 2000. Rumsfeld, another signatory of PNAC's founding principles, is a long-time associate of the Center for Security Policy (CSP) and winner of its 1998 'Keeper of the Flame' award.

This is not to suggest the existence of a grand design or right-wing conspiracy, far from it, but simply to highlight the historic interconnectedness of a discrete group of individuals who share a cohesive staunchly conservative view of US foreign and defence policy and have interacted with one another, some more than others, through the Ford, Reagan and George H. W. Bush administrations, in Congress and Congressional commissions, and in think-tanks such as PNAC, AEI, CSP, JINSA and others.

Policy review

The Bush administration inherited the Clinton administration's containment-plus strategy developed through 1999–2000 after Operation Desert Fox. As described in Chapter 2, this comprised five main elements: aggressive action against Iraq's radar and anti-aircraft facilities when provoked in the no-fly zones and the right to take military action against any suspected WMD facilities; development of smart sanctions to target the regime and relieve the suffering of the Iraqi people as much as possible; efforts to install UNMOVIC inspectors in Iraq; efforts to reduce humanitarian suffering by expanding the oil-for-food programme and lifting restrictions on how much oil Iraq could export but retaining UN controls on oil revenue; and a formal policy of regime change as an explicit long-term goal of US foreign policy.

The Bush administration adhered to this strategy while it reviewed its long-term policy on sanctions and the no-fly zones and investigated, as Powell put it, 'whether or not there are organizations and people out there who are committed to a free Iraq, who might want to participate in activities that would lead to a change of regime'.[3] The review involved the State Department, the Department of Defense, the Commander in Chief (CINC) of Central Command, the Joint Chiefs of Staff and the National Security Council (NSC), with National Security Advisor Condoleezza Rice looking at the administration's overall policy.[4]

The review began almost immediately when Bush met with the principals (the heads of relevant government departments and agencies) of his National Security Council for the first time. Iraq and the regime's destabilising activities in the Middle East were on the agenda. Discussions focused on Iraq's WMD programmes, strategies for pressuring the regime and US military support for the Iraqi opposition. The reported outcome of the meeting was that Powell would draw up a new sanctions regime to replace the current one that was deemed ineffective and damaging to perceptions of the US in the region. Rumsfeld and Joint Chiefs of Staff Chairman General Hugh Shelton would re-examine the Pentagon's military options in Iraq.[5] It was apparent at this early stage that the administration was intent on moving beyond Clinton's containment-plus and adopting a more aggressive policy toward Saddam Hussein. Ron Suskind reported that the next meeting of NSC principals took place on 1 February 2001 with a review of current US policy in Iraq and examination of options on the agenda.[6] A further meeting occurred on 16 May. By then the State Department had produced a number of reports on the situation in Iraq, the Pentagon had explored a range of military options, and CIA director George Tenet had presented intelligence findings on Iraq's WMD, which he reportedly declared were only speculative.[7]

The review took many months and it is not clear if it was completed by 11 September. By August 2001 the administration's official position was that it had not yet fashioned a new policy on Iraq.[8] The only significant change was that the Bush administration actively pursued actions associated with the containment-plus strategy that the Clinton administration had put aside, such as supporting the Iraqi opposition with funds released under the ILA and developing a smart sanctions proposal to put to the UNSC.

Two processes were therefore at work during the first six months of the Bush administration. One was a continuation of the containment-plus strategy supported by Powell and to a certain extent by Rice and Bush. The second was a policy review that entailed examination of regime change strategies developed by conservative intellectuals in Washington's think-tanks, some of whom were now in the administration. This approach was championed by Wolfowitz and to a certain extent by Cheney and Rumsfeld. Cheney, for example, shortly before the presidential election in November 2000, volunteered that it might be necessary 'to take military action to forcibly remove Saddam from power'. This potential course of action was evidently in the Vice President's thoughts when the Bush administration entered the White House a few months later.[9]

Support for a full policy review that would lead to a firm policy of regime change flowed from conservative think-tanks and senior members of Congress. Mainstream press reports regularly interpreted statements on Iraq from the senior ranks of the Bush administration and military actions in support of the no-fly zones as evidence that the administration was planning to remove Saddam Hussein from power. Underlying the administration's review, as well as think-tank and Congressional support for regime change, were two assumptions. The first pervasive assumption – then reported as fact – was that Saddam Hussein still possessed weapons of mass destruction, retained functioning programmes to build more and was expanding those programmes as the sanctions regime deteriorated. The second was an assumption that the status quo could not continue. If the containment-plus strategy did not change Saddam Hussein's behaviour or lead to his regime's demise in the near future, and it was widely believed that it would not, then a serious strategy of regime change would be developed and implemented. Otherwise a WMD-armed Saddam would emerge to threaten the United States and its interests. Indefinite containment was dismissed as an illusion.

Powell and containment-plus under Bush

Powell did not advocate an aggressive strategy to remove Saddam Hussein from power; instead he promoted the containment-plus approach. He did this not just because wider Iraq policy was under review and containment-plus was all the administration had to work with, but because he favoured such an approach as the administration's permanent policy. Using language similar to that of his predecessor, Madeleine Albright, Powell argued that containment was a successful strategy that could continue to work. In his confirmation hearing before the Senate in January 2001 Powell argued that the United States should be 'steadfast in our policy towards Saddam Hussein' while supporting opposition efforts. This suggested a continuation of containment while providing limited support for the INC through the Iraq Liberation Act.[10]

Powell was later more explicit about his support for continued containment and his view that the INC might only be effective in the long term. On the former Powell stated in February 2001 that 'Iraq is pretty much contained right now, and we're going to keep it that way',[11] and that 'we have kept him contained, kept him in his box'.[12] Furthermore Powell suggested that containment would eventually result in the Iraqi leadership's enlightenment and cooperation. He suggested that 'containment has been a successful policy, and I think we should make sure that we continue it until such time as Saddam Hussein comes into compliance with the agreements he made at the end of the war',[13] and that 'he has to be contained until he realizes the errors of his ways'.[14] On the latter he said the INC could only be useful in terms of 'some of the public diplomacy actions they have undertaken, in broadcasting or getting information to the Iraqi people' and 'in terms of providing humanitarian relief', but not, it would seem, in terms of bringing down the regime.[15] In March he repeated the Clinton administration's formulation that 'hopefully, the day will come when circumstances will allow, permit, or it will happen within Iraq, [when] we see a regime change that will be better for the world'.[16] In stark contrast to Clinton's critics in Congress and conservative think-tanks, Powell mirrored his predecessor's approach by saying nothing about moving beyond a containment strategy or arming the INC and supporting its actions with US firepower.

Powell also downplayed the threat from Iraq, stating in February 2001 that Saddam had 'not developed any significant capability with respect to weapons of mass destruction. He is unable to project conventional power against his neighbors.'[17] Powell also maintained, as one might expect of the Secretary of State, that the United States should work with its allies to deal with Iraq through the UN, insisting that he and the President 'will be working with our friends in the region and our friends in the United Nations to hold them [the Iraqi leadership] to account for the obligations they made'.[18]

Bush seemed to support a continuation of containment for the time being, describing Saddam Hussein in August 2001 as a 'menace' that his administration would keep 'in check'.[19] Just how much support the President was willing to give Powell on the containment-plus strategy was not clear, but he did endorse Powell's development of a smart sanctions proposal that was a crucial part of the containment-plus strategy.[20]

Smart sanctions

The smart sanctions initiative involved tightening sanctions on military hardware, particularly those related to WMD, while removing most restrictions on materials for civilian use, including many items previously proscribed because of their 'dual-use' status as items that might be used in Iraqi WMD programmes.[21] The review and development of the sanctions regime was left in Powell's hands. In fact, this approach was decided before the administration entered office, with Powell stating in December 2000 and again at his confirmation hearing that the new administration planned to work with its allies to 're-energize the sanctions regime'.[22] Powell argued that reconfiguring sanctions would help to contain Iraq.[23] He acknowledged that the sanctions regime was in serious danger from smuggling and significant leakage when he took over, but he did not accept that the sanctions regime had collapsed, as many of Clinton's critics had argued.[24] 'It hasn't broken up, it hasn't fallen apart,' he stressed. 'A few planes going in from time to time does not cause this to be a failure. In fact, it's been quite a success for ten years...'[25]

In February 2001 Powell toured the Middle East to discuss Iraq and rally support for the smart sanctions initiative. He visited Egypt, Jordan and Syria to discuss means of tightening access into Iraq and to reach agreement on how to modify the sanctions regime through the UN Sanctions Committee.[26] By April, Powell was pleased with how far the sanctions policy review had gone and the new ideas that had been developed.[27] However, he had difficulty securing support from regional allies and other Arab countries and UNSC members. Several governments in the Middle East said they did not want to discuss Iraq and sanctions while the Palestinian al-Aqsa intifada that erupted in September 2000 continued, and voiced concerns about the apparent double standard regarding US policy towards Israel and its policy towards Iraq.[28] Nevertheless, throughout May 2001 Powell's team worked at the UN to reach agreement on reforming the sanctions regime. In June the UNSC reached agreement by a 15–0 consensus vote to continue the existing sanctions regime, while increasing the quantities of civilian goods allowed into Iraq. This would come into effect on 4 July for six months. As far as the new smart sanctions proposal was concerned, agreement had been reached and all that had to be worked out for the new regime to come into force was a new reduced list of proscribed items. It was agreed that this task would be completed in 30 days, but it proved to be far from simple.[29]

Despite the political consensus in the UNSC, Powell, to his frustration, encountered a host of bureaucratic obstacles to agreeing the new sanctionable items list.[30] Obstruction came in particular from Russia. Moscow had economic and commercial interests in Iraq and wished to see sanctions lifted altogether, rather than just reconfigured. Deputy Foreign Minister Sergie Ordzhonikidze rejected any reference to smart sanctions in the June resolution that kept the original sanctions package in place.[31] When it came to agreeing the new list to allow the new smart sanctions regime to come into effect at the start of July 2001, the US could only muster 14 votes, with Russia refusing to support the revised sanctions regime. In the end, the UNSC voted to keep the old regime in place for a further five months and try to reach an agreement during that period.[32] Naji Savri, Iraq's Minister of State for Foreign Affairs, described the postponement of the smart sanctions regime as a 'defeat for the Anglo-American policy against Iraq'.[33] Sanctions without end or without incentives faced increasing opposition not only from Russia, but from two other Security Council members, France and China.[34]

UNMOVIC

The issue of inspections remained in the background during the first eight months of the new administration. Bush insisted that Saddam Hussein re-admit UN weapons inspectors and 'open his country up for inspection, so we can see whether or not he's developing weapons of mass destruction',[35] and Powell called on Iraq to 'allow inspectors in so that they can verify that these weapons are no longer there, that they claim are no longer there'.[36] However, the administration was adamant that this time it would not plead with Iraq to let inspectors in, this time it was up to Iraq to cooperate fully: 'rather than us begging him to let the inspectors in, the burden is now on him'.[37] Condoleezza Rice was circumspect in her appraisal of the value of further inspections, arguing that whilst tough inspections unchallenged by Saddam Hussein would be a 'helpful step forward', this was an unlikely prospect since the US had 'been down this road before, and there is nothing in Iraq's past or present that suggests that they're serious about weapons inspections that would make clear that they have no weapons of mass destruction'.[38] For Rice, then, UNMOVIC did not have a central part to play in the administration's Iraq policy.

The bottom line of the containment-plus strategy remained the same for the Bush administration as it had for Clinton: on no account would it be acceptable for Saddam Hussein to have full access to oil revenues or full access to international markets through which he could develop WMD while he remained in violation of UNSC resolutions. That, in essence, meant that a credible sanctions regime had to remain in place until Saddam Hussein was removed from power or, in the unlikely event that Hussein lent full cooperation to UNMOVIC, for a sustained period of time to the satisfaction of the US government, after which a review of the sanctions regime might be warranted.[39]

Powell, however, suggested on several occasions that there was a way out for Saddam Hussein, perhaps indicating his preference for containment and hope of some form of long-term peaceful resolution of the enduring crisis with Iraq. He suggested that Saddam could find a way out if he would only allow inspectors to go back in: 'If the inspectors get in, do their job, we're satisfied with their first look at things, maybe we can suspend the sanctions. And then at some point way in the future, when we're absolutely satisfied there are no such weapons around, then maybe we can consider lifting.'[40] Powell, however, continued to make it quite clear in his statements that his brief focused only on the UN track of the administration's Iraq policy. His actions and statements did not reflect the second track of an overall review of the administration's Iraq policy and possible strategies for regime change. 'I will be concentrating on the UN part of the policy', he said, 'as opposed to the United States bilateral relationship with respect to Iraq and our other activities in the Gulf and with the Iraqi opposition.'[41]

Weapons of Mass Destruction

The administration believed that the threat to the United States posed by Iraq's WMD was clear and serious, as Clinton had done. Statements by administration officials suggested an enduring assumption that Iraq had WMD, or at the very least was actively pursuing WMD programmes. In March 2001 Condoleezza Rice argued 'there is a reason that Saddam Hussein does not want weapons inspections in Iraq … obviously he's got something to hide'.[42] Secretary of Defense Donald Rumsfeld was convinced in February 2001 that Iraq was developing WMD, or at least intended to develop them at the first opportunity: 'There's no question but that Saddam Hussein and his regime have had an enormous appetite for nuclear, chemical and biological weapons over a sustained period of time. There's nothing new about this. They have been, in varying degrees, successful in developing those types of capabilities.'[43] The potential threat from Iraq's ballistic missile programme was also cited by the Pentagon as a major justification for the development of a national missile defence system, based on the possibility that Iraq could build and deploy long-range ballistic missiles capable of reaching the United States in the future.[44]

The assumption that Iraq had or was developing WMD was reinforced by a number of reports and articles in late 2000 and in 2001. These intimated that Iraq's nuclear weapons programme, the most potentially devastating of Saddam's WMD programmes, was operational and successfully concealed. In November 2000 Iraqi defector Khidir Hamza, a nuclear weapons expert, insisted that Iraq was only months away from making a nuclear bomb if it could get hold of the necessary fissile material.[45] In January 2001 an Iraqi defector claimed that Saddam Hussein had two fully operational nuclear weapons and was working to construct others.[46] In addition, the conclusions of the UN's Amorim report remained valid since there had been no new inspections or actions by Baghdad to address disarmament issues deemed outstanding by UNSCOM before it left Iraq.

Of all the senior members of the administration's foreign and defence bureaucracies only Powell articulated a more moderate interpretation of the threat from Iraq's WMD. He too concluded that 'we have to assume that he has never lost his goal or gone away from his goal of developing such weapons [of mass destruction]'[47] and that 'we know he is working on weapons of mass destruction, we know he has things squirreled away.'[48] But despite his conviction that Saddam was developing WMD, he was equally convinced that threat from these programmes was small:

> even though we have no doubt in our mind that the Iraqi regime is pursuing programs to develop weapons of mass destruction – chemical, biological and nuclear – I think the best intelligence estimates suggest that they have not been terribly successful. There's no question that they have some stockpiles of some of these sorts of weapons still under their control, but they have not been able to break out, they have not been able to come out with the capacity to deliver these kinds of systems or to actually have these kinds of systems that is much beyond where they were 10 years ago.[49]

Bush and regime change

President Bush supported the containment-plus strategy and Powell's efforts to restructure the sanctions regime while the major review of policy on Iraq was under way. Nevertheless, long-term containment appeared far from his mind at the start of 2001 when he said 'No one had envisioned Saddam – at least at that point in history – no one envisioned him still standing. It is time to finish the task.'[50]

Before becoming National Security Advisor, Condoleezza Rice set out her views on foreign policy under a Bush government during the election campaign in 2000. In an article for the journal *Foreign Affairs*, which covered a range of subjects, including Iraq, Rice lent unqualified support to the goal of regime change, arguing that Saddam Hussein was 'determined to develop WMD. Nothing will change until Saddam is gone, so the United States must mobilize whatever resources it can, including support from his opposition, to remove him.'[51] Nevertheless, she considered this a long-term goal, arguing in August 2000 that 'The containment of Iraq should be aimed ultimately at regime change' and that by strengthening sanctions, using force aggressively when provoked and lending full support to the INC, then 'in the long run, you should succeed in creating a Saddam-free Iraq'.[52] This was, in essence, Clinton's containment-plus policy. Upon her appointment to the White House, Rice lent qualified support to the containment-plus strategy while arguing that such an approach could not, and would not, continue indefinitely. With the administration's review firmly under way, Rice stated in March 2001 that Bush had 'put the world on notice that the status quo with Iraq is not acceptable ... this is a regime that continues to threaten its neighbors, threaten its own people and threaten world peace and stability. And so it isn't a situation that can continue forever ... This is a problem the world had better get serious about very soon.'[53] In July 2001, paraphrasing the President, Rice said Saddam Hussein remained a persistent threat to the region and international security, and asserted that Bush had 'reserved the right to respond when that threat becomes one that he wishes no longer to tolerate,' hinting at the possibility of unilateral action in the future. 'The world can be certain of this,' she went on to say, 'Saddam Hussein is on the radar screen for this administration.'[54] At this early stage Bush suggested he would only take military action to remove the regime if Iraq were demonstrably developing WMD: 'if I found in any way, shape or form that he was developing weapons of mass destruction, I'd take him out'.[55]

The group of conservative national security experts brought in by Bush did not support the containment-plus option favoured by Powell and continued to push for a more aggressive strategy of regime change. Many of these were in the Defense Department. At the NSC principals' meeting in February 2001 Rumsfeld reportedly argued that 'sanctions are fine ... but what we really want to think about is going after Saddam'.[56] Wolfowitz was more explicit about regime change. In July 2001 he also described Saddam Hussein as 'a menace' who was only interested in 'overthrowing his neighbors' and 'acquiring weapons of mass destruction'. When asked whether the US should 'go after him', Wolfowitz replied 'When we find the right way to do it, I believe we should.'[57] He was supported by the Chair of the Defense Policy Board, Richard Perle, who insisted in January 2001 that 'What we have in mind is making it clear to Saddam and the world that we're in favor of seeing this regime change.'[58] He was even more explicit before the Senate in March 2001, arguing that US military force combined with the INC could remove Saddam from power. According to Perle, the

United States could do 'really quite extraordinary things with air power' in Iraq; 'this is not as daunting a prospect as people say it is'.[59] Perle was deeply sceptical of Powell's sanctions initiative and warned that smart sanctions would be interpreted as American weakness in the face of pressure. 'We don't have an effective policy now and the changes [Powell is proposing] won't be effective, either,' he said. 'We will not be protected from [weapons of mass destruction] as long as Saddam Hussein is in power', Perle insisted, 'We should concentrate our efforts on one policy that will work in removing him.'[60]

A number of conservative intellectuals in the administration, particularly those in the Defense Department, saw the removal of the regime in Baghdad as the key to resolving other problems in the Middle East. Following NSC discussions in the first half of 2001, Bush's Treasury Secretary Paul O'Neill reportedly stated that 'from the start we were building that case against Hussein and looking at how we could take him out and change Iraq into a new country. And, if we did that, it would solve everything. It was all about finding *a way to do it* [emphasis in the original].'[61]

The Pentagon was strongly in favour of regime change, and both Bush and Rice agreed that containment would not continue indefinitely. Meanwhile Powell and much of the State Department advocated the continuation of containment. This led to a serious division in the administration on the future of Iraq policy and the outcome of the policy review. In April 2001 it was reported that Richard Haass, Director of Policy Planning at the State Department and head of an interagency working group on Iraq policy, prepared a report outlining a set of options for US policy towards Iraq. One option, supported by Rumsfeld, Wolfowitz and Cheney's national security team, involved US backing of a military coup led by the INC, a plan similar to that developed by Wolfowitz and others towards the end of the Clinton administration. However, many State Department and CIA officials, it was reported, doubted the efficacy of the INC's plan to create a military opposition inside Iraq and opposed such a venture.[62]

From the start of Bush's term in office Iraq dramatically increased its attempts to shoot down British and American warplanes patrolling the northern and southern no-fly zones as the low-intensity conflict continued. Coalition aircraft routinely responded to Iraqi missile and anti-aircraft artillery fire by attacking individual weapons and radar sites. The Bush administration sanctioned more aggressive retaliation, in line with Clinton's containment-plus strategy. Nevertheless, Iraq was quick to repair any damage. In February 2001 coalition aircraft staged a large-scale attack on Iraqi early-warning radar and command-and-control sites near Baghdad, but by July it was reported that much of Iraq's air defence system had been rebuilt.[63] The increasing number of attacks reinforced sentiment in the Bush administration that the status quo was not an acceptable long-term proposition, and the February air strikes, the first time Baghdad had been hit since Operation Desert Fox, were viewed as a significant increase in pressure on Saddam Hussein.[64] After the air strikes Richard Perle advocated INC-led regime change as the only solution, confessing 'I don't see any other way of doing it. Sanctions can't be made tough enough. The West is not prepared to send in ground troops. It's got to be done by Iraqis.'[65] The February air strikes deepened the rift between America's European and Middle East allies over Iraq. In particular, both Germany and France denounced the February air strikes as illegal. Even at this stage it was clear that if the US was going to use force to remove Saddam Hussein it would be doing it either alone or with only Britain by its side.[66]

Conservative think-tanks

The conservative think-tanks that lambasted Clinton's Iraq policy continued to push the new Bush administration to aggressively pursue regime change in Baghdad. In the run-up to the November election Richard Perle, then resident scholar at AEI and one of Bush's 'Vulcans', when asked by Senator Sam Brownback how Bush would deal with Iraq should he become president, replied

> Governor Bush has said that we should, and he would, fully implement the Iraq Liberation Act. I think we all understand what that means. It means a serious and sustained effort to assist the opposition with a view to bringing down Saddam's regime. I am confident that when the Governor says that would be his policy, he means what he says.[67]

In January 2001 a Center for Security Policy decision brief gushed that it was

> enormously heartening, therefore, that senior ranks of the incoming Bush–Cheney Administration are likely to be populated by individuals who have, in the past, condemned the feckless Clinton effort to 'contain' the Butcher of Baghdad – and advocated a dramatically different approach aimed at ending Saddam's misrule and the threat it poses to his own, long-suffering people and others beyond his borders.[68]

The conservative think-tanks fully expected Bush to go after Saddam.

But as the administration's review process continued into the summer of 2001 some think-tanks began to lose heart. Tom Donnelly, deputy executive director of PNAC, for example, wrote in July 2001,

> George W. Bush came to office declaring he would 'defend America's interests in the Persian Gulf' by reviving 'the vision' of his father's 'Gulf War coalition'. But more was promised ... It now appears that those campaign promises aren't likely to be fulfilled ... In the wake of the failure of the 'smart sanctions' policy, it is increasingly difficult to countenance the fiction that Saddam Hussein remains safely 'in his box'. If the Bush Administration compounds the problem by embracing a defense review that takes a regime-changing 'ground option' off the

table, Saddam will not only be free of the threat of removal from power, but will have little to deter him from renewed trouble-making and oppression in the region.[69]

The Center for Security Policy also expressed its confusion about the Bush administration's Iraq policy, but urged the new government to pursue regime change:

> While the messages sent by various statements about smart sanctions and renewing international inspections of Iraqi weapons of mass destruction programs have been confusing, to say the least, the sorts of steps long advocated by senior members of the new Bush team would – if adopted as part of a comprehensive effort – have the greatest chance of undermining and ultimately bringing an end to the Iraqi despot's hold on power.[70]

The conservative think-tanks remained resolute in their prognosis of the threat posed by Saddam Hussein. Writing in the *Weekly Standard* in May 2001, PNAC's Reuel Marc Gerecht asked, 'Once Saddam has his nuke – as he inevitably will if he stays in power – will Washington gird its loins again, even if Saddam has not lately invaded any neighbors?' The solution remained INC-led regime change backed by US ground troops that were 'the key to instigating insurrection against the Ba'ath party'.[71] The think-tanks were deeply critical of the smart sanctions initiative, given the difficulty of securing Russian support and then gaining Syrian and Iranian cooperation to enforce the new regime should it be agreed by the UNSC. On 9 August 2001 WINEP's Michael Rubin warned that 'the State Department has proposed to revise sanctions to try to undermine Saddam Hussein's propaganda, but the approach is little more than appeasement'.[72] They also doubted the utility of further UN inspections and urged Bush to abandon this approach. WINEP's Patrick Clawson, for example, stressed that arms inspections should not constitute the 'centerpiece of U.S. Iraq policy' and that Bush 'should not sacrifice the goal of replacing Saddam in order to restart arms inspections, which experience suggests may no longer be particularly productive'.[73] Other analysts, such as Daniel Byman of RAND's Center for Middle East Public Policy, maintained that 'the return of UN arms inspectors would do more harm than good ... the nominal success of inspections today would give Saddam a free hand to develop WMD programs tomorrow'.[74]

Michael Ledeen of the AEI, who served as a consultant to both Reagan's national security adviser and defence secretary from 1982 to 1986, sounded the call to arms in the *National Review* in March 2001. He proclaimed that

> Bill Clinton squandered our great victory in Desert Storm, and Iraq once again threatens our national interests. We will not be able to reassemble the war party, and we will not have the support of our previous Middle

East allies until and unless they see that we are again serious in our resolve. That means taking the fight to Saddam. It means arming and training his democratic enemies, even though we can have no certainty about the outcome, and cannot be sure the struggle will be brief ... it is a brave strategy, altogether worthy of an outstanding leader. Let him pronounce the final words: We're going to fight, and we're going to win.[75]

Five months later, on August 30, 12 days before 11 September, Ledeen repeated his call, insisting that 'Saddam should have been driven from power, a disgraced and broken tyrant, long ago, and we should signal our intention to engage him by supporting the people he most fears ... [the President] should tell State and the Pentagon to give the Iraqi National Congress the wherewithal to fight'.[76]

Congress

A number of senior and influential Republican Senators and Representatives continued to push for a more aggressive strategy. In March 2001 Senator Sam Brownback, Chairman of the Senate Foreign Relations Committee's Subcommittee on Near Eastern and South Asian Affairs, cautioned against a new sanctions initiative. 'We have to bite the bullet,' he argued, 'and admit that sanctions have not achieved their desired goal ... the only answer is getting Saddam Hussein out of power.'[77] In March 2001, at a Senate hearing on US policy toward Iraq, former Senator Bob Kerrey pushed the Bush administration to implement the Wolfowitz regime change plan and recognise a provisional opposition government in Iraq, protect the northern and southern safe havens, lift sanctions on the liberated areas and back the INC with US military force.[78]

Rhetoric against Saddam Hussein continued to flow from Congress throughout the new administration's first eight months. For example, on 11 January Senator Jesse Helms declared

For the last eight years, we have watched as the Clinton administration has presided over the collapse of our Iraq policy. The Clinton people have abandoned weapons inspections, abandoned sanctions and ultimately, abandoned the people of Iraq themselves. We must have a new Iraq policy, and such a policy must be based on a clear understanding of this salient fact: Nothing will change in Iraq until Saddam Hussein is removed from power. Almost a decade has gone by since the United States liberated Kuwait from Saddam Hussein. The time has come to liberate Iraq as well.[79]

On 19 March 2001 Congressman Henry Hyde urged the Bush White House to 'actively embrace a policy to liberate Iraq and replace the regime of Saddam Hussein',[80] and on 30 July Representative Mark Kirk stressed that

Saddam Hussein was 'becoming an increasing security threat to the international system'.[81]

However, the Republican Party suffered a slight reversal in its fortunes in mid-2001 when Vermont Senator Jim Jeffords defected from the party and established himself as an independent Senator. The Senate had been split 50–50 between Republicans and Democrats, with the Vice President having a casting vote in the event of a split vote on an issue. With Jeffords gone, the Republicans' numbers fell to 49, giving the Democrats a majority of one and, more crucially, chairmanship of the Senate's powerful committees. With less support among Democrats for an aggressive regime change strategy, Jeffords's defection may have affected the administration's future Iraq policy, but with a razor-thin majority, Congressional Democrats could exert only minimal additional pressure for their agenda.

Conclusion

President Bush came into the White House determined to review Clinton's Iraq policy and pursue a more aggressive strategy against Saddam Hussein. He appointed a number of people with hard-line conservative views on national security and foreign policy to senior positions within the administration, a number of whom had developed and promoted strategies for regime change. A significant number had also signed the three letters to Clinton, and to Gingrich and Lott. They were bitterly critical of Clinton's containment and insisted before the 2000 election that it simply could not continue. It was an unsustainable illusion, a failure of US policy symptomatic of the weaknesses inherent in the Clinton administration's liberal internationalist worldview. They hoped that change was on its way in the form of a more forceful policy that, in all likelihood, could only result in a new confrontation between the Bush White House and Saddam Hussein within a few years, if not sooner. They resolutely advocated regime change, not as a supplement to the containment strategy, but as a wholesale replacement.

As the administration reviewed its Iraq policy, Bush and Rice supported the efforts of Secretary of State Colin Powell to implement the containment-plus approach inherited from the Clinton administration. This focused solely on the UN dimension of the administration's Iraq policy, through the restructuring of the sanctions regime with the smart sanctions initiative taking priority. Bush did not support the containment-plus policy as an enduring strategy for his administration; instead he lent it provisional support until the internal review was completed that would articulate a new and potentially more aggressive strategy to replace containment-plus. Cheney and Rumsfeld seemed prepared to tolerate this until the review was complete. They, and other senior members of the administration, considered the sanctions regime unworkable, a view compounded by Russian intransigence, and held the view that UNMOVIC inspections would be of little use. Both seemed to favour a forceful regime change strategy involving full support for the INC as the ultimate outcome of the review process. The escalating clashes in 2001 between US and UK aircraft patrolling the no-fly zones and Iraqi anti-aircraft batteries reinforced this view.

Bush, Rice, Cheney and Rumsfeld assumed that Saddam Hussein possessed WMD, or at the very least continued aggressive programmes to develop them, and that the containment-based status quo could not endure for much longer. Powell shared some of these views, but he also gave full support to the containment-plus strategy. He considered it a success and thought it should be continued, evidenced in language very similar to that of his predecessor, Madeleine Albright. This led to serious divisions in the administration on its long-term policy towards Iraq that were played out in the review process.

Throughout the Bush administration's first eight months, support for regime change continued to pour forth from conservative think-tanks in Washington and members of Congress who had been deeply critical of Clinton's 'illusory' containment. Nevertheless, the Jeffords defection in Congress shifted the balance of power in the Senate and tempered Congressional support for the new administration's agenda. After an initial surge of optimism, the absence of immediate action against Saddam Hussein, plus presidential support for Powell's smart sanctions initiative and the seemingly endless internal review of Iraq policy, began to deflate conservative think-tank support for the administration and their hopes of regime change.

By September 2001, however, the smart sanctions initiative was losing ground, there was no sign of a resumption of UN inspections and serious doubts had been raised in the administration as to their intrinsic utility. Many in the administration remained convinced that Saddam was a serious threat who had to be decisively dealt with at some point during the Bush presidency. As the policy review ground on, Baghdad remained defiant and continued to emerge from its political and economic isolation. It seemed likely that the policy review would come down on the side of Rumsfeld and Cheney. A new confrontation with Iraq was probable, either via a major military and economic commitment to the INC or through demands for renewed UN inspections that Saddam would undoubtedly refuse. If this happened, the ardent supporters of an aggressive strategy to remove Saddam's regime that were brought into the administration were prepared with a ready-made solution to topple the regime, a solution that would enjoy significant Congressional approval. Then 9/11 occurred and the threat from Iraq took on a new light.

Part II

REGIME CHANGE

5

9/11 AND IRAQ

Introduction

The following chapters explore the contention that military-led regime change in Iraq was inevitable after 9/11. The evidence to support this argument comes from statements made by senior members of the administration, statements by Congressional leaders, and statements from influential conservative think-tanks. Government statements demonstrate that a post-9/11 security paradigm was constructed by the Bush administration that left Saddam Hussein little or no realistic room to manoeuvre. Confrontation was coming, the administration was determined to control and manipulate the national discourse on Iraq, it was prepared to bring the full force of the US military to bear, and the Iraqi regime's history left little doubt that it would refuse to comply with US demands. The post-9/11 paradigm and its path to confrontation with Iraq enjoyed the full support of Congressional leaders. Dissenting opinion was found in both Houses, but these voices had little impact. The administration's policy was supported and pushed by Washington's network of conservative think-tanks which had a close relationship with senior figures in government. This combination of government policy, Congressional support and think-tank drive, plus a body politic still reeling from the 9/11 attacks, led to widespread support from the nation's media networks for a new confrontation with Iraq. This closed off other possible avenues for addressing the threat posed by Saddam Hussein and subdued critical analysis and dissenting opinion.[1]

This chapter looks at the statements by senior members of the administration, in particular Bush, Cheney, Rice, Powell, Rumsfeld and Wolfowitz. Analysis of these statements reveals an immediate focus on Iraq after 9/11 and again after the war in Afghanistan. It uncovers the construction of a post-9/11 national security paradigm that rapidly evolved through a number of stages to take the administration from the attacks of 9/11 to war with Iraq. The evolution of this paradigm was not necessarily deliberate or linear, but neither was it accidental or random since a confrontation between the Bush administration and Iraq was likely even if 9/11 had not occurred.

Iraq and the new global war on terror

The terrorist attacks on 11 September stunned George W. Bush as they stunned much of the world. His immediate response was uncertain and his address to the nation on the evening of the attacks was unexceptional. Nine days later, however, in an assured speech before Congress, Bush seemed a president transformed.[2] In that intervening period a broad strategy had been developed, one that already involved Iraq.

Addressing the problem of the Iraqi regime was an important and enduring foreign policy issue for the Bush administration. For others in the US government and influential opinion-formers in Washington, Iraq was an urgent priority. After 9/11 the Bush White House began to adopt this view, a view compounded by Powell's stuttering smart sanctions initiative, the escalation of the low-intensity air war over the no-fly zones since the start of the administration and, most importantly, a new resolve after 9/11 to deal with foreign policy issues differently and jettison old rationalisations and ways of thinking.[3]

An immediate focus on Iraq

After 9/11

The review of Iraq policy initiated by Bush in January 2001 had not reached any conclusions by 9/11. The attacks, however, transformed and hastened the review process. Decisions now had to be taken about Iraq in the context of the war on terrorism – in particular whether or not Iraq should be part of this new war and, if so, at what stage it should be confronted.

The day after the attacks, the National Security Council principals met. During the meeting Rumsfeld raised the question of whether the US should go after Iraq as part of its response to the attacks.[4] Whether Rumsfeld was specifically advocating such an approach, or merely raising it as a discussion point, is difficult to say – Rumsfeld kept his cards close to his chest in most of his public statements on Iraq. However, notes taken by an aide on 9/11 suggest that targeting Saddam Hussein was at the very forefront of his thinking, quoting Rumsfeld as saying he wanted 'best info fast. Judge whether good enough hit S.H. [Saddam Hussein] at same time. Not only UBL [Usama bin Laden].'[5] Wolfowitz was not convinced that al-Qaida had planned and conducted the attacks alone, but was certain instead that a state had assisted the terrorists and that the state involved was probably Iraq.[6] Wolfowitz also thought that Iraq had somehow been involved in the first terrorist attack on the World Trade Center in 1993.[7] At the end of the meeting Bush, according to the administration's counter-terrorism coordinator Richard Clarke, asked Clarke and others to 'go back over everything, everything. See if Saddam did this. See if he's linked in any way…'[8] Attacking Iraq as part of the response to 9/11 was a serious consideration from the outset.

Four days after the attacks, Bush brought his senior advisers together at Camp David to discuss the administration's response. Bush had ordered the Defense Department to come armed with a range of military options for Afghanistan and, if necessary, Iraq.[9] During the discussion Wolfowitz argued strongly for expanding the war on terrorism to other 'rogue' states involved in terrorism, specifically Iraq. He claimed that an attack on Iraq would be easier than invading Afghanistan and estimated that there was a 10 to 50 per cent chance that Baghdad was directly involved in the 9/11 attacks.[10] Bush had reservations about this approach, as did Cheney. Cheney did, however, voice deep concerns about Saddam and said he would not rule out going after him after Afghanistan.[11] Powell argued strongly for only attacking Afghanistan and maintained that 9/11 did not necessitate a renewed confrontation or war with Iraq.[12]

Consensus was finally reached to attack al-Qaida in Afghanistan and if necessary destroy the Taliban regime. But within 12 days of the attacks it became apparent that the administration would not stop once al-Qaida's infrastructure in Afghanistan had been destroyed. Powell reported on 23 September that Bush had decided to pursue the al-Qaida network but that 'He has not ruled out what we might do in later phases.'[13] According to Wolfowitz, the real issue at stake in the discussion immediately after 9/11 was whether Iraq would be part of a larger strategic objective in the war on terrorism. He contended that 'the president came down on the side of the larger goal'.[14] Bush was clear that there was going to be a phase two, and in the administration's post-9/11 discussions Iraq was already the prime target.

The Defense Department continued to advocate regime change in Iraq as part of the new war on terrorism. This view continued to come from Secretary of Defense Donald Rumsfeld and Deputy Secretary of Defense Paul Wolfowitz who, according to journalist Bob Woodward, was 'the intellectual godfather and fiercest advocate for toppling Saddam'.[15] The Pentagon's leaders were wholeheartedly supported by the outspoken and influential figure of Richard Perle, Chair of the Pentagon's Defense Policy Board, and Washington's conservative national security think-tanks. On 19 and 20 September, a few days after the Camp David meeting, the Pentagon's 18-member Defense Policy Board met together with Rumsfeld, Wolfowitz and Ahmed Chalabi, head of the Iraqi National Congress, to discuss the option of taking military action against Iraq.[16] Wolfowitz was adamant that the war on terrorism move beyond al-Qaida and Afghanistan. 'It's not just a matter of capturing people and holding them accountable', he said at the end of September, 'but removing the sanctuaries, removing the support systems, ending states who sponsor terrorism.'[17] Powell, however, was disconcerted by the Pentagon's eagerness to expand the war on terrorism to Iraq and other hostile states.[18]

The divide on Iraq policy between those in the Pentagon pressing for regime change and the more pragmatic realists around Powell had characterised the Iraq policy review process since the start of the Bush administration. Within 10 days of 9/11 it had surfaced again in the *Los Angeles Times*:

The policy divide, the most serious to date within the young administration of President Bush, has played out most visibly on the decade-old challenge of Iraq and, to a lesser degree, other state sponsors of terrorism, according to administration and other well-placed sources. And in what is becoming a hallmark of the Bush foreign-policy team, it pits the views of the nation's top diplomat, Secretary of State Colin L. Powell, against the Pentagon's key strategist, Deputy Defense Secretary Paul D. Wolfowitz.... 'Iraq is unfinished business, and this is an opportunity to finish it. He and others in the Pentagon have long had a vendetta about getting rid of Saddam and they believe that irrespective of what happened on Sept. 11, he has to be removed,' said a source familiar with the debate who asked to remain anonymous. 'They think now's the moment to push for it again'.[19]

After Afghanistan

After 9/11 the Bush administration embraced a new way of looking at the world and new strategies for dealing with the problems perceived through that worldview – in essence a new national security paradigm. The first part of the new paradigm was based on attacking and eradicating al-Qaida in Afghanistan. In October 2001 the United States attacked Afghanistan to destroy al-Qaida's network of training camps and facilities. A direct consequence of this was the elimination of the Taliban regime, which controlled much of that country and had refused to surrender Osama bin Laden and his deputies.

This led, almost immediately after 9/11, to the second part of the paradigm – the expansion of the new war on terrorism to states that harboured and assisted terrorist organisations as well as operations targeting the terrorist organisations themselves. This second step explicitly linked terrorist groups that threatened the United States with the governments that supported them. In his address to the nation on the night of 11 September, Bush had stated that he would 'make no distinction between the terrorists who committed these acts and those who harbor them'.[20] He made that broad commitment to pursue not only terrorist organisations but also those that sponsored them without consulting his senior national security advisers. However, this initial reaction was elevated to a key plank in the war on terrorism. 'Afghanistan', the President said on 10 November, 'is still just the beginning. If anybody harbors a terrorist, they're a terrorist. If they fund a terrorist, they're a terrorist. If they house terrorists, they're terrorists.'[21] The symbiotic relationship between the Taliban and al-Qaida was translated into a universal principle of the war on terrorism, a principle applicable to all those on the US State Department's list of state sponsors of terrorism.

This second step was a significant break with previous policy, which had tended to draw a sharp distinction between terrorist groups and the governments of the countries that harboured them. Such regimes would now be indistinguishable from and accountable for the actions of any terrorist groups they supported.

In November and December the President expressed his clear determination to do precisely that: 'For every regime that sponsors terror, there is a price to be paid, and it will be paid';[22] 'Every nation now knows that we cannot accept and we will not accept states that harbour, finance, train or equip the agents of terror... Those nations that violate this principle will be regarded as hostile regimes... They have been warned. They are being watched, and they will be held to account.'[23] Very early on, then, Iraq was legitimised as a potential target in the war on terror as one of the State Department's designated state sponsors of terrorism.[24]

Weapons of mass destruction

By December 2001 the administration had outlined the third step in the post-9/11 paradigm: the inclusion of weapons of mass destruction – chemical, biological and nuclear weapons and their means of delivery, particularly ballistic missiles. This step highlighted the dangerous potential for some states with WMD programmes to directly or indirectly provide such weapons to terrorist groups. Bush assured the world that those developing such weapons 'to terrorize nations' would be held to account,[25] and that 'America's next priority in the war on terrorism is to protect against the proliferation of weapons of mass destruction and the means to deliver them.'[26] As the administration's policy solidified, Powell declared that future phases in the war on terrorism would involve going after 'those countries that harbor terrorism, or those countries that develop weapons of mass destruction that can be used by terrorists'.[27]

Only a few months after 9/11, the United States had manifestly demonstrated its intent in Afghanistan to use military force, including substantial numbers of ground troops, in its new war on terrorism and categorically stated that this war would have a second phase. The question now was who would be next.[28] The new paradigm meant that states defined by the US State Department as sponsors of terrorism with active or suspected weapons of mass destruction programmes and with a historically hostile relationship with the United States were prime candidates for aggressive US action in 'phase two' of the war on terrorism. A number of countries fitted the phase two criteria, such as Yemen, Sudan, Syria, Iran and even Cuba. There was also talk of pursuing Islamic terrorist groups in Somalia, Sudan and the Philippines. Iraq, however, found itself at the top of the list with its post-Gulf War history of unfulfilled UN Security Council resolutions and an enduring sentiment among senior members of the Bush administration and Congressional leaders that the status quo in Iraq could not continue indefinitely. Iraq was singled out by Bush on 10 November: 'As for Mr. Saddam Hussein, he needs to let inspectors back in his country, to show us that he is not developing weapons of mass destruction.'[29] As for the consequences of refusal, the President warned, 'he'll find out'.[30] Bush repeated this insistence and warning once more, on 16 January.[31] The anthrax-laced letters sent to US business and political leaders in October and November 2001 heightened awareness of the risk of WMD terrorism, with Iraq initially suspected as the source of the attack.[32]

The Defense Department

The senior civilian leadership within the Defense Department consistently and forcefully pushed the case for regime change in Iraq. In particular the Pentagon persistently asserted that Saddam Hussein was in league with al-Qaida, and cast serious doubt on the utility of further coordinated action through the UNSC, particularly a new round of weapons inspections. According to the Treasury Secretary Paul O'Neill's account through journalist Ron Suskind, Rumsfeld and Wolfowitz saw Afghanistan as essentially a 'demonstration model' of what other countries might face in the war on terrorism, 'pointing to the ease with which the Taliban had fallen as evidence of how do-able Iraq would be'.[33] In October 2001 Rumsfeld reiterated that Iraq was an enemy of the United States, accused it of harbouring and facilitating terrorists, and named Iraq as one of the few countries in the world with active chemical and biological weapons programmes and a relationship with terrorist networks.[34] In November Rumsfeld began to set out the case for confronting Iraq by declaring that Saddam Hussein was 'proceeding apace with his ... weapons of mass destruction efforts' with little interference,[35] and arguing that 'the likelihood of Iraq transforming itself is zero'.[36] Having linked the pursuit of WMD by unsavoury regimes to the war on terrorism in the new post-9/11 paradigm, Rumsfeld branded Iraq a WMD state, firmly linked it to international terrorism (though not at this stage directly to al-Qaida) and dismissed the notion that diplomacy, or any other strategy, could force Saddam to change his ways.[37]

Wolfowitz was unambiguous in his desire for the parameters of the war on terrorism to cover terrorist groups, rogue states and WMD. In testimony before the Senate Armed Services Committee in October 2001 he linked all three of these components:

> The terrorist movements and totalitarian regimes of the world have a variety of motives and goals. But the same thing unites our enemies today, as it did in the past: a desire to see America driven into retreat and isolation. Usama bin Laden, Saddam Hussein, Kim Jong Il and other such tyrants all want to see America out of critical regions of the world, constrained from coming to the aid of friends and allies, and unable to project power in the defense of our interests and ideals.

He went on to argue, 'It is no coincidence that the states harboring, financing and otherwise assisting terrorists, are also in many cases the same states that are aggressively working to acquire nuclear, chemical and biological weapons of mass destruction, and the means to deliver them.' For Wolfowitz this was a threat as great as any faced during the Cold War.[38]

Wolfowitz and Rumsfeld were determined to find evidence linking Iraq to 9/11, and soon after the attacks they sent Defense Policy Board member and former Director of Central Intelligence, James Woolsey, on a mission to gather evidence linking Saddam Hussein to the 9/11 attacks and to develop plans to depose him.[39] Two months after 9/11 Woolsey revealed that he was investigating Saddam Hussein's possible role in the attacks on behalf of the Bush administration. Woolsey argued that Saddam Hussein was involved in the attempted bombing of the World Trade Center in 1993, that he was probably behind the postal anthrax attacks from September to November 2001 and that Iraqi intelligence agents met with al-Qaida operatives in the months leading up to 9/11.[40] Shortly after 9/11, on 13 September, Woolsey suggested that 9/11 was 'sponsored, supported, and perhaps even ordered by Saddam Hussein'.[41] He was convinced that Baghdad should be the next target in the war on terrorism.[42] 'Once we bring about a regime change in Afghanistan', he said on 10 November 2001 in an interview for *PBS Frontline*, 'I think we ought to very seriously consider moving toward a regime change in Iraq and getting rid of the bad regime of Saddam's.'[43]

For the White House, evidence of Saddam's involvement would have provided sufficient justification for an immediate attack on Iraq, but the absence of evidence did not quell the Pentagon's determination. For Wolfowitz the world had changed after 9/11 and Saddam now categorically had to be removed even if he was not involved in 9/11, a theme that would recur throughout 2002 as the administration constructed its case for war with Iraq. 'The events of September 11th', he said in November 2001 during a roundtable with European journalists,

> make it clear that what might in the past have been regarded as nasty behavior but one of those kinds of nasty things you live with in international affairs, I think September 11th took all of that stuff to the level of the intolerable ... that kind of behavior that condones terrorism, that treats terrorism as just another instrument of national policy is just not acceptable any more.[44]

A *USA Today* report on 19 November stated that the Pentagon was

> building a case for a massive bombing of Iraq as a new phase of President Bush's war against terrorism, congressional and Pentagon sources say. Proponents of attacking Iraq, spearheaded by Deputy Defense Secretary Paul Wolfowitz, are now arguing privately that still-elusive evidence linking Iraqi leader Saddam Hussein's regime to the terrorist attacks Sept. 11 is not necessary to trigger a military strike ... Pentagon officials say Iraq should be a target because it supports terrorism, is trying to build nuclear, biological and chemical weapons and has refused to admit U.N. weapons inspectors for nearly three years.[45]

Like Wolfowitz, Defense Policy Board Chair Richard Perle turned his attention to Iraq shortly after 9/11, placing Saddam Hussein at the centre of the new war on terrorism. On 8 November 2001, in an interview for PBS *Frontline*, he stated that Saddam Hussein was 'probably the most dangerous individual in the world today', and went on to argue that

> The question of Saddam Hussein is at the very core of the war against terrorism. There can be no victory in the war against terrorism if, at the end of it, Saddam Hussein is still in power ... to leave him in place and wait for him to take action against us is simply too dangerous.

For Perle, Iraq should have come before Afghanistan: 'I would have gone about this differently. I would have gone after Iraq immediately. I would not have relegated it to some subsequent phase.'[46] Once the war against the Taliban had ended, Perle was unequivocal that 'Iraq should be the principal next target because it poses the biggest threat to the United States',[47] and that 'at the top of the list for phase two is Iraq'.[48]

Powell and Rumsfeld's views were both known. Powell favoured a war on terrorism that would pursue Islamic terrorist organisations through judicial, intelligence, diplomatic, economic and limited military means. Rumsfeld and Wolfowitz, plus Cheney's powerful Chief of Staff I. Lewis Libby, favoured a far more assertive war on terrorism that would aim to eradicate terrorism from Middle Eastern politics through primarily military means, with its main focus on the regime in Baghdad.[49] By the end of 2001 Bush, Rice and Cheney had moved to the more forceful camp.[50]

Support from the think-tanks

The conservative think-tanks that had pilloried Clinton's Iraq policy and urged a new and aggressive policy of regime change at the end of Clinton's presidency and throughout the first eight months of the George W. Bush administration saw the attacks of 9/11 as ever more reason to take down the regime in Baghdad. They lent full support to those in the administration that shared this view, with whom they had close connections.

Just nine days after the 9/11 attacks the *Weekly Standard* published an open letter to the President arguing that Iraq should be attacked and that the INC-led regime change plan should be fully implemented:

> Even if evidence does not link Iraq directly to the attack, any strategy aiming at the eradication of terrorism and its sponsors must include a determined effort to remove Saddam Hussein from power in Iraq. Failure to undertake such an effort will constitute an early and perhaps decisive surrender on the war on international terrorism. The United States must therefore provide full military and financial support to the Iraqi opposition. American military force should be used to provide a 'safe zone' in Iraq from which the opposition can operate. And

American forces must be prepared to back up our commitment to the Iraqi opposition by all necessary means.[51]

The letter was signed by the same group of people that had signed the 1998 letters to Clinton and to Gingrich and Lott, though without the names of those now in the administration, such as Wolfowitz and Rumsfeld.

The American Enterprise Institute's Newt Gingrich and Jeffrey Gedmin were firmly in favour of regime change in Iraq as part of the war on terrorism. In October 2001 Gingrich maintained that the first targets in this war should be 'dictators determined to obtain weapons of mass destruction, like Saddam Hussein', insisting 'at the same time we are replacing the Taliban, we should be replacing Saddam Hussein in Iraq as well'. International terrorist organisations such as al-Qaida were not the priority.[52] Three weeks after 9/11 Gedmin wrote, 'There is probably no better way to deliver a major setback to the terrorist threat – and restore America's standing in the Middle East – than to reconstitute the anti-Saddam coalition of 1991. This time, though, the objective must be putting an end to the dictator's blood-soaked rule.'[53]

The Heritage Foundation was equally forceful in arguing for regime change in Iraq after 9/11 over and above the elimination of al-Qaida. In October 2001 Heritage's James Phillips asserted that 'The concept of fighting a war against international terrorism is stillborn without the goal of removing terrorist regimes... Even if Osama bin Laden should disappear tomorrow, terrorist attacks against America will continue as long as the terrorist regimes in Kabul and Baghdad remain in power.'[54] 'Saddam', he argued, 'poses a greater threat to U.S. national security than bin Laden.' PNAC's William Kristol and Robert Kagan were in full agreement. The United States, they argued, could and should go after Iraq at the same time as pursuing Osama bin Laden and stabilising Afghanistan: 'none of this precludes dealing with Iraq, or makes the obligation of dealing with Iraq less urgent. The United States can, after all, walk and chew gum at the same time.'[55]

Continued containment

After 9/11 Secretary of State Colin Powell argued that Iraq need not be confronted as part of the war on terrorism, insisting instead that the containment strategy was sufficient: 'Iraq is a country we have had on our list of nations that sponsor terrorism, its an enemy we keep well contained with the strong support of our British friends and others. We have contained them for ten years and we will continue to do so.'[56]

Cheney and Rice seemed to agree with Powell in the first few months after the attacks, indeed Cheney kept a relatively low profile in the months after 9/11. With the nation on high alert he was reported to be at an 'undisclosed location' to ensure continuity of government should the President be killed or incapacitated in a terrorist attack. Cheney may have been convinced that Iraq was a problem that would have to be addressed by the administration, possibly with military force, but in the aftermath of the 9/11 attacks he leaned towards Powell's view. 'The focus is over here on al-Qaida and the most recent events in New York', he stated on 16 September 2001, 'Saddam Hussein's bottled up, at this point, but clearly, we continue to have a fairly tough policy where the Iraqis are concerned.' The implication is that Cheney was not convinced that Iraq should constitute a central or immediate part of the war on terrorism. Similarly, National Security Advisor Condoleezza Rice advocated adherence to a containment approach while continuing to review the administration's Iraq policy. On 16 October she highlighted Powell's smart sanctions initiative as the focus of the Iraq policy, stating that the government was concentrating on changing the sanctions regime to target Saddam's government and relieve pressure on the Iraqi people and that the administration would 'watch and monitor Iraq'. Iraq was certainly a significant concern for Rice – 'we worry about Saddam Hussein', she said. 'We worry about his weapons of mass destruction.'[57]

In November, as the President turned his attention to Baghdad after the Afghan War, Cheney insisted that Iraq was developing WMD and therefore constituted a threat to the US, although it is not clear whether he considered, at this stage, the threat markedly different to that before 9/11: 'There's every reason to believe, since he kicked out the inspectors, that he did that specifically because he wanted to develop further his capabilities in this area, so-called biological, chemical agents and nuclear weapons'; Saddam Hussein 'continues to be a significant potential problem for the region, for the United States, for everybody, with interests in the area'.[58] Rice used similar language on 11 November, labelling Saddam a direct threat 'to the region and a threat to us because he is determined to acquire weapons of mass destruction', implying that he did not yet possess them.[59] Powell continued to play down the WMD threat and in October he again stated that Iraq was contained and, as far as WMD were concerned, Iraq was only 'fiddling with weapons of mass destruction'.[60] This was a cautious approach towards Iraq similar to that articulated before 9/11. The confrontational rhetoric of the Pentagon stressing the immediacy of the threat from Iraq had not yet taken full hold in the White House.

Confrontation decided

It is difficult to gauge when Bush took a decision to confront Saddam Hussein as part of the war on terrorism, even if that meant outright war, partly because such a decision can be defined in a number of ways and partly because only the President truly knows. For some it is the point at which he ordered troops to invade, or the point at which he decided to seek formal endorsement from Congress. For others it is the point at which the President decided to comprehensively challenge the status quo over Iraq in the full knowledge that the ultimate conclusion to the process could well be war. Exactly a year after 9/11, *USA Today* reported that Bush had decided 'Saddam must go' in November 2001.[61] This coincided with a report from British newspaper *The Observer* on 2 December 2001 that the President had ordered the CIA and senior military commanders to draw up plans for an attack on Iraq.[62] This was later supported by Bob Woodward's account of the build-up to the war in *Plan of Attack*. Woodward reports that on 21 November 2001 Bush asked the head of US Central Command, General Tommy Franks, to look at the Iraq war plan and what it might take to remove Saddam from power. This was followed two weeks later by a formal request from Rumsfeld to Franks to produce a 'commander's estimate' for a new war plan to destroy the regime in Baghdad and Iraq's WMD. This request came at the height of the war in Afghanistan.[63] The contention that Bush made his decision in November or December 2001 is further supported by White House speech writer David Frum's recollection of being asked in late December to 'sum up in a sentence or two our best case for going after Iraq' for the forthcoming State of the Union Address.[64]

In December both Cheney and Rice stepped up their rhetoric against Iraq. The *New Republic* reported that Cheney had 'slowly come around to his staff's view that Iraq should be targeted. "What [Cheney] had a problem with was the timing, not the issue of confronting [Saddam]," insists an official close to the vice president. "He follows the president's lead and had no desire to get out ahead on this".'[65] The President's expansion of the post-9/11 security paradigm to link WMD, hostile 'rogue' states and terrorist groups was supported by Cheney in December in the specific context of Iraq. 'The evidence is conclusive', he argued definitively, 'that the Iraqis have harboured terrorists. Saddam has had a robust biological and chemical weapons programme.'[66] With no evidence of Saddam's involvement in 9/11, Cheney focused on Iraq's WMD programmes. Iraq, he said, was a problem because of 'Saddam Hussein's behavior over the years and with his aggressive pursuit of weapons of mass destruction'.

Having insisted that Iraq re-admit inspectors and having had that proposal rejected by Baghdad, Cheney was careful not to volunteer details on how the administration might respond. 'We've not yet made a decision about how best to proceed', he said on 9 December,[67] but warned two days later that if 'I were Saddam Hussein, I would be thinking very carefully about the future, and I would be looking very closely to see what happened to the Taliban in Afghanistan'.[68] Rice compounded this view on 18 December by insisting that Iraq would remain a threat as long as Saddam remained in power, reinforcing the view that regime change in one form or another was the only effective solution.[69] By January 2002, Cheney too was persuaded that Iraq should be the overwhelming focus of phase two of the war on terrorism. Having intimated his willingness to use US military forces against Baghdad, announced his conviction that Iraq had WMD and active WMD programmes and placed Iraq in the post-9/11 security paradigm, Cheney added his weight behind the President's drive towards confrontation with Iraq.

By the end of 2001 Bush, Cheney and Rice seemed convinced that action was needed to confront Saddam Hussein and remove him from power, this time as the next step in the war on terrorism. Rumsfeld and Wolfowitz needed no convincing, leaving Powell relatively isolated in his view that Iraq could still be successfully contained. The end of this first stage in the post-9/11 road to war, which saw the evolution of the post-9/11 paradigm and the emergence of a clear conviction in the Bush White House that Saddam Hussein could now no longer remain in power, was marked by the President's State of the Union Address in January 2002.

That address was delivered on 27 January 2002. It set out the full logic of the post-9/11 security paradigm that later became known as the Bush doctrine. The doctrine initially targeted terrorist groups before progressing to target states sponsoring or harbouring terrorist groups. It then evolved to target those states that had active WMD programmes, before finally its sights settled on those states that had WMD programmes, links to international terrorism and a history of hostility towards the United States. The doctrine branded these states a serious threat to the US and presented pre-emptive military action as a valid response. The State of the Union Address systematically linked the new paradigm to Iran, North Korea and Iraq, paying particular attention to the Iraqi regime and its past transgressions:

- On terrorism the speech declared that Iraq continued 'to support terror'.
- On the link between terrorist groups and states: 'States like these [Iran, Iraq and North Korea], and their terrorist *allies*, constitute an axis of evil, arming to threaten the peace of the world.' [Emphasis added]
- On WMD: 'The Iraqi regime has plotted to develop anthrax, and nerve gas, and nuclear weapons for over a decade. This is a regime that has already used poison gas to murder thousands of its own citizens', adding emotively 'leaving the bodies of mothers huddled over their dead children'.
- On state WMD programmes and terrorist groups: 'They [Iraq, Iran and North Korea] could provide these arms to terrorists, giving them the means to match their hatred.'
- On past transgressions and UN inspections: 'This is a regime that agreed to international inspections – then kicked out the inspectors. This is a regime that has something to hide from the civilized world.'
- On hostility and threat: 'Iraq continues to flaunt its hostility toward America ... By seeking weapons of mass destruction, these regimes pose a grave and growing danger ... They could attack our allies or attempt to blackmail the United States.'
- On the need to act pre-emptively: 'In any of these cases, the price of indifference would be catastrophic ... We'll be deliberate, yet time is not on our side. I will not wait on events, while dangers gather. I will not stand by, as peril draws closer and closer. The United States of America will not permit the world's most dangerous regimes to threaten us with the world's most destructive weapons.'[70]

By the end of January 2002 Iraq had emerged as the predominant focus of phase two in the war on terrorism and a decision had been taken by the White House to initiate a far more vigorous challenge to Saddam Hussein.[71] Iran and North Korea would be dealt with differently. Before 9/11 the new administration's main challenge to Baghdad was a more rigorous implementation of Clinton's containment-plus strategy until the White House policy review on Iraq was completed. By January 2002 the nature of that challenge and its ultimate objective had been transformed. In the absence of compelling evidence of Baghdad's involvement in 9/11 the White House sought to legitimise a renewed confrontation with Iraq as part of the war on terrorism by positioning it at the centre of the post-9/11 security paradigm – exemplified in the State of the Union Address.

The strategy for confrontation would focus on Iraq's suspected WMD programmes and the re-admission of UN weapons inspectors, as Cheney had intimated in December 2001. This was, to an extent, a calculated strategy to allow the United States to use established procedures that could deliver international legitimacy for armed action in the name of enforcing UNSC disarmament resolutions. Wolfowitz acknowledged this in a revealing interview with *Vanity Fair* in May 2003. Speaking about the reasons for going after Iraq, Wolfowitz explained, 'for reasons that have a lot to do with the U.S. government bureaucracy we settled on the one issue that everyone could agree on which was weapons of mass destruction'.[72] Baghdad's refusal to comply with US demands and UNSC resolutions was expected, and military planning was initiated in anticipation of Saddam's intransigence. The ultimate objective was regime change, either through coercive transformation of the existing regime via full compliance with US demands and UNSC resolutions, or forced removal of the existing regime and its replacement with a more favourable alternative. This strategy was reported in *The Observer* article on 2 December 2001[73] and in *Newsweek* on 28 January 2002.[74]

The administration therefore sought to justify a confrontation and possible war with Iraq on two fronts. Domestically it presented the threat from Iraq as a vital part of the war on terrorism, the nation's response to 9/11. Internationally it presented a renewed confrontation as a necessary means of enforcing UNSC resolutions. The administration's determination to oust Saddam had solidified and would prove unbreakable. After the President's State of the Union Address the White House worked hard to develop, package and present the case against Iraq on both fronts throughout 2002. This culminated in the President's speech at the United Nations in September 2002, the period explored in the next chapter.

6

CONSTRUCTING THE CASE: FROM THE 'AXIS OF EVIL' TO THE UNITED NATIONS

Introduction

By the start of 2002 the Bush administration had decided to pursue regime change as part of the war on terrorism. From the President's State of the Union Address in January 2002 to his presentation at the United Nations in September 2002, the administration tenaciously constructed a case for war with Iraq. The administration's strategy involved a period of consultation with other governments, a determined and consistent elaboration of Iraq's position at the heart of the war on terrorism, and the issuing of demands to Iraq.

The consultation period spanned the first six months of 2002. The aim of the consultation exercise was to convince sceptical allies of the need to confront Saddam Hussein and forcibly remove his regime if he did not fully comply with UNSC resolutions. Cheney's tour of the Middle East in February and March 2002 was a key part of this process. The administration worked hard to place Iraq at the centre of the post-9/11 nexus of WMD, terrorism and rogue states that now constituted the prevailing threat to the US. Bush and other senior members of the administration forcefully expressed their determination to prevent that threat materialising in Iraq. The threat from Iraq's WMD was considered overwhelming and growing. Senior members of the administration stated that they did not believe Iraq's claims that it no longer possessed any WMD and insisted on nothing less than total cooperation and full WMD disarmament. Only Powell espoused a less alarmist view.

As the administration constructed its case it also pursued two different policy paths. The first involved Powell's continuing work on smart sanctions in the hope that containment could be made to work. The second involved the development of military plans and military preparations for war. Powell continued to differentiate between the UN track of the administration's policy toward Iraq and its own independent US policy, with growing disparity between the UN objective of a peaceful resolution of outstanding disarmament issues and the White House objective of confrontation and regime change.

At this stage the administration had a number of options for regime change. It could pursue the strategy developed and advocated by conservative think-tanks in the late 1990s and train and arm the Iraqi National Congress (INC) and use US military force to establish a series of enclaves in Iraq around southern and northern oil fields to gradually squeeze Saddam's regime to breaking point. Following 9/11 and the subsequent determination to confront Saddam Hussein sooner rather than later, this strategy was dismissed by the administration as too slow, uncertain and dangerous. Another option was an internal coup to overthrow Saddam, something the CIA had attempted to engineer in the early 1990s without success. At the start of January 2002 Cheney asked the CIA to brief him on what they could accomplish in Iraq. The deputy chief of the CIA's Near East Division told him that covert CIA action would not remove Saddam Hussein.[1] The third alternative option was an armed invasion. With the chances of a successful coup considered slim, the administration focused on this option.[2] During the first half of 2002 the Pentagon developed detailed plans for such an invasion at the President's request. A full plan was presented to the President in August 2002 after a number of iterations, with war planned for February 2003.

In August 2002 Bush decided to take the case against Iraq to the UN to gain international support and legitimacy for regime change. The President's determination to remove the regime found expression in his insistence that the UN process would not derail the administration's strategy. Cheney and Rumsfeld were against going to the UN, and in August Cheney made two major speeches outlining the threat from Iraq, the need for regime change and the irrelevance of any further UN inspections. Once the President had taken the case to the UN, Powell came fully behind the White House case and embraced the administration's rhetoric on the threat from Iraq and the need to remove Saddam Hussein from power.

Consultation

Iraq was the highest priority for the administration after the 2002 State of the Union Address.[3] In the first few months of 2002 Rice indicated that the administration was reviewing its Iraq policy in the light of 9/11 and consulting with its allies, while insisting that the current situation in Iraq was no longer tolerable to the US government. 'The status quo is not acceptable,' she said in February, 'we're going to have broad-gauged policy against Iraq', stating that the world would be a far safer place when the regime in Baghdad had been dismantled.[4] She indicated that the administration was looking at all options for deposing the regime in Baghdad, including assisting the INC and other opposition groups and using US military power. In May she repeated the White House position that 'We're in consultation with our friends and allies … the president felt that it is extremely important to make clear that the status quo is not acceptable with this regime.'[5]

In July 2002 Powell remarked that the President was consulting widely with other government leaders, particularly the G8 and Arab leaders, a steady stream of whom had been through the White House. But, as Powell's interviewer, ABC's

Ted Koppel, suggested, the consultation had tended to involve disagreement and frustration on the part of foreign leaders. Powell replied that whereas the President was 'interested in their perspective' and had 'listened carefully to them', it was really a task of persuading them to see the situation from America's view since 'he [the President] believes regime change is the right way to go'.[6] In fact a few days after that interview Powell described the consultations not as two-way discussions on how to deal with Iraq, but as 'making the case to our friends, and it's a case that is increasingly hard to deny, that this regime is a real and present danger to the world'.[7]

Cheney's concern about WMD, in the hands of both 'rogue' regimes and terrorist groups, intensified after 9/11.[8] This was reflected in his first major speech on the post-9/11 security paradigm at the Council on Foreign Relations on 15 February 2002. He argued that 9/11 had forced the US to consider its vulnerability to international terrorism and 'the possibility that terrorists may someday gain access to the weapons of mass destruction'. He pointed to evidence in Afghanistan that al-Qaida was seriously interested in nuclear, biological and chemical weapons to support this assertion. He went on to state that the United States must work to 'prevent regimes that sponsor terror from threatening America or our friends and allies with chemical, biological or nuclear weapons – or allowing them to provide those weapons to terrorists', singling out Iraq as the administration's main concern.[9] The Vice President had by now swung fully behind the need to deal with Iraq in phase two of the war on terrorism and played a vital role in constructing the case for confrontation and war.

Soon after this speech, the President sent Cheney on a tour of the Middle East to gain support for military action against Iraq. In the President's words, 'The Vice President can deliver the message to many important world leaders that our government is absolutely committed to fighting terror, and we expect people to join us in doing so ... the Vice President I think is going to be very effective at convincing – at convincing our friends we mean business.'[10] The purpose here was not to consult but to sell the administration's post-9/11 paradigm abroad with Iraq at its core, and to convince sceptical friends and allies, reflecting Powell's response to Ted Koppel's questions a few months later. Whilst Bush did not explicitly state that Iraq was the focus of Cheney's trip, Rice reportedly stated that Cheney 'will want to talk to our friends and allies about how we deal with the threat of Iraq' on the tour that included Egypt, Saudi Arabia, Turkey, Kuwait, Bahrain, the United Arab Emirates, Jordan, Qatar and Oman.[11] In fact Bob Woodward later reported that Cheney was briefed by the head of US Central Command, General Tommy Franks, on what was needed from countries in the region to support a war against Iraq so that Cheney could gauge each leader's response and increase the pressure for cooperation.[12] The Vice President himself said he spent 'a lot of time on the Iraqi situation, and Saddam Hussein's development of weapons of mass destruction'.[13]

Reports of the Vice President's trip suggested that many of his discussions were dominated by the ongoing Palestinian al-Aqsa intifada rather than the case for action against Iraq, for which Cheney found little support.[14] The ongoing Israeli–Palestinian violence was not, according to the Vice President, going to prevent the administration from addressing Iraq. 'The U.S. doesn't have a choice of saying, well, we're going to worry about Israeli–Palestinian peace or we're going to worry about Saddam Hussein', he said on 24 March 2002. 'We've got to do it all.'[15] For Cheney, the tour signalled the end of further consultation. On his return he reiterated the President's unequivocal determination to decisively address the threat posed by the possibility of terrorist organisations linking with hostile, WMD-armed 'rogue' states, particularly Iraq.[16] His determination was reflected in a *Time* magazine online article which reported that on his return from the Middle East Cheney explained in confidence at a Republican policy lunch that it was no longer a question of *if* the US would attack Iraq, but *when*.[17]

Iraq at the heart of the war on terrorism

The President's State of the Union Address introduced the concept of a nexus or a web of hostile 'rogue' states, weapons of mass destruction, and terrorist groups with an international reach. A combination of any two of these constituted a significant threat, but the possibility of all three combining and conspiring against the United States was a threat of far greater magnitude. The potential for terrorists groups to acquire WMD from a hostile state and to collaborate with that state to deliver them against the United States existed well before 9/11. The new paradigm, however, recast that potential as an unacceptable threat that had to be dramatically reduced, if not eliminated. Throughout the first half of 2002 Bush used the consultation process to make other government leaders understand his determination to take action against Baghdad and to persuade them to join him.

The administration tirelessly placed Iraq at the centre of the war on terrorism and branded Saddam's regime the source of the greatest threat after 9/11. Bush remained convinced that Iraq had ongoing WMD programmes, concluding in March 2002 that Iraq's refusal to cooperate with the UN meant that Saddam had 'obviously got something to hide'.[18] Iraq's suspected WMD programmes were the crucial factor that allowed the United States to place Baghdad at the centre of the nexus. As far as the White House was concerned the burden of proof lay with Baghdad, and Bush demanded that Saddam had to prove that he wasn't developing weapons of mass destruction.[19] The logical conclusion here is that if Saddam could not prove that he *did not* possess WMD or active WMD programmes, then the United States would use force to change the regime.

Bush stated on a number of occasions that he could not allow the potential threat to materialise – it was simply not permissible. 'Our mission', he said in February 2002, 'includes countries which develop weapons of mass destruction, nations with a history of brutality. If they're ever able to mate up with terrorist organizations, the free world will be threatened. And this President is not going to allow regimes such as Iran, Iraq and North Korea to threaten our way of life.'[20] In March he insisted that 'We cannot allow nations that have got a history of totalitarianism, dictatorship – a nation, for example, like Iraq that poisoned her own people – to develop a weapon of mass destruction and mate-up with terrorist organizations who hate freedom-loving countries.'[21] In April, with British Prime Minister Tony Blair at his side, he declared, 'the worst thing that can happen is to allow this man [Saddam Hussein] to abrogate his promise, and hook up with a terrorist network ... We can't let it happen, we just can't let it happen.'[22] More emphatically, he declared in an interview with British television network ITV on 4 April 2002 that he had decided that Saddam had to be removed.[23]

Rice echoed this sentiment. On 29 April she explained how 9/11 underscored

the need to deny terrorists and hostile states the opportunity to acquire weapons of mass destruction. The world's most dangerous people simply cannot be permitted to obtain the world's most dangerous weapons. And it is a stubborn and extremely troubling fact that the list of states that sponsor terror and the lists of states that are seeking to acquire weapons of mass destruction overlap substantially.[24]

By using the language of allowing or not allowing this threat to be realised, Rice and Bush implied that the United States could and would use every means at its disposal to prevent it occurring.

The President's determination to act was intimated in a series of veiled threats to the Iraqi regime in the first half of 2002 that suggested the United States was prepared to use military force if Iraq did not comply with US demands. 'Saddam Hussein', the President warned, 'needs to understand I'm serious about defending our country ... these nations they've got a choice to make. And I'll keep all options available if they don't make the choice.'[25] In March he said that Saddam was a problem that his administration was going to deal with,[26] reiterating in April that 'the policy of my government is the removal of Saddam and that all options are on the table'.[27]

The President's determination that the war on terrorism be prosecuted to a conclusion that involved confronting Iraq was also couched in terms of the weight of history. Here was the United States, the most powerful country the world had ever known. The 9/11 attacks had highlighted the terrifying possibility that Saddam Hussein might provide a terrorist group with chemical, biological or even nuclear weapons to detonate in a US city. The historical record, Bush suggested, would not look kindly on the President that failed to prevent such a threat materialising. It was history, he argued, that had 'called this nation into action'.[28] Furthermore, he was determined to 'seize this moment for the good of the world, for peace in the world and for freedom'.[29]

The focus on Iraq at the heart of the war on terrorism was about more than just the President's personal determination not to allow a particular threat to materialise; it was more than a straightforward policy choice. It was portrayed as an obligation that reflected but also went beyond the President's personal principles: it was a presidential duty, a moral imperative for the nation that he, as president, could not and would not shy away from. Furthermore, the President insisted that the passage of time would not diminish his resolve, assuring his audience in March 2002 that 'this distance between September the 11th is not going to cause me to weaken in my determination to defend our country and to fight for freedom'.[30] This heightened the sense of inevitability that the road to war would be taken.

However, the potential for a concrete threat to emerge from a nexus of hostile states, terrorist groups and WMD is a qualitative, subjective judgement based primarily on intelligence data and analysis. It is not open to quantitative assessment and it is therefore difficult to measure how, if or when the potential for Iraq to provide WMD to 'an al-Qaida type organisation' to use against the United States could have been reduced to an extent to which Bush might no longer have considered it necessary to use military force against Baghdad.[31] It was and remained the President's call, and he clearly saw a threat and could not understand why others did not.[32] A confrontation and a final conclusion to Washington's decade of conflict with Saddam Hussein appeared inevitable.[33]

This was encapsulated in the President's major policy speech at the US Military Academy at West Point on 1 June 2002. The speech reinforced the post-9/11 security paradigm described in the State of the Union Address but further stressed the need to act pre-emptively in relation to the threat from hostile regimes, terrorists and WMD:

> The gravest danger to freedom lies at the perilous crossroads of radicalism and technology. When the spread of chemical and biological and nuclear weapons, along with ballistic missile technology – when that occurs, even weak states and small groups could attain a catastrophic power to strike great nations ... We cannot put our faith in the word of tyrants, who solemnly sign non-proliferation treaties, and then systemically break them. If we wait for threats to fully materialize, we will have waited too long ... We must take the battle to the enemy, disrupt his plans, and confront the worst threats before they emerge. In the world we have entered, the only path to safety is the path of action. And this nation will act ... We will not leave the safety of America and the peace of the planet at the mercy of a few mad terrorists and tyrants. We will lift this dark threat from our country and from the world.[34]

Cheney fully supported this approach, declaring in late June that 'wars are not won on the defensive', and adding, a 'regime that hates America must never be permitted to threaten Americans with weapons of mass destruction'.[35] By June there was no doubt that Iraq was the next target in the war on terrorism and that the United States was prepared to take pre-emptive military action. A decision had been made to remove Saddam Hussein from power and it would not be overturned.[36]

The Pentagon

Senior and influential leaders in the Pentagon fully endorsed the case for war with Iraq. For Rumsfeld, Iraq was a clear threat. He insisted that the US government knew that Iraq had weaponised chemical weapons and had active nuclear and biological weapons programmes.[37] Furthermore, there was little that could be done diplomatically to reduce that threat. Throughout the first half of 2002 Rumsfeld insisted that containment and UN initiatives simply would not work, and was deeply sceptical as to whether UN inspections could disarm Iraq of its WMD or build any confidence that Baghdad did not have WMD programmes.[38] He cited a number of reasons for this: first, the 'greater degrees of mobility' of Iraq's WMD, particularly its biological weapons programme, meant that inspectors would not be able to find anything;[39] second, the fact that Saddam Hussein's regime was replete with 'accomplished liars'.[40] When asked in June 2002 what he made of the statement by the Iraqi government that it had no WMD and was not developing any, Rumsfeld replied: 'They are lying. Next';[41] and third, the fact that for inspections to have any chance of working, a much more intrusive regime with many more inspectors would be required that Iraq would simply not acquiesce to.[42] Rumsfeld said he had 'looked at inspection regimes and it's hard for me to fashion one in my mind that's sufficiently intrusive that would give one high confidence that they would not be able to measurably improve their circumstance each year with respect to WMD'.[43]

Rumsfeld was equally doubtful whether Powell's smart sanctions initiative would prevent Iraq developing WMD, and said so explicitly in June 2002.[44] Finally, he saw absolutely no hope of any form of internal regime change.[45] When asked whether he expected to see regime change in Iraq during his tenure as Secretary of Defense he replied 'Oh, I would certainly hope so.'[46] Rumsfeld's deputy, Paul Wolfowitz, shared his perception of the threat and insisted that 9/11 signalled the time to confront Iraq once and for all.[47] He too maintained that countries such as Iraq, developing WMD, supporting terrorism and hostile to the United States had to be dealt with because they now constituted 'a deadly mixture that we can't continue living with indefinitely'.[48]

The Chair of Rumsfeld's Defense Policy Board, Richard Perle, went even further. He claimed in July 2002 that 'It is likely that chemical weapons, biological weapons in the possession of the Iraqis derived during the cold war from the Soviet Union are now being disseminated to terrorists.' As a result of this assumed activity Perle alarmingly insisted that 'every day we wait is a day during which a plan may well be forming that could result in the deaths of a great many Americans. Time is not on our side ... we have no time to lose, and I think the president understands that and it's probably taken too long already, but I don't think it'll be much longer.'[49]

Powell, on the other hand, presented a less alarmist view of the threat posed by Saddam Hussein. His view in December 2001 was that Iraq's nuclear capability had been capped, that Iraq still had some stocks of chemical weapons and that

Baghdad might be trying to generate a biological weapons capability again. Saddam was considered only 'a *potential* danger to the *region*' (emphasis added), rather than an imminent threat to the United States.[50] This threat assessment differed markedly from that of other senior officials. In February Powell again presented a much more moderate view of the threat from Iraq, arguing that there was no link between Iraq and 9/11 and that Iraq remained contained, or 'bottled up'.[51] Nevertheless Powell did maintain that Iraq had WMD and was continuing to develop them, and he too linked Iraq to the war on terrorism, stating 'we should be fearful too because the weapons he is developing could well fall into the hands of terrorists who might be able to use them'.[52] As for other senior officials, 9/11 had shifted Powell's views on Iraq.[53]

Military planning

Military planning for a war with Iraq was initiated by Bush in November 2001. From the President's State of the Union Address to his UN speech the planning process rapidly gathered momentum. Concerns about a war were raised by the Joint Chiefs of Staff, who were wary of becoming immersed in urban warfare against a regime that might use WMD as a last resort. The civilian leadership in the Pentagon, however, remained determined to pursue regime change.[54]

At the end of December 2001, General Tommy Franks requested permission to begin a series of preliminary tasks to improve the US military position in the Gulf region with a view to a war with Iraq. Bush approved them all. The tasks included building up forces in Kuwait from 500 to 3,000 troops and building a command-and-control facility in Qatar. This would be done incrementally to avoid provocation and speculation.[55] In February 2002, Franks presented Rumsfeld with the fourth iteration of the Iraq war plan with substantially lower numbers of troops.[56] At this stage, it was later reported, planning and preparations for a war with Iraq began to hinder US actions against Osama bin Laden and the Taliban in Afghanistan, findings that suggested the administration's overriding priority in the war on terrorism was now Iraq.[57]

The war plan was finally presented by Franks to Bush and the National Security Council on 5 August 2002. The plan had undergone radical changes and detailed analysis, the service commanders had been briefed, and the Joint Chiefs of Staff had conducted a tabletop exercise, called Prominent Hammer, to assess the plan's feasibility.[58] It had been decided that the operation to depose Saddam Hussein would begin with a massive air offensive, Special Forces operations aimed at weakening Iraqi air defences, covert CIA actions to foment a coup in Iraq and prepare for military strikes, and land and sea-based forces attacking Iraq from the north, south and west. The war plan was now highly evolved and working its way through the relevant military channels.[59]

By now the views of Middle East government leaders had been canvassed by the Vice President and a range of further preparatory tasks were under way. These included the rapid expansion of the al-Udeid air base near Doha, Qatar, to handle a hundred or more strike aircraft,[60] large-scale servicing of US Army military trucks, enquiries about the availability of oil tankers needed to transport aviation and other fuel to the Gulf for use by US forces,[61] and requests to the British government to build special shelters on the Indian Ocean territory of Diego Garcia to accommodate B-2 stealth bombers.[62] The White House was fully prepared for a war, and the provisional date was February 2003.[63]

Not only had the US developed a comprehensive military plan and begun military preparations for war, but it also began low-level military operations against Iraq under the guise of enforcing the no-fly zones. Throughout 2002, US and UK warplanes significantly increased the number of bombing raids against Iraq. British Secretary of State for Defence Geoff Hoon was cited in a leaked Downing Street memo of 23 July 2002 that the US had begun 'spikes of activity' in its bombardment to put pressure on Iraq.[64] This included a substantial strike on Iraq's H-3 airfield, a major air defence installation in western Iraq, by 100 American and British warplanes at the start of September 2002. This was the first time warplanes had attacked a target in western Iraq while patrolling the southern no-fly zone. It was reported that the operation 'seemed designed to destroy air defenses to allow easy access for special forces helicopters to fly into Iraq via Jordan or Saudi Arabia to hunt down Scud missiles before a possible war within the next few months'.[65]

Powell and smart sanctions

As the administration attacked the Taliban and al-Qaida in Afghanistan and reviewed its strategy on the war on terrorism and revised its military plans for Iraq, the State Department continued its work on smart sanctions. In November 2001 the Security Council voted unanimously to approve the smart sanctions programme (resolution 1382) to come into effect by 30 May 2002, and Powell stated that the administration believed smart sanctions were the way forward.[66] These sanctions, Powell argued, would supply more goods to the Iraqi people but 'at the same time make sure that the Iraqi regime is contained with respect to the development of weapons of mass destruction'. Agreement was eventually reached and the UNSC passed resolution 1409 formally adopting the new export control system. Regime change, however, was not part of Russian Foreign Minister Igor Ivanov's plan. He viewed the new sanctions regime, plus the return of UN inspectors, as the route to 'the final removal of sanctions against Iraq'.[67] Powell conversely stated that even though a new sanctions regime had been agreed, he found it 'hard to imagine that we will ever find a solution to this problem with Saddam Hussein sitting at the head of that regime ... what we have to do is persuade the international community that this is a real and present danger requiring political, diplomatic and perhaps military action to resolve'.[68]

Despite his considerable efforts to shore up containment through the smart sanctions initiative, Powell now seemed to accept that regime change was the only viable solution to the problems posed by Saddam Hussein. Bush later suggested that Powell's smart sanctions initiative had little impact on his regime change policy and were part of the old defunct containment strategy: 'prior to September the 11th,' he said on 30 January 2003, 'we were discussing smart sanctions. We were trying to fashion a sanction regime that would make it more likely to be able to contain somebody like Saddam Hussein. After September the 11th, the doctrine of containment just doesn't hold any water, as far as I'm concerned.'[69]

As the United States' principal diplomat, Powell continued to tread a difficult path balancing US support for UNSC resolutions and the peaceful disarmament of Iraq's WMD on the one hand, with the administration's policy of confrontation and regime change on the other. The friction between these two aspects of the administration's Iraq policy was exemplified by the issue of UN inspections. In December 2001 Powell declared that the only way to resolve whether or not Iraq was developing WMD was to 'send the inspectors in'. But he differentiated this approach from US policy, stating that 'the United States still continues to believe as a separate matter that it would be better to have a different regime in Iraq... It is a goal of the United States. But the United Nations' goal is the inspectors and getting rid of those weapons of mass destruction.'[70] Powell stated on a number of occasions that inspectors should be re-admitted to Iraq because of the useful role they could play, but said that regime change remained the policy of the United States 'regardless of what the inspectors do'.[71] This reinforced the view that a renewed round of inspections would serve only as a diversion from or a means of facilitating the administration's policy of regime change. Concerted action to support the UN's goals, as described by Powell, was never really part of the Bush administration's strategy.

Taking the case to the United Nations

During the second half of 2002 the White House made two important decisions. The first was to go to Congress and seek formal endorsement for the use of military force against Iraq if that proved necessary, and the second was to go to the UN to seek a new resolution sanctioning the use of force should Iraq continue to abrogate existing UNSC resolutions. To succeed in both these tasks the administration increased the level and vigour of its rhetoric against Baghdad to convince members of Congress and the UNSC of the need to confront Saddam Hussein and remove him from power if he refused to accede to US demands and UNSC resolutions. Former Treasury Secretary Paul O'Neill recounts that the administration sharpened its language in August and began to close 'the gap between what had long been clear inside the White House and what was being revealed to the public'.[72] August also saw the creation of the White House Iraq Group (WHIG), established by the President's Chief of Staff Andrew Card to sell the war to the US public.[73] The group included Condoleezza Rice, Bush's political guru Karl Rove, his powerful communications director Karen Hughes, Cheney's Chief of Staff I. Lewis Libby, and Deputy National Security Advisor Stephen

Hadley. There was no going back but the timing was crucial, as Card remarked on the administration's Iraq strategy, 'From a marketing point of view you don't introduce new products in August.'[74]

In August the President decided to make his case to the UN. Not all members of the administration wanted to take this route, but the President was under pressure to seek international legitimacy from a number of quarters. Secretary of State Colin Powell, British Prime Minister Tony Blair, important members of Congress in the House and Senate, and senior conservative Republican voices, including Brent Scowcroft and James Baker, National Security Advisor and Secretary of State to George H. W. Bush respectively, all wanted the President to exhaust all diplomatic options and build a coalition to disarm Iraq if it refused to comply with UNSC resolutions. A coalition would require legitimacy, which meant going through the UN Security Council. Exhausting all diplomatic avenues to ensure British and, more importantly, unqualified Congressional support also meant going to the UN. Powell finally persuaded Bush on 5 August 2002 that international backing would be crucial for both the war and post-war reconstruction.[75] Opinion polls also indicated that many Americans favoured seeking a UN resolution and international support.[76] Warnings from the likes of Scowcroft and Baker not to rush down a unilateral path to war had a marked effect, but it is important to note that neither Scowcroft nor Baker was against regime change.[77]

By taking the issue to the UN, the administration could temper its critics, gain a degree of international support and possibly a UN seal of approval. However, the UN route could potentially have derailed the administration's now considerable momentum behind a war to remove Saddam from power. To mitigate this, the President set a number of explicit and implicit conditions on UN actions.

Bush explicitly stated that he expected a quick resolution on the issue and reiterated his conviction that Saddam would not meet his or the UN's demands.[78] The United States had its own timetable for action in the face of Saddam's intransigence that would not accommodate a drawn-out debate in the UN or a prolonged period of renewed inspections. The President and his senior foreign policy advisers agreed on a strategy that would not allow the UN to delay or dictate the terms of a war. Inspectors would be given one last brief opportunity to test Saddam's will and the international community's resolve to deal with the threat from Baghdad.[79]

Bush implicitly maintained that the US position was not open for negotiation. He was determined to confront and if necessary remove Saddam Hussein in the very near future, and the US would not be swayed from its course. The US analysis of the threat and appropriate response was correct, and the UNSC could 'show some backbone and resolve' and 'show its relevance' only by concurring with the White House. This was reflected in the President's ultimatum that 'if the United Nations Security Council won't deal with the problem, the United States and some of our friends will'.[80] This was the UN's opportunity to get behind the US position rather than the United States' opportunity to accommodate the concerns of the UNSC. Countries that joined the United States were defined by the President as those 'which long for peace and care about the validity of the United Nations', implying that those who opposed the White House had no concern for peace.[81]

Both Cheney and Rumsfeld were wary of becoming mired in a prolonged negotiation and inspection process and strongly urged the President not to ask the UN to produce a new resolution.[82] They thought that forces in and outside government sought to divert, slow or halt the drive to war by entangling US policy in UN bureaucracy and negotiations. To counter these forces Cheney made two significant policy statements in August to place the nexus of Iraq, WMD and al-Qaida at the heart of the war on terrorism and advocate imminent regime change. In a dramatic escalation of rhetoric, Cheney insisted on 26 August that 'The risks of inaction are far greater than the risk of action. If the United States could have preempted 9/11, we would have, no question. Should we be able to prevent another, much more devastating attack, we will, no question. This nation will not live at the mercy of terrorists or terror regimes.' He reiterated the post-9/11security paradigm by stating 'Deliverable weapons of mass destruction in the hands of a terror network, or a murderous dictator, or the two working together, constitutes as grave a threat as can be imagined.'[83]

Iraq's WMD programmes and Baghdad's intentions were now presented as categorical facts: 'there is no doubt that Saddam Hussein now has weapons of mass destruction. There is no doubt he is amassing them to use against our friends, against our allies, and against us', and, more alarmingly, 'Many of us are convinced that Saddam will acquire nuclear weapons fairly soon.' As the President decided to take the issue to the UN, Cheney left no doubt as to the administration's position on further inspections as a response to Iraq's WMD programmes. Inspections, he declared, would not work because 'Saddam Hussein had sought to frustrate and deceive them at every turn, and was often successful in doing so'; sending in inspectors would provide 'false comfort that Saddam was somehow "back in his box" '. Cheney dispelled any hope that the United States might be prepared to revert to a tougher version of containment and abandon the goal of regime change by insisting that containment was simply not possible 'when dictators obtain weapons of mass destruction, and are prepared to share them with terrorists who intend to inflict catastrophic casualties on the United States'. In a similar policy speech on 29 August Cheney argued that the 'old doctrines of security' of containment and deterrence were no longer valid.[84]

On 12 September 2002 Bush addressed the UN in New York. In the weeks before his speech he continued to make the case against Iraq in the context of the war on terrorism.[85] In particular the President expanded the parameters of the war on terrorism to include 'nations that have proven themselves to be bad neighbors and bad actors'.[86] This meant that Iraq's war with Iran, the invasion of Kuwait, the missile attacks on Israel and Saudi Arabia during the 1991 Gulf War, the gassing of the Kurds in Halabja in 1988, the brutal repression of the Marsh

Arab uprising in 1991 and the general viciousness of the Iraqi regime could all be brought to bear in the case against Iraq.

In his address to the United Nations General Assembly, the President restated that Iraq had weapons of mass destruction and that this was a serious threat that the US was no longer prepared to endure:

> We know that Saddam Hussein pursued weapons of mass murder even when inspectors were in his country. Are we to assume that he stopped when they [UN inspectors] left? The history, the logic, and the facts lead to one conclusion: Saddam Hussein's regime is a grave and gathering danger. To suggest otherwise is to hope against the evidence. To assume this regime's good faith is to bet the lives of millions and the peace of the world in a reckless gamble. And this is a risk we must not take.

Here the President presented Iraq's possession of WMD as a solid fact and rested his argument on two important assumptions: that Baghdad began producing WMD after inspectors left the country in 1998 and that Baghdad would be wholly uncooperative. Valid as these assumptions were, based on the historical record and intelligence assessments, they were still assumptions rather than irrefutable facts.

The President, like Cheney, proclaimed that containment had failed: 'We've tried sanctions. We've tried the carrot of oil for food, and the stick of coalition military strikes. But Saddam Hussein has defied all these efforts and continues to develop weapons of mass destruction', implying that this was now the end of the line. It would require Iraq's full cooperation or military force to remove the regime. And for the White House, full cooperation meant *total* cooperation. Only by meeting five conditions set out in previous UNSC resolutions could Baghdad hope to avoid military action, and it was highly unlikely that Saddam would meet any of them. These were listed as: (1) to disclose, remove and destroy all WMD, long-range missiles and associated material; (2) to stop supporting terrorism and actively suppress it; (3) to stop persecuting the Iraqi population; (4) to account for all Gulf War personnel missing in action, return stolen property and accept full liability for losses stemming from its invasion of Kuwait, and cooperate fully with the UN on these matters; and (5) to end all illicit trade outside the oil-for-food programme.[87]

These five demands were similar to those set out in the Clinton administration's 1999 State Department report *Saddam Hussein's Iraq*. The previous consequence of non-compliance was a permanent sanctions regime that Baghdad was increasingly able to circumvent and a low-intensity air war with US and UK warplanes patrolling the no-fly zones. Now the consequence would be a direct attack on Saddam Hussein and his regime, and Bush asked the UNSC for a new resolution to approve this course of action.

After the UN speech Cheney, according to Woodward, suggested that a new UNSC resolution would facilitate a US-led attack on Iraq no matter what the outcome. The full declaration of WMD and WMD activities requested of Iraq in the resolution would

> require Saddam to submit a detailed 'declaration' after a resolution was passed. Iraq would have to give a full accounting of all programs to develop chemical, biological and nuclear weapons ... it was designed more or less as a trap for Saddam. He would claim that he had no WMD and that lie would be grounds for war. Or Saddam would confess he had WMD, proving he had lied for 12 years. As Cheney framed it, 'That would be sufficient cause to say he's lied again, he's not come clean and you'd find material breach and away you'd go'.[88]

September was a turning point for Powell. When Bush went to the UN, the tension between the two strands of US policy toward Iraq – the administration's support for UN-led containment carried forward by Powell and the administration's wider policy of regime change – was resolved: containment-plus was now truly finished. Powell did not place the potential nexus of Iraq, WMD and terrorism at the heart of his arguments as the President and other members of the administration did. For him disarmament was the issue and always had been.[89] This could be achieved through the UN route and weapons inspectors *or* through regime change. Doing nothing was not an option, for Powell it was now one or the other. When Bush went to the UN, the Secretary of State appeared to accept that the latter was the most likely outcome and swung fully behind the White House position.[90]

This was signalled by a number of comments by Powell shortly before Bush's UN speech. In an interview with *Fox News* he firmly reiterated the administration's main arguments in the case against Iraq: the inspectors were not going to disarm Iraq, 'you should have a skeptical attitude as to how much inspections can do, particularly in the presence of a regime that's going to do everything they can to hide things from inspectors'; there was a relationship between Iraq and al-Qaida, we 'know that there is some al-Qaida presence in Iraq'; attacking Iraq was part of the war on terrorism, 'consideration of what to do about Saddam Hussein is very consistent with the war against terror ... to continue our campaign against terrorism, it's absolutely correct for us to be looking at Saddam Hussein and his regime as well'; and time was running short: 'It is not in our interest to let this issue linger indefinitely, as it has lingered for the last several years'.[91]

Conclusion

In the first half of 2002 the Bush administration developed its case against Iraq by placing Saddam's regime at the very heart of the war on terrorism. The White House remained convinced that Iraq was a dangerous and impending threat, and was determined to act. As the White House tried to convince allies and other governments in the Middle East of its case, it also developed comprehensive plans for war.

The President's determination was undeniable: he would not allow the potential threat represented by the nexus to occur and he would do all he could to prevent it occurring. This was an obligation that went beyond his personal conviction. He issued threats to Baghdad, confirmed the US policy of regime change and demanded Iraq prove a difficult negative in terms of its assumed WMD programmes.

The perceived need for international legitimacy persuaded Bush to take the case against Saddam Hussein to the United Nations, but on the President's terms. This was an opportunity for others to get behind the United States. It was not an opportunity to alter the administration's strategy, temper its determination to act or extend its timetable for war in the event of Iraqi non-compliance. As Bush, Rumsfeld and Cheney continued to push for regime change, Powell successfully implemented the smart sanctions initiative. However, as the Secretary of State acknowledged, actions such as these in support of containment now held little currency in a White House geared up for confrontation and war. With the chances of Saddam Hussein complying with the President's demands remote and serious military preparations for war under way, conflict was virtually inevitable. Richard Clarke, the administration's counter-terrorism coordinator, argued that the decision to go to the UN was a major turning point in the road to war, but that 'all along it seemed inevitable that we would invade. Iraq was portrayed as the most dangerous thing in national security. It was an *idée fixe*, a rigid belied, received wisdom, a decision already made and one that no fact or event could derail.'[92] The next chapter explores how the administration stepped up its rhetoric after the UN speech and refused to accommodate any form of compromise.

7

FROM THE UNITED NATIONS
TO WAR

Introduction

After Bush presented his case against Iraq to the UN, the White House was keen to secure a new UNSC resolution. The months after the speech saw senior administration officials escalate their rhetoric against Saddam Hussein and the severity of the threat he represented, supported by Washington's conservative think-tanks. The administration insisted that the world had changed and that the containment of Iraq was no longer feasible or acceptable. The position of Iraq at the centre of a deadly nexus of WMD, terrorist organisations and rogue states hostile to the US was reinforced. The administration was adamant that a firm relationship existed between Saddam Hussein and al-Qaida, and that it was inevitable that Iraq would eventually supply WMD to al-Qaida to be used against the United States. Furthermore, this threat could materialise in the form of a nuclear weapon if it was not dealt with immediately. The threat from Saddam Hussein was therefore portrayed as urgent and unique. With containment and deterrence no longer applicable, a pre-emptive attack was presented as the only reliable way of reducing the threat – a threat that had shifted in the administration's rhetoric from a possibility to a probability to a categorical certainty.

UN inspections could play no useful role in ameliorating this threat other than by verifying Iraq's total cooperation and compliance with the administration's demands. In October 2002 Congress voted to give Bush full authorisation to take action against Iraq, and in November the UNSC unanimously passed resolution 1441 that threatened 'serious consequences' if Iraq continued to violate its obligations. This reinforced the President's demand for unequivocal compliance. By this stage the only option for the White House in the face of Iraqi intransigence was a US-led military invasion. A long period of inspections was dismissed and the option of arming the INC was no longer seriously considered. This chapter explores the administration's heightened rhetoric and the foreclosing of options other than a military invasion after the UN speech and the administration's unequivocal determination to destroy Saddam Hussein's regime.

The world has changed and containment will not work

One of the administration's central arguments after the UN speech was that the world had changed after 9/11 to the extent that containment could not work and the present situation with regard to Iraq was totally unacceptable.[1] On 8 October 2002 Bush forced home his message that the world had changed: 'People are concerned about Saddam, and I understand that', he said. 'But a lot of Americans have understood that the dynamics have shifted since 11 years ago, because of what happened on September the 11th. No longer are we secure.'[2] On 14 October he stated that 'after September the 11th we've entered into a new era and a new war'.[3] Bush also continued to assert that Iraq's active WMD programmes proved that containment had failed.[4] In his January 2003 State of the Union Address Bush proclaimed once more that Iraq could no longer be contained:

> Before September the 11th, many in the world believed that Saddam Hussein could be contained. But chemical agents, lethal viruses and shadowy terrorist networks are not easily contained. Imagine those 19 hijackers with other weapons and other plans – this time armed by Saddam Hussein. It would take one vial, one canister, one crate slipped into this country to bring a day of horror like none we have ever known. We will do everything in our power to make sure that that day never comes.[5]

In testimony before the House Armed Services Committee in September 2002 Rumsfeld argued that the US perception of the international security paradigm changed irrevocably after 9/11, necessitating a new focus on the potential nexus between terrorist networks and 'rogue' states: 'What has changed is our experience on September 11th. What has changed is our appreciation of our vulnerability – and the risks the U.S. faces from terrorist networks and terrorist states armed with weapons of mass destruction.'[6] Rumsfeld described the post-9/11 security environment as 'possibly the most dangerous security environment the world has known', insisting that the gravest danger lay in the risk of not acting against known threats.[7]

In testimony before the Senate Foreign Relations Committee on 26 September 2002 Powell explained that 9/11 had changed the security calculus of the administration: 'a new reality was born', he said. 'We now see that a proven menace like Saddam Hussein in possession of weapons of mass destruction could empower a few terrorists with those weapons to threaten millions of innocent people.' For that very reason this time Iraq had to comply with UN resolutions or face 'decisive action to compel compliance.[8]

The deadly nexus

The administration's second principal argument was that Iraq remained at the heart of the war on terrorism and the post-9/11 paradigm it had constructed. In statements by Bush, Cheney, Rumsfeld and Wolfowitz the potential nexus between Iraq, WMD and terrorist groups evolved into a concrete nexus between Iraq, WMD and al-Qaida itself, rather than just 'an al-Qaida-type organisation'. The possibility that Baghdad would actively team up with an international terrorist organisation such as al-Qaida was increasingly presented as fact, and strong claims were made about the relationship between them. The threat posed by this nexus was restated time and again as the UN and governments around the world debated the US case for confronting and attacking Iraq.

On 23 September Bush described Saddam as a 'man who would use weapons of mass destruction at the drop of a hat, a man who would be willing to team up with terrorist organizations with weapons of mass destruction to threaten America'.[9] Three days later the President insisted, 'The regime has long-standing and continuing ties to terrorist organizations. And there are al-Qaida terrorists inside Iraq.'[10] In October Bush depicted Saddam as 'addicted' to weapons of mass destruction. He claimed that 'Iraq and al-Qaida have had high-level contacts that go back a decade', that 'Iraq has trained al-Qaida members in bomb-making and poisons and deadly gases', and that 'confronting the threat posed by Iraq is crucial to winning the war on terror'.[11] This escalated further when the President argued that Saddam 'is a man who would like nothing more than to team up with a terrorist network; a man who could use a terrorist network perhaps to use the weapons of mass destruction he's developed',[12] and that Saddam 'would like to use al-Qaida as a forward army'.[13] He went on to contend that Iraq had provided al-Qaida with chemical and biological weapons training and was 'harboring a terrorist network, headed by a senior al-Qaida terrorist planner'.[14]

The perceived threat posed by the potential nexus of WMD, Saddam Hussein and al-Qaida was no longer a possibility that the US had to guard against; it was now a probability that would almost certainly occur if the US did not act. Bush went on to make over twenty speeches around the US throughout October and November 2002 setting out the case that Iraq had WMD and a relationship with al-Qaida, that it could, and probably would, provide WMD for terrorists to use against the United States, and that the US could not afford to wait and must act now.[15]

Cheney was equally eager to link Iraq, WMD and al-Qaida: 'We've already found confirmation that the Al-Qaida terrorists are pursuing weapons of mass destruction. At the same time there's a danger of terror groups joining together with the regimes that have or are seeking to build such weapons. In Iraq, we know that Saddam Hussein is pressing forward with these capabilities', he said in October 2002, asserting that Iraq was 'producing chemical and biological weapons and aggressively pursuing a nuclear weapons program while also working to develop long-range missiles'.[16] He repeated this assertion in December, stating that there was 'a grave danger that al-Qaida or other terrorists will join with outlaw regimes that have these weapons to attack their common enemy, the United States of America. That is why confronting the threat posed by Iraq is not a distraction from the war on terror. It is absolutely crucial to winning the war on terror.'[17] Bush and Cheney were joined by Rice who claimed that there was a concrete relationship between Iraq and al-Qaida and that Iraq provided training to al-Qaida in chemical weapons development.[18]

The White House was fully supported by the Pentagon, not least by Rumsfeld. As far as the Defense Secretary was concerned there was no doubt that Iraq had WMD and a relationship with al-Qaida. On WMD he said in September 2002 that 'There's no debate in the world as to whether they have those weapons. There's no debate in the world as to whether they're continuing to develop and acquire them... We all know that. A trained ape knows that.'[19] Iraq, Rumsfeld argued, had 'massive tunnelling systems' for concealing WMD programmes, mobile biological capabilities, and unmanned aerial vehicles for delivering WMD.[20] On al-Qaida he insisted that 'We know that al-Qaida is operating in Iraq today',[21] and described the contention that Saddam was not aware of their presence and what they were doing as ludicrous.[22] For Rumsfeld, the nexus between 'rogue states', WMD and terrorist networks was a reality rather than a possibility: 'after September 11th, they ['rogue' states] have discovered a new means of delivering these weapons – terrorist networks'.[23]

Rumsfeld was convinced that attacking Iraq was central to the war on terrorism and not a distraction from it: 'Iraq is a part of the Global War on Terror – stopping terrorist regimes from acquiring weapons of mass destruction *is* a key objective of that war.' In testimony before the House and Senate Select Committee on Intelligence, Wolfowitz was equally resolute: 'separating out the issue of Iraq as not part of the war on terrorism is a mistake... They really are part of a piece.'[24] In October he professed:

> It is hard to see how we can expect to be successful in the long run if we leave Iraq as a sanctuary for terrorists and its murderous dictator in defiant safety. Saddam Hussein supports and conspires with our terrorist enemies. He lends them both moral and material support. Disarming Saddam Hussein and fighting the war on terror are not merely related, they are one and the same. If we can defeat a terrorist regime in Iraq it will be a defeat for terrorists globally.[25]

Washington's conservative think-tanks were in no doubt that confronting Iraq was at the centre of the war on terrorism. In December 2002 William Kristol asserted: 'Regime change in Iraq and the destruction of al-Qaida are two related fronts in one war, and both fronts should be prosecuted aggressively and simultaneously.'[26] Meanwhile the Center for Security Policy insisted there was a concrete link between Iraq and al-Qaida: 'there is considerable evidence that Saddam Hussein has long been associated with and been willing to support, facilitate and otherwise exploit terrorist organizations like al-Qaida'.[27] The Center suggested that Iraq was linked to the bombing of the Murrah Federal Building in Oklahoma City in 1996 and the bombing of the World Trade Center in 1993, and that 'another government played an indispensable role in planning, facilitating and executing the September 11th attacks: Saddam Hussein's regime in Iraq'.[28]

The administration's insistence on a relationship between Iraq and al-Qaida was informed and supported by CIA Director George Tenet, who provided a letter at the request of Senator Bob Graham, Chair of the Senate Select Committee on Intelligence, on 7 October 2002 detailing Iraq's links to al-Qaida.[29] The administration's claims were refuted by respected scholars and US and British intelligence officials (see Chapter 9).[30]

A nuclear nightmare

The ultimate catastrophe that could potentially emanate from this nexus of 'rogue' states, WMD and international terrorism was the detonation of an Iraqi nuclear weapon in a US city by a terrorist group allied with Saddam Hussein at some point in the future. The President used just such disturbing imagery to convey his view of the threat from Iraq and the need for a military response: 'The regime is seeking a nuclear bomb, and with fissile material, could build one within a year... Each passing day could be the one on which the Iraqi regime gives anthrax or VX – nerve gas – or some day a nuclear weapon to a terrorist ally.'[31] Rice supported this assertion: 'We do know that he is actively pursuing a nuclear weapon', she said. 'We know that he has the infrastructure, nuclear scientists to make a nuclear weapon.'[32]

Bush went even further in October, saying 'Saddam Hussein has held numerous meetings with Iraqi nuclear scientists, a group he calls his "nuclear mujahideen" – his nuclear holy warriors... Facing clear evidence of peril, we cannot wait for the final proof – the smoking gun – that could come in the form of a mushroom cloud.'[33] He claimed that Baghdad 'has the scientists and facilities to build nuclear weapons, and is seeking the materials needed to do so'.[34] By describing Saddam's nuclear scientists as 'mujahideen' Bush merged the two powerful images of Saddam's WMD and Islamic terrorism into one. White House claims about the extent of Iraq's nuclear weapons programme were supported by Tenet. Tenet claimed in February 2002 and again in September 2002 that 'Saddam never abandoned his nuclear weapons program. Iraq maintains a significant number of nuclear scientists, program documentation and probably some dual-use manufacturing infrastructure that could support a reinvigorated nuclear weapons program.'[35]

This was the Vice President's foremost concern. After his tour of the Middle East at the start of 2002, Cheney's concern about WMD in the post-9/11 security paradigm narrowed to a specific focus on nuclear weapons, particularly the vital importance of preventing Iraq from developing nuclear weapons, a capability he insisted Baghdad was actively pursuing.[36] 'We do know, with *absolute certainty*, that he [Saddam Hussein] is using his procurement system to acquire the equipment he needs in order to enrich uranium to build a nuclear weapon [emphasis added],'[37] he said in September 2002, insisting that Saddam had 'reconstituted his nuclear program to develop a nuclear weapon'.[38] In the days before the war Cheney again warned that it was only a matter of time until Saddam acquired nuclear weapons and for that reason alone he had to be disarmed and deposed.[39] These claims were based on inconclusive intelligence (see below) and were contrary to statements by the IAEA. But Cheney was not for turning, and a few days before the war he declared on NBC's *Meet the Press* that 'we believe he has, in fact, reconstituted nuclear weapons', claiming that the IAEA's assessment that Iraq had no residual nuclear weapons programme was 'frankly wrong'.[40]

The possibility of Baghdad supplying one of a few precious nuclear weapons to a terrorist group to detonate in the United States wasn't Cheney's only nuclear concern. The prospect of a Saddam 'Armed with an arsenal of these weapons of terror, and seated atop ten percent of the world's oil reserves', was equally alarming. From there, 'Saddam Hussein could then be expected to seek domination of the entire Middle East, take control of a great portion of the world's energy supplies, directly threaten America's friends throughout the region, and subject the United States or any other nation to nuclear blackmail'.[41] The United States, Cheney argued, would not allow Saddam 'to dominate the Middle East and threaten the United States'.[42]

The administration used two important pieces of evidence for Iraq's nuclear weapons programme. The first was documents received by US intelligence agencies in October 2001 purportedly showing that Iraq had purchased significant quantities of uranium oxide from Niger in 1999.[43] Through a series of complex industrial processes uranium oxide can be made into highly enriched uranium for use in a nuclear weapon. This material, plus additional documentation and analysis, was presented in a Defense Intelligence Agency (DIA) report in February 2002.[44] Later that month Joseph Wilson, a retired US diplomat, was sent to Niger by the CIA to investigate the case. Wilson concluded that the report was false and that no such deal had been reached between Iraq and Niger.[45] This information was relayed to the FBI, the Justice Department, the Joint Chiefs of Staff and the DIA in March 2002. Nevertheless, Wilson's report was not conclusive and a few days later the CIA issued a third intelligence report stating that Niger had agreed to provide Iraq with 500 tons of uranium oxide per year. The claim continued to be supported by the CIA, the DIA and by the British government in its 24 September 2002 White Paper on Iraq's WMD, which said 'there is intelligence that Iraq has sought the supply of significant quantities of uranium from Africa'. The claim was presented as fact by the US and UK despite serious doubts as to its veracity. In October 2002 the IAEA concluded that the documents were forgeries.

The second piece of evidence was a claim that aluminium tubes purchased by Iraq were of a type specifically suited to making centrifuges. Centrifuges are the key component in the main industrial process for enriching uranium to a level suitable for use as nuclear fuel or for use in a nuclear weapon. Evidence that Iraq was purchasing such tubes was cited by the United States as proof that Iraq had an active nuclear weapons programme.[46] It was later shown conclusively that the tubes were part of a conventional Iraqi rocket programme.[47] Nevertheless, the United States continued to assert that Iraq had an active nuclear weapons programme.

An urgent threat and pre-emptive action

With containment unconditionally ruled out and Baghdad at the centre of a nexus that could result in a covert nuclear attack on US soil, Iraq was increasingly proclaimed a unique and urgent danger that required pre-emptive action. 'The danger to our country is grave. The danger to our country is growing', Bush said in September 2002. 'The dangers we face will only worsen from month to month and from year to year. To ignore these threats is to encourage them.'[48] The pre-emption argument was bolstered further here as the President argued that doing nothing about the potential threat from a terrorist group armed with Iraqi WMD would actually encourage the realisation of that threat. The following month he described Iraq as 'a threat of unique urgency'[49] and claimed that 'while there are many dangers in the world, the threat from Iraq stands alone'.[50] Time was running out for Iraq, Bush insisted. The urgency of the threat demanded immediate action because 'delay, indecision and inaction could lead to a massive and sudden horror. By timely and resolute action, we can defend ourselves and shape a peaceful future.'[51] Powell, who was now firmly taking the administration's line, agreed: 'The more we wait, the more chance there is for this dictator with clear ties to terrorist groups, including al-Qaida, more time for him to pass a weapon, share a technology, or use these weapons again.'[52]

For Rumsfeld the threat from Iraq was also urgent and unique. In testimony before Congress in September 2002 he set out the case: 'There are a number of terrorist states pursuing weapons of mass destruction – Iran, Libya, North Korea, Syria, to name but a few. But no terrorist state poses a greater and more immediate threat to the security of our people, and the stability of the world, than the regime of Saddam Hussein in Iraq.' Iraq, Rumsfeld argued, was unique,[53] and a 'classic example of the nexus between a terrorist state and well advanced weapons of mass destruction programs and relationships with terrorists'.[54]

Rumsfeld also maintained that the threat was so urgent that it required pre-emptive action. He argued that the potential for a material threat to emerge from the nexus of WMD-armed 'rogue' states and terrorists now had to be considered inevitable rather than just probable or possible, and because it was considered inevitable it could happen at any time. Therefore this threat, by definition, had to be considered one of constant urgency and imminence: 'we have to recognize that terrorist networks have relationships with terrorist states that have weapons of mass destruction, and that they inevitably are going to get their hands on them, and they would not hesitate one minute in using them. That's the world we live in.'[55] Wolfowitz agreed that the United States *had* to assume that Iraq would join forces with al-Qaida, stating that 'The most dangerous assumption of all ... is the assumption that Saddam would *not* use terrorists as an instrument of revenge [emphasis added].'[56]

Four months later Rumsfeld insisted that such attacks could not be deterred, essentially necessitating and legitimising pre-emptive action.[57] 'If they believe they can conceal their responsibility for an attack, then they would likely not be deterred', Rumsfeld argued in September 2002. 'Do you believe it is our responsibility to wait for a nuclear, chemical or biological 9/11? Or is it the responsibility of free people to do something now – to take steps to deal with the threat *before* we are attacked?'[58] In the case of Iraq, Rumsfeld assured members of Congress in September 2002 that 'the Iraqi regime poses a growing danger to the safety and security of our people, and of the world',[59] maintaining a week later that 'time is not on our side here. He's got the oil revenues, he's buying additional weapons, he's moving his weapons of mass destruction programs forward, he's dealing with terrorists. And every week month and year that go on he's going to be more of a threat not less of a threat.'[60]

Wolfowitz wholeheartedly agreed with the case for pre-emptive action against Iraq, maintaining that 'the risks of inaction are the continuing and growing danger that tens of thousands, or even hundreds of thousands, of Americans will die in some catastrophic attack with a biological weapon, or if we wait long enough, a nuclear weapon. So the risks of inaction are severe.'[61]

> The more time passes the more time Saddam Hussein has to develop his deadly weapons and to acquire more [he argued]. The more time he has to plant sleeper agents in the United States and other friendly countries or to supply deadly weapons to terrorists he can then disown, the greater the danger... We cannot afford to wait until Saddam Hussein or some terrorist supplied by him attacks us with a chemical or biological or, worst of all, a nuclear weapon, to recognize the danger that we face.[62]

The doctrine of pre-emptive attack against hostile WMD-armed adversaries was formalised in the National Security Strategy (NSS) published by the White House in October 2002. The NSS restated that the administration made no distinction between terrorists and those who harboured or supported them, and maintained that it would continue to focus on the nexus of terrorist organisations and their sponsors that threatened the US and had or were developing WMD. It went on to declare that the US would take pre-emptive action against 'rogue states and their terrorist clients before they are able to threaten or use weapons of mass destruction'.[63] This was reinforced two months later in the administration's National Strategy to Combat Weapons of Mass Destruction, which stated the need to 'defend against WMD-armed adversaries, including in appropriate cases through preemptive measures'.[64] The argument that containment no longer worked and that Iraq posed a unique and imminent threat led inexorably to the solution of a pre-emptive attack set out in the NSS. Pre-emption was the new mindset. As Rice, who was heavily involved in drafting the two documents, commented, 'as a matter of common sense, the United States must be prepared to take action, when necessary, before threats have fully materialized'.[65]

UN inspections

Given the urgent nature of the threat and the assumption that Baghdad would remain defiantly mulish, the administration had a dim view of UNSC calls for a renewed inspections process after the President's UN speech. Bush had already said that inspections and UN debate could not go on for long. After the passage of UNSC Resolution 1441 he put strict conditions on further inspections, stipulating that Saddam had to hand over all of Iraq's WMD and associated material that US and other intelligence agencies insisted Iraq still possessed, and that there could be no negotiations with Baghdad about the nature of the inspections regime and the obligations on Iraq.[66] To that end, the administration argued that the UN inspectors had a narrowly defined function as recipients and verifiers of this process, their responsibility 'simply to confirm the evidence of voluntary and total disarmament. It is Saddam Hussein who has the responsibility to provide that evidence as directed, and in full.'[67]

Rumsfeld, Wolfowitz and Perle insisted that inspections would not work. Rumsfeld was adamant that inspections could only occur with a cooperative country, otherwise there was no point: 'an inspection really is not designed for a hostile environment. It just isn't, that isn't how its supposed to work.'[68] In September 2002 he condemned inspections as a waste of time in which Iraq goes 'week after week after week stiffing the international community, the UN and others'.[69] Wolfowitz reinforced this view, claiming in December 2002 that 'It is not and cannot be the responsibility of the inspectors to scour every square inch of Iraq. It cannot be their responsibility to search out and find every illegal weapon or system. That would be a task beyond their means. Nor is it their responsibility to disarm Iraq.'[70] Perle maintained that it was 'simply not possible to devise an inspection regime on territory controlled by Saddam Hussein that can be effective in locating, much less eliminating, his weapons of mass destruction',[71] later claiming that the United States 'would be fools to accept inspections, even an inspection regime far more ambitious than anything the UN contemplates'.[72]

The outcome of a new inspections process would have little effect on the administration's regime change policy. This view was epitomised by John Bolton, Under Secretary of State for Arms Control and International Security Affairs. Bolton was a staunch ally of Wolfowitz and Cheney, regarded as the number three in the State Department's policy-making machinery and a firm advocate of regime change. He stated in August 2002: 'Let there be no mistake. While we also insist on the reintroduction of the weapons inspectors, our policy at the same time insists on regime change in Baghdad. That policy will not be altered whether the inspectors go in or not.'[73] Rumsfeld was also of the view that regardless of what weapons or WMD programmes UN inspectors uncovered, US policy would remain one of regime change.[74]

If Saddam refused to comply by insisting that there were no WMD or WMD programmes in Iraq, he would not be believed – 'Should he again deny that this arsenal exists, he will have entered his final stage with a lie',[75] said Bush; 'if they continue claiming that they don't have these weapons when we have multiple indications that they do then clearly their attitude has not changed',[76] argued Wolfowitz – and would consequently be found to be in 'material breach' of existing and any new UN resolutions. Iraq had to prove that it did not have WMD or WMD programmes and no amount of inspections would be enough to convince the administration that Iraq did not have WMD. Just because inspections did not find anything did not mean the WMD were not there.[77] Iraq's failure to *prove* its full compliance would result in military action. All Iraq had to do, Powell said in January 2003, was 'come forward with the evidence for that truth and lay it out before the world, lay it out before the inspectors to verify, and there will be no war'.[78] But Iraq did not take that step. Of course, if Iraq genuinely had no WMD or WMD programmes, then there was little it could do to avoid war.[79]

The conservative think-tanks were categorically opposed to UN inspections. Frank Gaffney, former Deputy Assistant Secretary of Defense for Nuclear Forces and Arms Control Under Assistant Secretary Richard Perle from 1983 to 1987 and founder and Director of CSP, was concerned that UN inspections could derail the administration's drive to war.[80] He argued:

> Even if, miraculously, every one of Iraq's secret weapons sites were found and their contents destroyed, as long as Saddam remains in power and has access to technicians, know-how and oil resources, it will be but a matter of months before he is back in the WMD business. In short, inspections without regime change amount to nothing more than an expensive, but ultimately futile postponement of the day of reckoning with Saddam Hussein.[81]

The Heritage Foundation's James Philips argued that inspections would be counterproductive because even if Baghdad surrendered all of its WMD, it could 'reconstitute its weapons programs in months, if not weeks, after the inspectors left. It has the scientists, the knowledge, and the technical base to regenerate prohibited weapons programs and the oil money to buy what it cannot make.'[82] Regime change was presented as the only solution.

UNMOVIC and IAEA inspectors entered Iraq on 25 November 2002 to begin inspections, and by the end of December over 100 inspectors were in the country. Hans Blix and Mohamed El Baradei delivered their verdict on Iraq's 12,000-page WMD declaration to the UNSC on 19 December and on 9 January 2003 delivered an interim report to the Security Council on progress to date, stating that no 'smoking gun' had been found. The inspection teams did go on to find a crate of warheads designed for chemical weapons. These had no chemicals in them but should have been declared. The inspectors also discovered that Iraq had tested ballistic missiles beyond the 150 km limit imposed by the UNSC and ordered the missiles to be destroyed, which Iraq did at the beginning of March. In total, over 70 Al Samoud 2 missiles were broken up at that start of 2003.[83] Blix reported once more to the Security Council on 27 January and declared that whilst there had been improved cooperation on the Iraqi side, there were still a number of 'unresolved disarmament issues'.[84] Blix and El Baradei gave their final reports to the Security Council on 7 March. Blix repeated that Iraq was cooperating but that the inspectors still needed either documentary evidence of the destruction of WMD or the WMD themselves to resolve all disarmament issues. Blix, in his own words, refused to assume that items unaccounted for must still exist as viable WMD. El Baradei stated that there was no evidence or plausible indication of the revival of Iraq's nuclear weapons programme.[85]

War plans

As the President went to the UN, plans for war accelerated. As far as the administration was concerned this was the only option. As Rumsfeld explained in September 2002, Saddam Hussein could go into exile, but 'he clearly won't do that out of choice'; Saddam might acquiesce in everything requested of him, but 'he's certainly given no indication of that in his background';[86] a popular uprising could occur, but 'it's a very repressive regime. It would be a very difficult thing to do'; or the United States could invade and change the regime.[87] The option of further inspections and sanctions was not an option for Rumsfeld, for whom 'every single approach that the world community and the United Nations have taken has failed'.[88] 'We've been trying political methods', Rumsfeld said on 25 September, 'we've tried economic sanctions, we've tried military activity in the Northern and Southern no-fly zones with our coalition partners, and none of them have worked. That is clear.'[89] A fifth option of arming the INC and pursuing the plan developed by conservative think-tanks during the Clinton administration had fallen by the wayside. General Richard Myers, Chairman of the Joint Chiefs of Staff, acknowledged in October 2002 that training the INC had not begun and that plans were still being evaluated because the government was only in the preliminary stages of examining that option.[90] According to Powell, most of the money available under the 1998 ILA had been distributed but not directly for the purpose of 'putting an armed opposition inside of Iraq'. Whilst this might happen at some point in the future, such plans were only at the 'feasibility study' stage.[91] A full-scale military invasion remained the government's only option.

A few days before his UN speech the President had been briefed by Franks and Rumsfeld on the latest war plan, and on 20 September White House and Pentagon officials publicly disclosed that the Defense Department had finished a highly detailed plan for attacking Iraq and delivered it to the President.[92] The following month, on 18 October 2002, Air Force Lieutenant General Michael Hayden, Director of the National Security Agency, briefed key members of his organisation via an NSA closed-circuit television to prepare for war in Iraq.[93] In October the Army's V corps and I Marine Expeditionary Force were ordered to deploy headquarters and staffs to Kuwait, the first non-routine dispatch of conventional ground forces to the Gulf.[94] By the end of November mobilisation deployment orders had been issued for war against Iraq, the first major step to implement the war plan. This led to a military planning exercise called Internal Look conducted from Central Command's new command-and-control facility in Qatar. It was a rehearsal for an invasion of Iraq.[95] On 23 January 2003 Franks delivered the final war plan to Rumsfeld and Myers, two days after the British government announced it was sending 30,000 troops to the Gulf.[96] By 28 February there were reportedly 200,000 troops in the region.[97] War was now imminent.

Military preparations for a large-scale ground invasion and air offensive began in early 2002 with a view to conflict towards the end of the year. The subsequent decision to take the confrontation with Iraq to the UN Security Council postponed conflict until early 2003 and allowed a greater build-up of forces in the region than might originally have been planned.

Demands and compliance

The President's determination to deal with Iraq once and for all resulted in a strict set of demands and an explicit stipulation of full compliance. The President continued to demand that Iraq comply with all UNSC resolutions and meet the five demands set out in his address to the UN General Assembly. 'The gathering threat of Iraq must be confronted fully and finally', he said on 10 October. 'There can be no negotiations. The days of Iraq acting as an outlaw state are coming to an end.'[98] On 16 October 2002, the President signed Congressional resolution H.J. Res. 114 into law as P.L. 107–243, the 'Authorization for Use of Military Force Against Iraq Resolution of 2002'. The resolution authorised Bush to use US armed forces to defend the United States against the threat posed by Iraq and to enforce UNSC resolutions regarding Iraq. On signing the resolution into law, Bush reiterated his five demands and explicitly set out the choice faced by Saddam Hussein: 'the days of Iraq flouting the will of the world, brutalizing its own people, and terrorizing its neighbors must – and will – end. Iraq will either comply with all U.N. resolutions, rid itself of weapons of mass destruction, and in its support for terrorists, or it will be compelled to do so.'[99]

After the UN Security Council unanimously passed resolution 1441 on 8 November 2002, Bush once more set out the stark choice faced by Baghdad and his determination to use military force to resolve the issue once and for all:

> Saddam Hussein must fully disclose and destroy his weapons of mass destruction. He must submit to any and all methods to verify his compliance. His cooperation must be prompt and unconditional, or he will face the severest consequences ... America will be making only one determination: is Iraq meeting the terms of the Security Council resolution or not? ... If Iraq fails to fully comply, the United States and other

nations will disarm Saddam Hussein... The outcome of the current crisis is already determined: the full disarmament of weapons of mass destruction by Iraq will occur. The only question for the Iraqi regime is to decide how. The United States prefers that Iraq meet its obligations voluntarily, yet we are prepared for the alternative.[100]

Powell concurred, maintaining that Saddam Hussein needed to make a 'strategic political decision to get rid of his weapons of mass of destruction'. If the US judged that he had not, then they would go to war: 'that's the question,' he insisted. 'There is no other question'.[101]

The administration now had a 'zero tolerance' view of Baghdad's actions.[102] Powell set out two criteria for avoiding imminent war: Baghdad had to make a comprehensive declaration of its WMD activities resolving the many suspicions and questions of US intelligence, and it had to give UN inspectors immediate, unimpeded, unconditional and unrestricted access.[103] If inspections were impeded or an inaccurate or incomplete declaration were submitted, then Bush would consider this 'further indication of the regime's bad faith and aggressive intent'.[104] This came to pass at the beginning of 2003 when Bush expressed his frustration at the 12,000-page declaration. No one seemed convinced by the declaration, including UNMOVIC Chair Hans Blix.[105] Bush labelled it '12,000 pages of deceit and deception',[106] and exclaimed that 'He [Saddam] must disarm. I'm sick and tired of games and deception.'[107]

By January 2003 time had run out for Saddam Hussein. Bush described Saddam Hussein as evil and said Iraq was not disarming but deceiving in his January 2003 State of the Union Address.[108] Cheney said that Iraq had 'absolutely no intention' of complying with UN demands for disarmament,[109] while Rice declared in February that 'it is time for this to end, enough is enough. Putting this off is not an option,' insisting that Saddam had 'weeks not months' to comply[110] and describing him as 'a serial liar'.[111] In January 2003 the White House published *What Does Disarmament Look Like?* setting out the three key expectations on Baghdad: high-level political commitment, national initiatives to dismantle WMD, and full cooperation and transparency. The examples of South Africa, Ukraine and Kazakhstan were provided to show what WMD disarmament should look like. The report insisted that Iraq was not following these examples but was instead engaged in 'highly organized concealment efforts' and 'national programs involving thousands of people to target inspectors and thwart their duties'. The report deemed Iraq's 12,000-page declaration incomplete and inaccurate because it did not provide information on, among other things, its efforts to procure uranium from abroad and its mobile biological weapons facilities, evidence for both of which was dubious at best and later shown to be completely unfounded.[112]

Pressure mounted for a second UN resolution to sanction the use of force, but the White House was not interested in this approach, despite the difficult predicament in which this placed his main ally, Prime Minister Tony Blair, who desperately needed a second resolution to satisfy British parliamentary and public critics of the impending war with Iraq.[113] Bush was satisfied that 1441 gave him authority to use military force without a second resolution.[114] As war beckoned on 6 March 2003, the President plainly stated his case and his views on Iraq's compliance with US/UN demands. He insisted that the inspectors did not need more time; Iraq was not disarming 'this is a fact. It cannot be denied'; another UN resolution was not required: 'when it comes to our security, we really don't need anybody's permission'; and the 'only way to disarm Iraq is through regime change'.[115] 'When people voted for 1441,' Rice observed, 'they voted for one final opportunity for Saddam Hussein to show that he made a strategic decision to disarm. He could do that tomorrow. He's not done it. He doesn't intend to do it. And what he intends to do is to keep stringing this down the road.'[116] All efforts to agree a second resolution collapsed on 14 March, with many UN Security Council members wanting to give inspections more time, a route the White House was simply not willing to take.

The only possible option open to Baghdad was exile. In January 2003 senior administration officials suggested that war could be avoided if Saddam Hussein and senior officials left the country. Powell, for example, said on CNN, 'I think the Iraqi people would be a lot better off, and this whole situation would be resolved, if Saddam Hussein ... his sons and the top leadership of the regime would leave.'[117] Woodward reports that Bush and the National Security Council discussed a formal 'Coup Scenario' paper on 14 February 2003 on what the US would do if Saddam left or if there was a coup in Baghdad. Woodward writes, 'a consensus soon emerged that they would not be able to wait to be invited: US forces would have to move in forthwith ... they determined that a coup, with all its imponderables, would not stop the military invasion'.[118] The administration insisted on full compliance with its demands and, as far as the White House was concerned, Iraq had failed to comply. This time there would be no second chance. On 17 March the President gave Saddam and his sons an ultimatum to leave Iraq within 48 hours.[119] They did not, and on 19 March war began.

Conclusion

The administration was determined to invade Iraq and remove Saddam Hussein from power, evidenced by the dramatic rhetorical escalation of the threat from Iraq in the administration's statements. The world had changed after 9/11 and the view from the White House was that Saddam Hussein could no longer be contained or tolerated. The administration insisted that Iraq had extensive WMD programmes despite the lack of evidence from UNMOVIC and IAEA inspections conducted between November 2002 and March 2003. It also insisted that Iraq had a working relationship with al-Qaida and would inevitably supply WMD to terrorist to use against the United States. The emotive image of a terrorist group detonating an Iraqi-supplied nuclear explosive in a US city was regularly employed by the administration. Iraq was now characterised as a unique and urgent threat, a view supported by Washington's conservative think-tanks. Bush set out a series of demands that it knew Iraq was extremely unlikely to ful-fil, and insisted on total compliance.

The United States was unwilling to compromise on its objectives and strategy, and was adamant that a pre-emptive military invasion was the only option that could neutralise the threat from Iraq and the certainty that Baghdad would sup-ply WMD to al-Qaida. The administration also made it clear that it had no patience for UN inspections and saw no need for a second UN resolution autho-rising force, regardless of the consequences. Saddam Hussein was running out of time and options. Baghdad's 12,000-page declaration of its WMD activities pre-sented to the UN in December 2002 was dismissed as wholly inadequate and a further example of Iraq's refusal to make a strategic decision to disarm. With opinion polls in the US showing full support for the administration's case and a pre-emptive military attack on Iraq, the Bush administration prepared for war. Regime change was a priority to be achieved using the full force of the US mil-itary if necessary. Talk of establishing more safe havens protected by US military force had faded from the discourse.

By the start of 2003 only irrefutable evidence of the destruction of WMD or the surrender of actual WMD could have prevented war. If Iraq had neither the documentation to prove the destruction of WMD or the destruction of materials used in WMD, nor any actual WMD to hand over and destroy, then there was nothing it could do to avert a military invasion.

8

UNQUALIFIED SUPPORT: CONGRESS AND WAR WITH IRAQ

Introduction

Towards the end of the Clinton administration support for a new US policy towards Iraq based explicitly on regime change gathered momentum. Senior and influential members of Congress became disillusioned with Clinton's containment and containment-plus policies and advocated radical change through the 1998 Iraq Liberation Act. As George W. Bush assumed the presidency Congressional supporters of the ILA continued to advocate aggressive action against Saddam Hussein. They beseeched the new administration to adopt regime change as the centrepiece of its Iraq policy and designate it an urgent priority.

After the attacks of 9/11 the debate on Iraq in Congress shifted, mirroring the shift inside the administration. For some members of Congress the threat from Saddam Hussein remained the same after 9/11, with the attacks simply reinforcing their argument that he urgently needed to be removed from power. They were joined by others who had supported the ILA in 1998 but had not pushed the case against Saddam Hussein because they were not as convinced of the immediacy of the threat. After 9/11 this group now saw the danger represented by the Iraqi regime in a new light and argued that the time had come to confront Baghdad. Although most members of Congress did not insist on regime change in Iraq as an immediate response to the 9/11 attacks, a consensus had emerged by September 2002 in both Houses of Congress that Saddam Hussein had to be confronted about his WMD programmes and his refusal to allow a robust UN inspections team back into Iraq. If he did not, then military force would be used to remove his regime. It was the willingness of Congress to sanction the use of military force *to attack and dismantle the regime* that marked the real significance of 9/11 for the ongoing Congressional debate on Iraq.

This chapter explores statements by senior and influential members of Congress immediately after 9/11, throughout 2002 and during the debate on the war resolution in September 2002. It argues that the Bush administration enjoyed widespread support for confronting Iraq as part of the war on terrorism, particularly after it announced that it would take its case to the UN.

114

After 9/11

Immediately after 9/11 Bush asked Congress to approve legislation to authorize him to use all necessary means against those responsible for the attacks, including force.[1] The Congressional debate on this resolution raised the issue of Iraq just days after the attacks. A number of senior Representatives and Senators urged the administration to confront Iraq as part of the new war on terrorism. Twelve days after 9/11 the Senate Republicans' elder statesman, Jesse Helms, declared on CNN that Iraq would be the target of US military action in the war on terrorism.[2] In October 2001 Senate Republican Leader Trent Lott advocated pursuing Iraq as phase two in the war on terrorism, reflecting the view in the White House.[3] In December Lott proclaimed: 'as we complete our work in Afghanistan and go to the next phase of fighting in a global way this terrorist problem, then we're going to have to look at how we deal with Iraq and their weapons of mass destruction'.[4]

Early pressure to target Saddam Hussein was not limited to senior Republicans. A month after the 9/11 attacks the Democrats' 2000 vice presidential candidate Senator Joseph Lieberman insisted that Iraq was a major threat to the US and called for Saddam's removal.[5] In November he argued that Iraq had chemical, biological and nuclear weapons programmes and that 'He will do us terrible damage unless we do him out of power.'[6] By December Lieberman had placed Iraq at the heart of the war on terrorism, arguing 'the war against terrorism cannot end before Saddam Hussein is out of power in Iraq, because he is the world's most powerful terrorist ... So we better get rid of Saddam before we declare victory in the war against terrorists.'[7]

In the House of Representatives the International Relations Committee debated the 11 September resolution to give Bush authority to pursue those responsible for 9/11. During this, and subsequent debates in December 2001, senior members of the committee banded Iraq and al-Qaida together as the primary focus of the emerging war on terrorism. Republican Henry Hyde, Chair of the Committee, argued in December 2001 that Saddam had WMD, that he would have no qualms about using them against the US and that al-Qaida was trying to get hold of WMD to use against the US. He went on to declare Iraq 'a mounting threat to our Nation, to our allies, and to international peace and security'.[8] Tom Lantos, senior Democrat member of the committee, also advocated taking the war on terrorism beyond Afghanistan to Iraq: 'Our Nation faces a critical terrorist threat that goes well beyond that posed by the Taliban and al-Qaida,' he argued, 'the threat is from Saddam Hussein's Iraq, a nation that is both a supporter and a generator of international terrorism and a proliferator of weapons of mass destruction.'[9] Benjamin Gilman, Chair of the Committee's Subcommittee on the Middle East and South Asia, said 'Hopefully, this resolution [11 September resolution] is an important first step in our renewed campaign against Saddam Hussein. Not only does he need to be stripped of his weapons of mass destruction, but he should be ousted from power.'[10] On 4 October 2001 he insisted 'While we are striking at other terrorists, we should end the regime of a master terrorist like Saddam.'[11] Republican Dana Rohrabacher declared that 9/11 signalled the time to 'finish the job' started in 1991 and eliminate Saddam Hussein's regime,[12] while Republican Lindsey Graham urged the administration to act now and get rid of Saddam. 'A failure to do so', he implored, 'and we will pay dearly later. Have we learned anything from September 11?'[13] He pressed the White House to insist on a new round of UN inspections and use military force if Baghdad refused.[14]

In January 2002 Republican Representative Chris Shays, Chair of the Committee on Government Reform's Subcommittee on National Security, Emerging Threats and International Relations, maintained that Iraq would have nuclear weapons within three to five years and that 'ultimately Iraq has to be dealt with' as part of the war on terrorism.[15] Similarly Representative Porter Goss, then Chair of the House Select Committee on Intelligence and later head of the CIA, argued 'You can't close the book on international terrorism without the chapter on Iraq being finalized.'[16]

In December 2001 Goss, Hyde and Graham introduced a resolution that would brand any refusal to admit UN weapons inspectors an act of aggression against the United States.[17] During the ensuing debate Representative Steve Chabot argued, 'if we are serious about ending, destroying and stopping international terrorism, we absolutely have to target Saddam Hussein … it is absolutely critical that we prevail in this war against terrorism. And I believe Saddam Hussein has to be a principal target of that war.'[18] The text of the bill was amended to declare that any refusal by Iraq would represent 'a mounting threat to the United States, its friends and allies, and international peace and security' rather than an act of aggression. It was then overwhelmingly passed by the House on 20 December 2001.[19]

The bill represented a powerful body of Congressional opinion that advocated targeting Saddam Hussein as part of the war on terrorism soon after the 9/11 attacks. It was articulated most forcefully in a letter to the White House in early December 2001. The letter, sent from Senators Trent Lott, Joseph Lieberman, John McCain and Jesse Helms and Representatives Richard Shelby, Harold Ford and Henry Hyde among others, argued that 'For as long as Saddam Hussein is in power in Baghdad, he will seek to acquire weapons of mass destruction and the means to deliver them. We have no doubt that these deadly weapons are intended for use against the United States and its allies. Consequently, we believe we must directly confront Saddam sooner rather than later.'[20]

Support in 2002: from the State of the Union address to the war resolution

After the President's State of the Union Address in January 2002 senior Republican and Democrat Senators and Representatives continued to argue that Saddam Hussein should be removed from power as part of the war on terrorism.

Many advocated regime change through military force as the appropriate method. In the Senate, for example, Sam Brownback urged Congress to take steps to depose Saddam.[21] Brownback was the senior Republican member and later Chair of the Foreign Relations Subcommittee on Near Eastern and South Asian Affairs when it reverted to Republican control following the November 2002 Congressional elections. Republican Arlen Specter, previously Chair of the Senate Intelligence Committee and later Chair of the Judiciary Committee in 2004, argued that 'Iraq is a real menace ... I think there are very strong United States national interests to topple Saddam Hussein.'[22] Republican Senator Richard Shelby insisted in August 2002 that Iraq was manufacturing WMD to the extent that 'Every month, every week, Saddam Hussein will have more weapons of mass destruction to use against us.' Accordingly he argued that removing Saddam Hussein was inevitable: 'it's not a question of if we invade Iraq. The question is do we wait until he continues to manufacture more weapons of mass destruction that can do us irreparable damage and our troops, or do we try to pre-empt some of this?'[23]

In the House, Republican Representative Joe Wilson, member of the House International Relations Committee and House Armed Services Committee, said 'Iraq poses the most serious threat to America's national security.'[24] August saw Republican Representative Tom DeLay, House Majority Leader, argue in *USA Today* that the US was already at war with Saddam Hussein, that there was ample evidence for going after him and that the US must 'seek a victory that cannot be secured at the bargaining table'.[25]

Throughout 2002 support for confronting Iraq became increasingly bi-partisan, with senior Democrats advocating regime change in Baghdad. In January 2002 Senator John Edwards, 2004 Democrat vice presidential candidate, argued that the United States could not allow Saddam Hussein to continue to develop weapons of mass destruction and that 'it's very difficult to imagine a situation where the world is secure, the United States is secure, while Saddam Hussein is still in power ... he's a very serious threat to the security of the United States', but cautioned that the US should only consider Iraq after the Afghan conflict had been fully resolved.[26] In February Senator Lieberman reiterated his hard line, insisting that 'Saddam can't remain in power' and that 'We know that he has weapons, chemical and biological weapons. We have reason to believe he is developing nuclear weapons.'[27] A few months later, in July, he asserted once more that 'Iraq is the most immediately menacing country to the security of the United States and the world ... The sooner we're able to dislodge Saddam the better.'[28] In October 2001 Senator John Kerry, 2004 Democrat presidential candidate, cautioned against taking action against Iraq during the war in Afghanistan but accepted that the United States would have to focus on Iraq in the long run.[29] By February 2002 Kerry was arguing that 'There's no question in my mind that Saddam Hussein has to be toppled one way or another, but the question is how', favouring using Iraqi opposition forces rather than US troops.[30] In June Democrat Dick Gephardt, House Minority Leader, argued that the United States should confront Saddam Hussein using 'diplomatic tools where we can, but military means where we must to eliminate the threat he poses to the region and our own security'.[31]

The war resolution

The Congressional debate on Iraq reached its climax in September 2002. On 19 September, five days after Bush addressed the UN, the White House presented a draft resolution to the Republican and Democrat leaders of the House and Senate to authorize the President to use military force against Iraq should it fail to relinquish its weapons of mass destruction and associated programmes.[32] This led to a number of debates and open and closed hearings in both Houses of Congress. A number of hearings on US policy towards Iraq had already taken place in August.[33]

The White House wanted a firm 'yes' vote on its resolution before the UNSC concluded its discussions on if, when and how to confront Iraq. Bush argued that he would have a better chance of securing a tough UN resolution against Iraq that could lead to the full disclosure and disarmament of Iraq's WMD programmes and possibly avoid a war if he had the full backing of Congress for military-led regime change in the event of Iraqi non-compliance. The original resolution from the White House was adjusted in Congress so that it only authorised the use of force against Iraq, and not any other state or organisation Bush might wish to target as part of the war on terrorism, and it required the White House to work through the UN to secure Iraqi compliance with UNSC resolutions.[34]

The debate in Congress revolved around three different perspectives that attracted varying degrees of support. Some argued in favour of regime change as part of the war on terrorism come what may: containment had failed; Saddam had had his last chance, there was no need to go to the UN; 9/11 meant that Saddam could no longer be tolerated, if left alone he would develop and deploy nuclear weapons leaving the United States hamstrung in the Gulf; he was definitely or probably in league with al-Qaida; he was comparable to Hitler; an ultimatum should be issued and in the absence of full compliance Iraq should be invaded and the regime overthrown.

A second group favoured granting Bush the authority to use military force against Iraq after all diplomatic possibilities had been exhausted. From this perspective 9/11 had genuinely changed perceptions of the threat from Iraq: the status quo with Iraq could not continue indefinitely; Bush should build a strong coalition; he should insist on UN inspections for one last time through a new UN resolution; and he should only invade Iraq in order to disarm the country should these attempts fail. Voting in favour of the resolution in Congress was supposed to send a strong signal to both the UN and Iraq that this time the United States was serious. Without such a signal, this group argued, the President's ability to secure a firm resolution at the UN would be diminished.

A final group argued that Bush did not have a robust case that Iraq was in league with al-Qaida, that it was aggressively pursing WMD programmes, that

Saddam Hussein was an imminent threat to US security, or that confronting Iraq was central to the war on terrorism. From this perspective it was feared that an invasion would be reckless, divisive, and counterproductive to the real war on terrorism against al-Qaida and its affiliates, of which the regime in Baghdad was not one.

The majority of senior Congressional Republicans and a significant proportion of senior Congressional Democrats fell into groups one and two, giving Bush ample support to demand action from the UN and Saddam Hussein.

Republican Congressional support

Senior Republicans in the Senate wholly supportive of taking the war on terrorism to Baghdad included Senate Republican Leader Trent Lott, Ranking Member of the Senate Armed Services Committee John Warner, the Senate Republicans' elder statesman Jesse Helms, Vice Chair of the Senate Select Committee on Intelligence Richard Shelby, Ranking member of the Senate Committee on Indian Affairs and 2000 Republican presidential contender John McCain, and Foreign Relations Subcommittee on Near Eastern and South Asian Affairs Ranking Member Sam Brownback.

McCain argued that the longer Saddam was left in power the more dangerous he would become because he was determined to develop nuclear weapons. Failure to end the regime made it more likely that Saddam would engage with al-Qaida, and that he would develop nuclear weapons and use them to control the region. Containment had failed, deterrence no longer worked and 'Giving peace a chance only gives Saddam Hussein more time to prepare for war'. According to McCain, then, 'In this new era, preventive action to target rogue regimes is not only imaginable but necessary.'[35] McCain later insisted that Saddam had to be removed; otherwise he could 'make a far worse day of infamy by turning Iraq into a weapons assembly line for al-Qaida's network'.[36] Immediately after the President's UN speech, Senators McCain and Lott, considered sometime rivals and 'an unlikely Republican team', came together to support the President, with Lott stating that war with Iraq was now almost inevitable.[37]

Senator John Warner stressed the risk that Saddam could form an alliance with terrorists and provide them with WMD to 'attack America without leaving any fingerprints'. He therefore insisted that 'confronting the threat posed by Iraq is crucial to winning the war on terror'.[38] Senator Pat Roberts, member of the Senate Armed Services Committee and currently Chairman of the Senate Select Committee on Intelligence, endorsed this argument and placed Iraq at the centre of the war on terrorism. He proclaimed that the government's foremost priority was to prevent terrorists using WMD, and this meant 'neutralizing' regimes like Saddam Hussein's.[39]

Other influential voices in favour of regime change as part of the war on terrorism were Senator Bill Frist, Chair of the National Republican Senatorial Committee from 2000 to 2002, who became Senate Majority Leader in

December 2002,[40] and Senator Mitch McConnell, Chair of the Senate Appropriations Committee Subcommittee on the State, Foreign Operations and Related Agencies, who became Senate Majority Whip in 2003.[41]

In the House of Representatives, Republican Whip Tom DeLay, Chair of the International Relations Committee Henry Hyde, and Chair of the House Intelligence Committee Porter Goss remained resolutely in favour of confronting and attacking Iraq. Many concurred with the administration's analysis that Iraq was at the centre of the war on terrorism, that it had extensive WMD programmes and that regime change was needed as soon as possible. Iraq's place at the heart of the war on terrorism was championed by Hyde, who suggested that the World Trade Center attack in 1993 and the anthrax letters of late 2001 might be linked to Iraq, and declared his belief that there was a direct connection between al-Qaida and Baghdad.[42] Representative Scott McInnis described al-Qaida and Iraq as 'comrades in arms' and said that instead of attacking the US directly, Saddam Hussein would hand his WMD out to al-Qaida terrorists.[43] Representative Felix Grucci argued that 'Americans will not be safe and the war on terrorism will not be won' until Saddam had gone,[44] while Representative Pete King of the International Relations Committee argued that removing Saddam Hussein from power and pursuing the war on terrorism were 'intertwined and connected. You cannot have one without the other.'[45]

The threat from Iraq's WMD was often characterised as a known certainty based on the irrefutable facts of their existence. Representative Gary Ackerman, for example, declared that Iraq continued with 'covert and comprehensive plans to acquire those weapons and the means to deliver them. All of these facts are established and known', while Democrat Representative, now Senator, John Thune insisted that 'we know that Iraq continues to attempt to develop nuclear weapons. These are not guesses. These are facts.'[46] McCain argued that 'Saddam Hussein continues to acquire, amass, and improve on his arsenal of weapons of mass destruction. He continues to attempt to acquire a nuclear weapon. These are all well-known facts.'[47]

Given the nature of the threat as perceived by members of the House, a number of Representatives urged the administration to remove Saddam sooner rather than later. Representative Illeana Ros-Lehtinen, member of the International Relations Committee and now Chair of its Subcommittee on the Middle East and Central Asia, outlined Iraq's WMD programmes and the reported relationship between Baghdad and al-Qaida and asked 'if we do not act now, when?'[48] Representative Darrell Issa vowed that 'we have an obligation to defend ourselves in the face of Saddam's threats. We cannot afford to remain silent while our enemies plot their next attack.'[49] Meanwhile Representative Howard Cable characterised Saddam Hussein as 'the modern day version of Adolf Hitler' and for that reason 'the time for us to act is now'.[50] Finally Representative Gilman urged the United States to 'take this threat seriously and take preventive action against the tyranny of the Iraqi Government and to order it to disarm before the events of September 11th are allowed to be repeated'.[51]

However, not all Republicans were in favour. House Speaker Dennis Hastert, a senior Republican figure, was not openly supportive of the war resolution,[52] while House Majority Leader Republican Dick Armey was not in favour at all and was personally lobbied by Cheney to secure support for the war resolution.[53] One senior Republican voice against a war with Iraq was Senate President *pro tempore* Robert Byrd, while others such as Senator Chuck Hagel cautioned against the White House's approach to dealing with Saddam Hussein.[54] However, a significant amount of the criticism from Congress was about the process rather than the content of the Bush administration's approach. 'We can't do this alone', said Hagel, arguing in favour of building a coalition through the UN. This reflected the caution and criticism from leading Republican figures from the administration of George H. W. Bush, such as Brent Scowcroft, who were not opposed to armed action against Baghdad *per se*, but urged the White House to build as strong a coalition through the UN as it could muster.

Democrat Congressional support

A number of senior Democrats were also in favour of the war resolution, particularly House Minority Leader Dick Gephardt, Senator Joseph Lieberman and Ranking Member of the House International Relations Committee Tom Lantos. Senators John Kerry, Joseph Biden, then Chair of the Senate Foreign Affairs Committee, and John Edwards were all in favour of confronting Saddam Hussein while insisting that Bush first exhaust all diplomatic avenues through the UN. Senator Carl Levin, Chair of the Senate Armed Services Committee, and other senior Democrats remained largely sceptical of the resolution and the apparent rush to war.

Lieberman in the Senate and Gephardt in the House lent full support to the White House war resolution, arguably undermining other senior Democrats who sought to dilute the resolution and limit the administration's authority to use force against Iraq. During the debate on the resolution Lieberman argued that the greatest threats faced by the US were 'al-Qaida and rogue regimes such as Saddam Hussein's' and gave full support to immediate military action against Iraq.[55] He insisted that all attempts to contain Saddam Hussein had failed, that he had been given his last chance and that it was too dangerous for him to remain in power.[56] In the House, Gephardt declared that 'Iraq's use and continuing development of weapons of mass destruction, combined with efforts of terrorists to acquire such weapons, pose a unique and dangerous threat to our national security' and advocated use of military force.[57] In October it was reported that Gephardt decided to back the resolution after concluding that the only chance of securing Iraqi compliance and averting war was through bi-partisan unity. His decision to support the President halted further debate in the Senate, where Democrat Senator Tom Daschle was pushing for a much more restrictive resolution.[58]

Senator Kerry argued that Saddam's behaviour and breach of international obligations were 'cause enough for the world community to hold him accountable by use of force, if necessary'. He also maintained there was little question that Iraq was pursuing a nuclear weapons programme, but cast doubt on Saddam's ability to acquire the necessary weapons-grade fissile materials. He agreed that Saddam must be confronted since his 'weapons represent an unacceptable threat', but insisted that the reason for going to war must be to disarm Iraq, rather than regime change.[59] On 2 October 2002 Kerry insisted 'I am willing to use force, but we should exhaust all possibilities first', declaring support for an invasion if weapons inspections were blocked.[60]

Senator John Edwards reiterated the White House argument that pre-emptive action was needed, that confronting Iraq was central to the war on terrorism, and that Baghdad could team up with terrorists and provide them with WMD:

> Thousands of terrorist operatives around the world would pay anything to get their hands on Saddam's arsenal, and there is every possibility that he could turn his weapons over to these terrorists ... we can hardly ignore the terrorist threat, and the serious danger that Saddam would allow his arsenal to be used in aid of terror.[61]

In the House Tom Lantos linked Iraq and terrorism and urged pre-emptive action: 'terrorists sharing his [Saddam's] anti-American hatred find refuge and resources under his wing', comparing the situation to Europe facing Hitler in 1939 and warning that 'if the costs of war are great, the costs of inaction and appeasement are greater still'.[62] Representative Gary Ackerman, Ranking Democrat on the International Relations Subcommittee on the Middle East and Central Asia, labelled Saddam Hussein 'pure evil' and 'an inveterate and dangerous gambler', and said that the United States could not 'simply hope that Saddam will not share weapons of mass destruction technology with terrorists. We know al-Qaida elements have already been at work soliciting Iraqi aid in this field.'[63]

A number of Democrats opposed the resolution, including Representatives Jim McDermott, David Bonior and Mike Thomson, who visited Iraq in October 2002 in an effort to undermine the White House case for war and faced ridicule from their colleagues.[64] Senator Biden took a more circumspect view. While supporting the White House effort to confront Iraq through the UN, he argued in February 2002 that a war could destabilise the region, stating, 'The easy part, if you will, is taking Saddam out ... The hard part is what you do after.'[65] In October 2002 he supported the war resolution on the basis that although Iraq did not at the time pose an imminent threat to the US, it soon would if left unfettered, and for that reason the US should compel Iraq to disarm through the UN.[66]

On 10 October, the House and Senate passed identical resolutions (H.J. Res. 114/S.J. Res. 45) authorising the use of force against Iraq. The final vote in the House was 296–133 for the resolution, and 77–23 in favour in the Senate. The joint resolution gave the White House broad authorisation to wage war against Iraq to disarm the regime of its weapons of mass destruction once all diplomatic avenues had been exhausted.

From the resolution to war

In November 2002 the UNSC passed resolution 1441, which required Iraq to re-admit UN inspectors and provide a complete declaration of all its WMD activities. As the inspections process in Iraq and deliberations at the UN in New York continued, senior members of Congress continued to push for a military confrontation, arguing that Saddam Hussein had failed to take the last opportunity offered to him by the UN, and that by failing to disarm he was in material breach of UNSC resolution 1441 and would face 'serious consequences'.[67] Senator John McCain, for example, argued that Bush had done all that was asked: he had pursued 'careful diplomacy ... refrained from using force unilaterally against Iraq ... was able to unite the Security Council behind our demand that Iraq disarm or be disarmed ... worked diligently to assemble a coalition'. With Iraq having failed to cooperate, McCain argued that the case for military action had not only become more compelling but that the administration had a duty to attack before it was attacked, comparing the situation to 'Winston Churchill's call to stand up to Adolf Hitler when Nazi Germany was still weak and millions of lives could have been saved by acting first'.[68]

Conclusion

After 9/11 a number of senior members of Congress in both Houses argued that Iraq should be targeted as part of the new war on terrorism. Throughout 2002 support for confronting Iraq became increasingly bi-partisan, with senior Democrats advocating regime change in Baghdad. In September 2002, when the White House submitted its draft war resolution to Congress, it found widespread support for action against Saddam Hussein, particularly if it took its case to the United Nations. The final resolution enjoyed considerable support from senior Republicans and Democrats. As the administration prepared for war at the start of 2003, senior Republican figures backed the President's assertion that Iraq showed no intention of complying with US demands and UNSC resolutions and that it was in material breach of those resolutions.

Powerful members of Congress shared the administration's view that confronting Iraq was key to the war on terrorism, that Baghdad was developing WMD and would soon have nuclear weapons, that it would readily share its WMD with al-Qaida, and that the threat was now so great that pre-emptive military action was required. The prospect of a nuclear-armed Iraq persuaded many members of Congress to support the White House drive to confront and destroy Saddam Hussein's regime.[69]

Without widespread support from Congress the White House would have faced a much more difficult task in persuading the American public to support military action against Iraq. It may have been forced to compromise, to allow inspections more time or to revert to the strategy set out in the ILA. But the cogent case put forward by the administration duly convinced Congress of the need to act and to act soon. The administration's case was based on an alarming analysis of the threat from Iraq. Following the failure to find any WMD after the invasion and charges that the administration exaggerated the intelligence on Iraq's WMD programmes and terrorist connections, some members of Congress have said they were misled by the administration, having now seen the evidence on which the administration based its claims.[70] The next chapter examines the administration's circumvention of traditional intelligence analysis procedures in an effort to find evidence of Iraq's WMD programmes and its links to al-Qaida.

9

FINDING THE EVIDENCE

Introduction

The absence of any evidence of weapons of mass destruction or ongoing WMD programmes in Iraq following the US-led invasion in March 2003 resulted in a number of government commissions and inquiries in the United States and the UK, and independent analysis in books and journals on the material presented by the Bush administration to justify the war. Evidence that has emerged since the war suggests that two important processes were at work. First, the US intelligence community operated on a number of false assumptions about Iraq's WMD programmes, leading to inaccurate analysis. Second, the Bush administration, particularly the senior leadership in the Defense Department, augmented the federal government's usual intelligence-gathering and analysis procedures. This was done for the specific purpose of finding evidence to support the administration's contention that a working relationship existed between Iraq and al-Qaida and that Iraq had active chemical, biological and especially nuclear weapons programmes, however ambiguous the evidence might be.

The contention explored in this chapter is that the administration was not content to rely on established methods of intelligence analysis on Iraq's WMD programmes and links to al-Qaida and sought to supplement, revisit and circumvent the standard procedures of the intelligence community precisely because it was so determined to pursue regime change. It was this determination that led the administration independently to scour all the available raw data in order to build as convincing a case as possible against Saddam Hussein and thus legitimise military action to remove the regime from power. These data would ordinarily be analysed by the intelligence community and then presented to the administration.

This is not to suggest that the administration fabricated or lied about intelligence or set out deliberately and knowingly to mislead Congress and the American public, but it is clear that a great many of the Bush administration's statements categorically maintained that Iraq possessed and was developing WMD, including a nuclear weapons programme, and that Iraq had extensive links with al-Qaida – statements that have turned out to be false. Had the administration not been so determined to depose Saddam and so convinced that Iraq had extensive WMD programmes and a concrete relationship with al-Qaida, a more objective analysis of available intelligence and the results of UNMOVIC and IAEA inspections conducted between November 2002 and March 2003 would have called into question the severity of the threat from Iraq and the need for a military invasion to disarm and destroy Saddam Hussein's regime.

After 9/11 the administration had to focus on the issue of WMD in order to place its policy of regime change in the context of existing UNSC resolutions and secure domestic and international legitimacy for confronting and, if necessary, attacking Iraq. The administration also sought to find evidence of Iraq's involvement in 9/11 immediately after the attacks, shown in Rumsfeld's instruction to get 'best info fast' on the attacks to judge whether the evidence was good enough to go after Baghdad, and Wolfowitz's request to former CIA Director and Defense Policy Board member James Woolsey to gather evidence on Iraq's involvement (see Chapter 5). This chapter details a number of processes, actions and issues that underscore the administration's determination to target Saddam as part of the war on terrorism.

The Counter Terrorism Evaluation Group and the Office of Special Plans

The US intelligence community comprises a number of agencies in several departments. The primary organisations are the State Department's Bureau of Intelligence and Research, the Central Intelligence Agency (CIA), and the Defense Department's National Security Agency (NSA), the Defense Intelligence Agency (DIA) and the National Reconnaissance Office (NRO).[1] The Director of National Intelligence is the head of the entire intelligence community. However, the three large intelligence organisations that are part of the Defense Department, together with the intelligence agencies of the armed services, give the Secretary of Defense significant authority over the United States' intelligence-gathering and analysis operations.

Throughout 2002 and 2003 it is reported that a rift developed between intelligence gatherers and analysts within the Department of Defense and those within the CIA and State Department. The activities of the Department of Defense are directed and managed by the Office of the Secretary of Defense in the Pentagon. After 9/11 new intelligence analysis activities were established in Pentagon offices under Douglas Feith, Under Secretary of Defense for Policy, part of the Office of the Secretary of Defense bureaucracy. Feith was the most senior of the four Under Secretaries of Defense. He was a protégé of Richard Perle and regarded as third in command in the department after Secretary Donald Rumsfeld and Deputy Secretary Paul Wolfowitz.[2] Feith fully supported taking the war on terrorism to Iraq. In October 2002 he too placed Iraq at the centre of the 'rogue' state–WMD–terrorism nexus, explaining that

The list of countries that support terrorists and the list of dangerous and irresponsible countries that are pursuing chemical weapons, biological weapons and nuclear weapons – those lists overlap. And the overlap represents a strategic threat of great importance. And we see now with the discussion of Iraq and the danger that the Saddam Hussein regime poses to the world a focus on precisely that nexus between state support for terrorism and the pursuit of weapons of mass destruction.[3]

In October 2001 a unit was set up in Feith's department to analyse existing documents and reports from the CIA, DIA, NSA and other intelligence agencies in order to study links between a range of terrorist organisations and states, including links between Iraq and al-Qaida.[4] The unit, known as the Counter Terrorism Evaluation Group (CTEG), produced an initial report on terrorist networks generally, and a second report in August 2002 on Iraq and al-Qaida. Feith and the DIA Director presented this report to CIA Director George Tenet, Deputy National Security Advisor Stephen Hadley and Cheney's Chief of Staff I. Lewis Libby.[5] The briefing was also given to National Security Council and Office of the Vice President staff members, apparently without Tenet's knowledge.[6] CTEG was run by David Wurmser, Director of Middle East Studies at the American Enterprise Institute and a firm advocate of regime change (who joined John Bolton's office in the State Department after CTEG was disbanded and later became Cheney's adviser on the Middle East), and F. Michael Maloof, a former aide to Richard Perle. The Group was disbanded in August 2002.[7]

Shortly after CTEG was disbanded another group was established under Feith by Wolfowitz called the Office of Special Plans (OSP). OSP was established as an expanded Northern Gulf Directorate, a directorate situated within the Office of Near East and South Asia (NESA) Affairs. NESA is one of four regional offices in Feith's policy department, the other three being Africa, Asia and Pacific, and Western Hemisphere. According to the Pentagon, OSP explored policy issues related to planning on Iraq and 'developed policy options for senior decision makers, coordinated those options within DoD and across the interagency, monitored the implementation of defense policy and recommended course corrections to defense policy'.[8] Senator John Kyl insists that OSP 'was not involved in intelligence collection, intelligence creation, or operational war planning'.[9] OSP was run by Abram Shulsky and NESA by William Luti, both firm supporters of war with Iraq.[10]

The creation of the OSP led to serious tensions with the CIA, described dramatically in several reports as a 'war' between the Pentagon and the CIA.[11] Rumsfeld and Wolfowitz, it is reported, were frustrated by the CIA and DIA mindset that there was no link between Saddam Hussein and al-Qaida, and wanted to re-examine undiluted intelligence. Members of the CIA and administration critics argued that the Pentagon was intent on finding intelligence to support preconceived ideas – in essence politicising the intelligence-gathering and analysis functions of the intelligence community.

It is asserted that CTEG and OSP relied on intelligence from the Iraqi National Congress (INC) and Iraqi defectors supplied by the INC to support the case for confronting Baghdad, sources that the CIA and State Department considered unreliable.[12] The CIA and State Department had serious concerns about INC leader Ahmad Chalabi's integrity. Information provided by defectors through the INC has proved incorrect. Information from two supposed Iraqi defectors supplied by the INC and interviewed by the DIA was initially taken very seriously. The most important information, it was reported, came from Adnan Ihsan Saeed al-Haideri, who claimed that Saddam had secret labs making biological, chemical and nuclear weapons hidden in underground wells, under villas, and beneath the Saddam Hussein Hospital in Baghdad. Nothing has been found to date to support these claims.[13] Another was Mohammad Harith who claimed on CBS's *60 Minutes* in March 2002 that he had purchased refrigerated trucks as an Iraqi intelligence operative for conversion into biological weapons laboratories. Two months later the DIA issued a 'fabricator notice' warning intelligence agencies that Harith was unreliable.[14] By early 2003, the *Independent* reported, the DIA had concluded that 'defectors introduced to US intelligence agents by the organization [INC] invented or exaggerated their claims to have personal knowledge of the regime and its alleged weapons of mass destruction'.[15]

A neo-conservative bias?

The main protagonists involved in the Defense Department's extra-curricular intelligence analysis activities, Wolfowitz, Feith, Wurmser, Luti and Shulsky, were all convinced that Iraq had WMD, that there was a relationship between Iraq and al-Qaida, and considered military-led regime change a necessity. It has therefore been claimed that CTEG and OSP produced and disseminated intelligence analysis on Iraq's WMD and its relationship with al-Qaida that reflected the bias in favour of regime change of those working for and overseeing the work of the two groups.

Vincent Cannistraro, a former senior CIA official and counter-terrorism expert, described material supplied to the OSP by the INC as propaganda telling the Defense Department what they wanted to hear and creating 'cooked information that goes right into presidential and vice-presidential speeches'.[16] Greg Theilmann, a senior official in the State Department's intelligence bureau until his retirement in September 2002 said 'They surveyed data and picked out what they liked ... The whole thing was bizarre. The secretary of defense had this huge defense intelligence agency, and he went around it.'[17]

Conversely, Richard Perle justified the approach taken by OSP and the Defense Department to revisit and re-analyse intelligence by arguing that

what we are now beginning to see is evidence that was there all along. It simply wasn't properly assessed. And the reason why it wasn't assessed, in my view, is that a point of view dominated the Intelligence Community, the CIA in particular, and that point of view held that a secular Ba'athist regime like that of Saddam Hussein would not cooperate with religious fanatics like al-Qaida. This was a theory. There was nothing to support it except the speculation of the intelligence officials who held that view. And as a result, they simply didn't look for evidence that there might be a connection.[18]

On 4 June 2003 Feith and Luti took the unusual step of calling a press conference to reject the allegations of bias made against OSP and CTEG.[19] Cheney has also vehemently denied that the administration in any way misled Congress or the US public in its intelligence analysis.[20]

An informal network

The determination of Feith's offices to find evidence to fit preconceived ideas lends considerable support to the contention that the administration was determined to go to war. This contention is supported by reports that the materials produced by CTEG and OSP were fed into the highest levels of policy-making in the White House through the small network of neo-conservatives in the administration.[21] This could not have been achieved, it is argued, without considerable support from Cheney and Rumsfeld, the two heavyweights of national security policy.[22] This adds further weight to the argument that Cheney and Rumsfeld, together with other influential neo-conservatives in the administration, shared OSP and CTEG's determination to find and use whatever evidence they could to construct the case for attacking Iraq and removing Saddam's regime.

This network, it is reported, comprised the Defense Policy Board, particularly members Richard Perle, Newt Gingrich, James Woolsey and Kenneth Adelman,[23] John Bolton at the State Department and his adviser David Wurmser, Office of Net Assessment Middle East specialist Harold Rhode, Deputy National Security Advisor Stephen Hadley, Cheney's chief of staff I. Lewis Libby and Eliot Abrams at the National Security Council, all major supporters of taking the war on terrorism to Iraq.[24] According to retired Lt-Col. Karen Kwiatkowski, who was assigned to NESA from May 2002 to February 2003, Feith and OSP/NESA communicated almost exclusively with this network of neo-conservatives rather than with other intelligence agencies such as the DIA, and preferred to work through Bolton's office at the State Department rather than the State Department's Bureau of Intelligence and Research or its Near Eastern Affairs bureau.[25] According to John Prados, senior fellow at Washington's National Security Archive, Bolton acted in parallel with the Office of the Vice President and the OSP to scour intelligence linking Iraq to al-Qaida and to extensive ongoing WMD programmes, while Cheney and Libby frequently visited CIA headquarters to press analysts on their data and conclusions.[26] This group of people knew each other well and many had worked together in previous administrations, or for the same Senators, on the same commissions, or for the same conservative think-tanks.[27]

Investigative journalist Seymour Hersh maintained that materials produced by CTEG and OSP were supplied directly to the Vice President and President outside the normal channels of communication between the White House and the intelligence community. This led the OSP to rival 'both the CIA and the Pentagon's own Defense Intelligence Agency, the DIA, as President Bush's main source of intelligence regarding Iraq's possible possession of weapons of mass destruction and connection with al-Qaida'.[28]

The contention here is that senior members of the US administration actively sought evidence to support preconceived ideas about Iraq's WMD programmes and ties to international terrorism and al-Qaida. They established or approved new intelligence analysis mechanisms to maximise the administration's ability to find such evidence and then they interpreted it in a manner conducive to their case and presented it in a sensationalist fashion. This is supported by statements from a number of important people. Hersh reports a conversation with former Senator Bob Kerrey stating that the administration had

> the intelligence on weapons and expanded it beyond what was justi-
> fied... It appeared that they understood that to get the American
> people on their side they needed to come up with something more to say
> than 'We've liberated Iraq and got rid of a tyrant.' So they had to find
> some ties to weapons of mass destruction and were willing to allow a
> majority of Americans to incorrectly conclude that the invasion of Iraq
> had something to do with the World Trade Center. Overemphasizing the
> national-security threat made it more difficult to get the rest of the world
> on our side. It was the weakest and most misleading argument we could
> use.[29]

Hans Blix, Chair of UNMOVIC, argued in October 2005 that the administration 'took things they saw as conclusive' and that 'they were not critically thinking. They wanted to come to these conclusions.'[30] Richard Clarke, formerly the administration's counter-terrorism coordinator, reports that Iraq and terrorism were nuanced issues that required critical thinking but 'Bush and his inner circle had no real interest in complicated analyses; on the issues that they cared about, they already knew the answers, it was received wisdom'.[31]

Finally, a leaked Downing Street memo of a British government cabinet meeting on 23 July 2002 to discuss the UK's role in the Bush administration's confrontation with Iraq reports that Sir Richard Dearlove, head of the British intelligence service MI6, stated that during his last visit to Washington he noticed a 'perceptible shift in attitude. Bush wanted to remove Saddam, through military action, justified by the conjunction of terrorism and [weapons of mass destruction]. But the intelligence and the facts were being fixed around the policy.'[32]

Investigating commissions

The evidence is compelling that the administration selectively used any and all available intelligence to make the case for war, however reliable or unreliable, but it is not conclusive. Proponents of this case have argued that pressure from Bolton, OSP and Cheney's office led to the 'politicisation' of the September 2002 CIA National Intelligence Estimate (NIE) on Iraq requested by Congress as it debated the war resolution and produced in a far shorter time than usual.[33] However, the conclusions of three important commissions have placed much of the blame for intelligence failure on the shoulders of the intelligence community, rather than on pressure and interference by administration officials. There can be no doubt that US intelligence agencies failed to critically re-examine their assumptions on Iraq's weapons of mass destruction programmes and failed to adequately manage their intelligence on Iraq. In particular it was assumed that Saddam's devious and obstructive actions meant that he was concealing WMD activities.

The President's *Commission on the Intelligence Capabilities of the United States Regarding Weapons of Mass Destruction* (the Robb–Silberman commission) placed the blame firmly with the intelligence agencies. In a letter to the President accompanying the report the panel said, 'The Intelligence Community was dead wrong in almost all of its prewar judgments about Iraq's weapons of mass destruction. This was a major intelligence failure.'[34] The panel, however, only had a mandate to examine the activities of the intelligence community. It did not address policy-makers' use of intelligence reports.[35]

The report on the *U.S. Intelligence Community's Prewar Intelligence Assessments on Iraq* by the Senate Select Committee on Intelligence concluded that most of the major key judgements in the Intelligence Community's October 2002 National Intelligence Estimate on *Iraq's Continuing Programs for Weapons of Mass Destruction* were overstated or not supported by intelligence, representing a serious failure by the community. The report stated that the assessments in the NIE that Iraq had reconstituted its nuclear programme, that it had been trying to procure uranium ore from Niger, that the aluminium tubes Iraq was trying to purchase were for centrifuges for a nuclear programme, that it possessed chemical and biological weapons, that it had an active offensive biological weapons programme, that it had mobile biological weapons facilities, and that it was expanding its chemical industry to support a chemical weapons programme were overstated, unsupported or incorrect.

It further maintained that the intelligence community 'did not accurately or adequately explain to policymakers the uncertainties behind the judgements' in the NIE and that it did not find 'any evidence that Administration officials attempted to coerce, influence or pressure analysts to change their judgements'. It too contended that the community suffered from a collective 'groupthink' assumption that Iraq had an active and growing WMD programme and too readily accepted information that reinforced it.[36]

A third report, this time commissioned by the CIA, recognised that there was pressure from policy-makers, but that 'serious pressure from policy-makers almost always accompanies serious issues'. It too placed the blame with the agencies that failed to exercise quality control checks on analysis in the face of daily briefings and contacts at the highest levels of government that led to the conveyance of intelligence 'unfettered by the formal caveats that usually accompany written production'.[37] The report argues that intelligence collection 'was not focused or conceptually driven to answer questions about the validity of the premise that the WMD programs were continuing apace'.[38] But there is also much to suggest that the administration was determined to use whatever intelligence it could and present it in as alarming a way as possible to support the political case for war. There was intense pressure on the agencies and a 'constant stream of questions aimed at finding links between Saddam and the terrorist network [al-Qaida]'. The agencies may have handled that badly in their intelligence collection and analysis, but the administration was looking hard for evidence to support its case.[39]

This is supported by a fourth investigation conducted by the Minority Staff of the Senate Armed Services Committee and led by Senator Carl Levin. The October 2004 Levin report, *Report of an Inquiry into the Alternative Analysis of the Issue of an Iraq–al-Qaida Relationship*, concludes that 'in the case of Iraq's relationship with al-Qaida, intelligence was exaggerated to support Administration policy aims primarily by the Feith policy office, which was determined to find a strong connection.' Analysis of this relationship by the intelligence community was much more cautious and Levin argues that the administration used analysis from Feith's office over analysis by the intelligence community in order to present a more startling case to Congress and the US public. Levin characterises the reports produced by Feith's CTEG as 'selective reinterpretations of intelligence', and presents evidence to support this. The fact that Feith's office conducted such an intelligence review rather than relying on the intelligence community, Levin argues, was symptomatic of the administration's determination to reach a particular conclusion.[40] In particular the administration appears to have made exaggerated claims about Iraq's nuclear weapons programme. It is clear from what is publicly available that evidence from the intelligence community was far from conclusive, yet the White House presented the existence of an active nuclear weapons programme as fact (see Chapter 7).

Conclusion

After 9/11 the administration was determined to target Saddam Hussein's regime as part of the war on terrorism. To gain Congressional, public and international support for this it needed evidence of Iraq's ongoing WMD programmes and/or its links to al-Qaida and even to 9/11 itself. The senior leadership in the Defense Department established CTEG and OSP to find this evidence by reviewing existing intelligence and new intelligence from Iraqi defectors. CTEG and OSP were run from Feith's Pentagon office and were staffed and overseen by officials determined to see Saddam's regime removed and who were convinced that Iraq had WMD programmes and a clear relationship with al-Qaida. This alone shows that the Pentagon was intent on seeing Saddam deposed and determined to find the evidence to support the case for regime change. But reports suggest that efforts to find evidence to fit the case went much further and that a small network of neo-conservatives in the administration supported and reinforced CTEG and OSP's work. Strong support from Rumsfeld and Cheney allowed the material produced by CTEG and OSP to gain entry to the highest levels of policy-making. A number of accounts also suggest that not only did the administration methodically look for intelligence data to support its preconceived ideas, but that it exaggerated available evidence and placed undue pressure on the intelligence community to produce results to fit the administration's case.

Formal reviews of pre-war intelligence have concluded that the intelligence community failed to challenge its own assumptions on Iraq. It is certainly clear that the administration's convictions were reinforced by the intelligence community whose own analysis suggested ongoing WMD programmes in Iraq and some degree of contact between Baghdad and al-Qaida. These reviews suggest that the administration fell foul of the intelligence community's failings. Other reports suggest that the administration did exaggerate and depict intelligence so as to support the case for a war it was determined to prosecute. A fifth report, the second from the Senate Select Committee on Intelligence, is expected to examine how the Bush administration publicly portrayed the intelligence on Iraq's WMD and, at the time of writing, is due to be published in 2006.[41] The Pentagon's inspector general's office has also reported that it is going to investigate the use of intelligence by Feith leading up to the invasion of Iraq.[42] Even if the administration did not deliberately exaggerate intelligence to support the case for war, the fact that the Pentagon established new offices and procedures to scour intelligence for supporting evidence, and that this process was supported and reinforced by other senior members of the administration supports the assertion that the administration was determined to see Saddam Hussein removed from power.

Part III

THE NEO-CONSERVATIVES

10

THE NEO-CONSERVATIVE
WORLDVIEW

Introduction

Before 9/11 there was strong pressure from senior officials within the Bush administration and opinion-formers outside government to depose Saddam Hussein. The most vociferous supporters of this goal were often those labelled 'neo-conservatives'. After 9/11 pressure from the neo-conservatives to use military force to change the regime in Baghdad increased and played a major role in the Bush administration's steadfast determination to confront and if necessary invade Iraq. Understanding contemporary neo-conservatism and its impact on the White House and the war on terrorism is crucial to understanding why the administration was so adamant about regime change.

The influence of neo-conservative policy-makers within the Bush administration, particularly the Pentagon, has been widely debated. Neo-conservatives and what might be described as a distinct neo-conservative worldview certainly had a crucial influence on the administration's determination to force regime change in Iraq, but neo-conservatives did not 'take over' the administration after the attacks of 9/11 or foist a radical new agenda on an unwitting administration as some have suggested.[1] This chapter explores neo-conservatism in the context of the war with Iraq. It examines the evolution of neo-conservatism, the main features of contemporary neo-conservatism's worldview, the impact of neo-conservatism on the Bush administration before 9/11 and its impact on White House after the terrorist attacks.

Grand strategies and worldviews

There are a number of broad schools of thought in the United States about how international politics operates and the role of the United States. These are often labelled 'grand strategies' and they each embody a distinct and coherent set of core foreign-policy ideas, values and goals based on a particular understanding of international politics, power and interests. They operate on many different levels and reflect enduring American political, religious, economic and social interests. Four grand strategies are commonly referred to in the US foreign-policy discourse: isolationism, liberal internationalism, political realism and primacy. Isolationism is a grand strategy that is rarely articulated in mainstream political discourse.[2] The other three have significant influence. These broad, prescriptive grand strategies provide a framework for directing and justifying actions, prioritising policy goals and allocating a government's resources.[3]

The key tenets of these grand strategies are not mutually exclusive and there can be areas of commonality between them as well as internal divergence. In addition a government rarely adheres regimentally to one of these 'ideal types' since a government is made up of many senior foreign-policy-makers of different shades of opinion who have different degrees of influence on different issues at different times. Nevertheless, they do provide a useful frame of reference for comparing and contrasting different broad approaches to foreign policy.

A distinct contemporary neo-conservative worldview that reflects much of the primacist grand strategy can be identified in the US foreign-policy discourse. This is explored in detail below. The Bush administration, however, came to power having articulated a worldview that had one foot in the political realist camp and the other in the primacist camp, a view that was characterised as hard-line realism or assertive nationalism. Both of these two worldviews – the neo-conservative primacist view and the George W. Bush assertive nationalist view – have much in common and reflect a number of enduring themes of US foreign policy. They both differ markedly from the liberal internationalism that typified the Clinton administration and diverge significantly from the cautious, pragmatic, internationalist realism that characterised the administration of George H. W. Bush.

The ideas, values and themes on which the neo-conservative and George W. Bush worldviews are based are not new and have a long tradition in US foreign policy. For example, the post-9/11 paradigm that took the United States to war with Iraq emerged from a number of long-term trends in US foreign policy, in particular an American nationalism with a unwavering belief in US exceptionalism at its core and a Wilsonian desire to extend the values of that nationalism abroad, such as democracy, individualism and free-market capitalism. What is new is the manner in which these ideas and values were articulated and the opportunities the second Bush administration has had to engage in activities that are informed by or seek to advance those ideas and values. The 2000 presidential election victory was the opportunity for Governor Bush and his advisers to implement their foreign policy based on their worldview. The attacks of 11 September 2001 were the opportunity for neo-conservatives within and outside the administration to affect the government's worldview and bring it much closer to their own.

We recognise that giving complex political views labels such as 'assertive nationalist' and 'neo-conservative' can be useful for conveniently delineating different perspectives but note that it can be potentially misleading because of the loss of nuance and subtlety between political viewpoints. Nevertheless, these are the two labels used here.

Neo-conservatism

Vietnam to glasnost

Neo-conservatism is a contested political label. Those often associated with neo-conservatism describe their perspective as democratic realism, democratic imperialism[4] or hard Wilsonianism.[5] Neo-conservatism is often referred to as an ideology, or a movement, whereas Irving Kristol, one of the original neo-conservative intellectuals, describes it as a 'persuasion'.[6] Neo-conservatism has much to say about domestic political issues such as labour policy, taxation and education; but it also expounds a particular approach to foreign policy. Neo-conservatism can be legitimately considered as a political movement advocating a distinct set of foreign-policy actions based on a particular interpretation of international politics, while acknowledging that neo-conservatism is a contemporary manifestation of enduring themes in US foreign-policy history and discourse.

The particular political perspective that became known as neo-conservatism emerged from the Democrat Party in the 1970s in response to both the liberal Democrat contention that the United States should scale back its overseas commitments following the Vietnam War and accept America's relative decline in international politics, and the conservative Republican *realpolitik* exercised by Secretary of State Henry Kissinger that favoured accommodation though 'peaceful coexistence' with the Soviet Union.[7] The group of scholars, academics and Democrat Party members that came to be labelled neo-conservative rejected these forms of foreign policy and asserted instead that the United States retain its commitments abroad, keep the Soviet Union firmly contained, and substantially rebuild its military forces. They condemned Kissinger's détente with the Soviet Union as a failure of nerve to stand up to an evil enemy regime. Fierce anti-communism, a strong nationalism backed by a powerful military and an assertive, internationalist leadership aimed at rolling back and eventually defeating communism underpinned this neo-conservative perspective.[8]

By the late 1970s the original group of neo-conservative scholars, such as Irving Kristol and Norman Podhoretz, had been joined by a number of young conservative foreign-policy intellectuals such as Richard Perle and Paul Wolfowitz. Disillusioned with the Carter administration, the neo-conservatives lent full support to influential Congressional Democrats such as Henry 'Scoop' Jackson, Hubert Humphrey and Daniel Patrick Moynihan, whose views reflected their own. They later abandoned the Democrat Party to support the Republican presidential campaign in 1980.[9]

Ronald Reagan's victory in the 1980 election had a dramatic impact on US foreign policy and the influence of the neo-conservative perspective. Reagan's first-term foreign policy was characterised by a massive nuclear rearmament and a sharp anti-communist rhetoric that branded the Soviet Union an 'Evil Empire'. This uncompromising approach resonated with the neo-conservatives, some of whom took up positions in the administration. Reagan's victory, it is argued, gave the neo-conservatives 'their most significant entrees to the citadels of US power', particularly with the appointment of neo-conservative Jeanne Kirkpatrick as Reagan's Ambassador to the UN.[10] Nevertheless, neo-conservatism by no means dominated Reagan's policies.[11]

Reagan's second term left neo-conservative hopes unfulfilled. The emergence of Mikhail Gorbachev as Soviet leader and his conciliatory *glasnost* (openness) and *perestroika* (reform) initiatives facilitated a second détente that would eventually lead to the end of the Cold War. Reagan's gradual engagement with Gorbachev and the pragmatism beneath the hard-line rhetoric dismayed many neo-conservatives. By 1985, as John Ehrman, author of *The Rise of Neoconservatism*, argues, the neo-conservatives' greatest period of influence was coming to an end as they became increasingly disenchanted with the Reagan administration.[12]

Neo-conservatives in the 1990s

The end of the Cold War was a time of great change domestically and internationally for the United States and it affected the neo-conservative movement deeply. Difficult questions were raised about the purpose of US foreign policy and the nature of America's national interests following the demise of the Soviet Union. President George H. W. Bush sought to meet the challenges of the post-Cold War world with a pragmatic, internationalist conservative realism, turning away from the stringent idealistic nationalism that characterised Reagan's first term and reflected the neo-conservative perspective.[13]

The political realist grand strategy that informed the George H. W. Bush administration contends that international politics is ultimately a game of survival, where military power is the only form of power that counts. National security sits firmly at the top of a government's agenda, and state behaviour is driven by the pursuit of national power, survival and self-interest. International order emerges from a balance of power between states as they seek to maximise their relative power in the international system and forge alliances with other states to balance stronger powers.[14] Such balance-of-power realism, often referred to as *realpolitik*, underpinned US foreign policy throughout much of the Cold War with its policies of nuclear deterrence and communist containment. In the post-Cold War era advocates of this grand strategy seek to preserve American overseas alliance commitments in order to reduce security competition in important regions such as Europe, East Asia and the Middle East. Political realism is an essentially pessimistic grand strategy that regards conflict as inevitable and sees little hope in the possibility of transforming the international system to the extent where conflict is no longer inevitable. Given the futility of such idealistic attempts at remaking the world, realism advocates only those foreign-policy actions that are of direct consequence to America's vital interests. Actions such as humanitarian interventions are not part of the cautious and conservative realist agenda. If, however, vital interests are threatened, realism advocates a strong defence.[15]

The political realist approach warns against allowing America's democratic spirit and enduring desire to spread democracy that has long pervaded the US foreign-policy discourse to impinge on foreign-policy actions. American values, political realists argue, should be subordinate to the pursuit of American interests, and American interests such as free trade, regional stability, access to vital resources and military power do not always coincide with American values of human freedom, liberty and democracy.[16] This pragmatic balance-of-power realism characterised the foreign policy of George H. W. Bush, together with a strong emphasis on maintaining and expanding a global economic system conducive to American interests.[17]

This, then, was a confusing and transitional period for the neo-conservative movement. The goal of defeating the Soviet Union and its communist ideology had been achieved and many original neo-conservatives merged with the larger mainstream pragmatic conservative movement. At the same time the movement was undergoing a generational change as younger neo-conservatives began to take up the leadership roles of the first generation and redefine neo-conservatism through a post-Cold War strategic vision for the United States.[18] For this second generation of intellectuals, scholars and policy-makers, the containment and defeat of Soviet communism was the first step towards the active promotion of democracy abroad through a global system that would be shaped by a militarily, economically and politically ascendant American hegemon.[19]

The first Bush administration's preference for a cautious realist foreign policy based on a balance of power between the world's great nations rather than an activist and more idealist foreign policy was criticised by neo-conservatives. In fact it led many of the second-generation neo-conservatives to turn towards Bush's 1992 presidential challenger, Bill Clinton.[20] The decision not to overthrow Saddam Hussein in 1991 was characterised as symptomatic of the Bush administration's preference for separating active promotion of American values and the exercise of US military power, in this case the spread of democracy in Iraq and emancipation of the Iraqi people.

As some neo-conservatives turned away from Bush and the political realism governing Republican foreign policy, Governor Bill Clinton began actively to engage them. Clinton's emphasis on spreading democracy and his expressed willingness to use military force to defend US vital interests abroad succeeded in attracting some neo-conservative support during his presidential campaign. Within a year of his victory, however, and with no appointments in the new administration, the neo-conservatives soon united against Clinton.[21]

Clinton's liberal internationalism and 'assertive multilateralism' were heavily criticised by mainstream conservatives and neo-conservatives alike. Liberal internationalism as a broad approach to foreign policy tends to accept that peace, security and stability cannot be achieved while tyrannical and dictatorial regimes exist. For the most part, however, liberal internationalists favour non-violent means of pursuing international change, primarily through the effects of political, economic and cultural globalisation that increasingly bind countries together in an interdependent web of governments, international treaties, agreements and regimes, and non-state actors such as international organizations and multinational corporations. Clinton advocated spreading democracy and political freedom worldwide, particularly human rights, and viewed these as legitimate and necessary issues to address with allies and adversaries alike, as did neo-conservatives. Clinton's preferred methods were economic globalisation and engagement with states through the growing network of international institutions, regimes and agreements since free trade, it was argued, would eventually lead to free politics.[22] For liberal internationalists, such a favourable framework of rules and institutions gave the exercise of US power its legitimacy.[23]

Liberal internationalism also maintains that global problems require global solutions based on collective security and absolute gain for all parties, rather than relative gain for a particular state. International institutions and multilateral cooperation, particularly through the United Nations, are considered the most effective means of addressing collective international problems, rather than the traditional competitive power politics represented by political realism.[24] Neo-conservatives, however, were deeply critical of Clinton's insistence on a UN mandate or broad support from allies and other nations before using US armed forces. They abhorred his ambivalence about using US military force as an instrument of policy, his underinvestment in the armed services, his deference to the United Nations and his undiminished belief in the utility of written agreements, treaties and international institutions. Inaction or multilateralism were perceived to be the choices of the Clinton team and neo-conservatives, together with mainstream conservatives, lamented his failure to act unilaterally when multilateralism foundered on important issues.[25] His 'wishful liberalism' was condemned as one that 'looks to the world community and its institutions as the ultimate source of international legitimacy, is profoundly uncomfortable with the unilateral assertion of American power, and tends to favor policies that rely heavily on the carrot rather than the stick'.[26] Criticism of Clinton's policy toward Iraq in this context was widespread (see Chapter 3).[27]

By the mid-1990s neo-conservatism was something of a political anachronism, but within a few years it had completed its long transition and began to re-emerge as a distinct voice in US political discourse.[28] This was facilitated by the resurgence of a more assertive conservatism in American politics following the 1994 Congressional elections that saw the Republican Party gain control of both Houses of Congress on a strongly conservative platform.[29] This was reflected in the conservative policies of 1996 Republican presidential candidate Bob Dole, policies that were influenced by neo-conservatives such as Paul Wolfowitz.[30]

This resurgent neo-conservative movement coalesced around a number of think-tanks in Washington, in particular the Center for Security Policy, the American Enterprise Institute, the Project for a New American Century, and the Jewish Institute for National Security Affairs. Prominent second-generation neo-conservatives (as well as many mainstream realist conservatives) populated these institutes and propagated neo-conservative views on domestic and foreign policy through magazines such as the *Weekly Standard*, conservative talk radio and television programmes and opinion pieces in the mainstream press.[31] The second generation of neo-conservatives includes current and former government officials, government advisers, members of research institutes, academics and media commentators.[32]

By the end of the 1990s the neo-conservatives had regrouped and formulated a radical agenda for US foreign policy that reflected an increasingly tough-minded mainstream conservative view of America's place and role in the world. Halper and Clarke contend that this new vision was something quite different from that espoused by the first generation of neo-conservatives and had no 'intellectual heritage anywhere among the first-generation neo-conservatives, the Reaganite Cold Warriors of the 1980s, or the congressional unilateralists of the 1990s'.[33]

The neo-conservative worldview

The neo-conservative worldview has gradually evolved into a distinct set of causal beliefs about how change can occur in the international system and normative beliefs about what the international system should look like, how that change should occur and how America should act.[34] It can best be described as a primacist grand strategy that acknowledges America's predominance in the international system and argues that the United States should do all it can to retain its position of strength, particularly its military supremacy, while pre-empting any conceivable challenges to the US-led international order.[35] Contemporary neo-conservatism has a disdain for the liberal internationalism of Clinton and the isolationist currents of US foreign policy represented by Patrick Buchanan in the 1990s. The amoral pragmatic conservative realism of Kissinger and the first Bush administration is acknowledged as 'a valuable antidote to the woolly internationalism of the 1990s' but, neo-conservatives argue, 'America cannot and will not live by *realpolitik* alone.'[36] It presents itself as a viable alternative to these three enduring themes or grand strategies of US foreign-policy discourse.[37] Contemporary neo-conservatism is a primacist grand strategy with a strong Wilsonian ambition to spread democracy far beyond America's shores and it is advocated by some of its adherents with a revolutionary zeal.[38] It is characterised by a thematic emphasis on military power, exporting democracy and unilateralism, and by a geographic emphasis on the Middle East and East Asia.

American hegemony and unilateralism

The neo-conservative primacist worldview argues that the United States should forego balance-of-power realism in favour of a preponderance of power based on military dominance and unfettered freedom of action in international politics.

Consequently neo-conservatives believe that international institutions, regimes and treaties that constrain US behaviour are unnecessary and damaging. They reject the idea that the United States should accept such constraints in return for support from other states and similar constraints on other states. The dominance they seek is not just an end, but a means to an end of expanding the zone of market-oriented democratic states to establish a truly American international order, an ambition it shares with liberal internationalism. Where it diverges from liberal internationalism is in its emphasis on the utility, and perhaps necessity, of military power as an instrument of policy and a view of America as the benign custodian of the international system legitimately residing above the constraints of international laws and institutions.[39]

Neo-conservatives insist that the United States is unique because it has overwhelming global power but no imperial ambitions and has found itself in the position of a global hegemon through 'pure accident of history'.[40] The prevailing view is therefore what is good for America is by definition good for the world because America seeks to create a benevolent imperium founded on what are commonly considered universal values of human liberty and democracy.[41] This is not seen as Wilsonian idealism by its advocates because it shares realism's focus on military power and largely rejects liberal internationalism's focus on multilateral cooperation and collective security. Instead it is branded as democratic imperialism, or democratic realism.[42] This benevolent American global hegemony is, according to neo-conservatives, the only thing that stands between peace and security and war and tyranny. Consequently the first objective of US foreign policy is to 'preserve and enhance that predominance by strengthening America's security, supporting its friends, advancing its interests, and standing up for its principles around the world'.[43] This view is not exclusive to neo-conservatives since the need to maintain predominance features widely in the US foreign-policy discourse. It is the purpose and methods of predominance that differ.

According to neo-conservatives, the United States quite legitimately requires complete freedom of action as a global hegemon and, whilst coalitions of the willing are important and useful, the United States should be willing and able to act unilaterally where and when it sees fit in order to safeguard its interests. Multilateralism is accepted when defined as persuading others to support America's agenda or forming useful alliances, with a little give and take. Neo-conservatives recognise that the United States needs support for the values and institutions of liberal democracy and free trade it advocates, but insists that support comes from active and determined US leadership.[44] Multilateralism that is seen to tie America's hands, mire issues in somewhat dysfunctional international institutions, and make the United States 'subservient to, dependent on, constricted by the will – and interests – of other nations' is dismissed entirely.[45] The United Nations in particular is often singled out for attack.[46] In January 2003 John Bolton, Under Secretary of State for Arms Control and International Security, epitomised the neo-conservative view of the UN: 'There is no such thing as the United Nations. There is only the international community, which can only be led by the remaining superpower, which is the United States.'[47] Bolton went on to become the US Ambassador to the UN.

Exporting democracy

Neo-conservatism is not a status quo ideology and it advocates change over stability. It contends that the world can only be made truly safe for America through the democratisation of dictatorial regimes and disarmament of hostile states that are arming themselves with WMD. These states may be able to deter US action to advance or defend its interests, however defined, at some time and place in the future, and that is not acceptable. Passive measures are not sufficient and neo-conservatives advocate active measures alone or with others to realise this fundamental goal of spreading democracy.[48] Exporting and defending democracy is considered an obligation, the moral duty of a unique and exceptional country, and the path to long-term security. As neo-conservative *Washington Post* columnist Charles Krauthammer argued in 2004, 'the spread of democracy is not just an end but a means, an indispensable means for securing American interests'.[49] Furthermore, the United States, according to Irving Kristol, will always be obliged to defend 'a democratic country under attack from nondemocratic forces, either external or internal', where possible.[50]

For neo-conservatives, the promotion of American values is in total accord with the pursuit of American interests, for only by promoting American values can the United States make a better and safer world: 'American foreign policy', Robert Kagan and William Kristol insisted in 1996, 'should be informed with a clear moral purpose based on the understanding that its moral goals and its fundamental interests are almost always in harmony.'[51]

The idea of American exceptionalism is a theme that runs right through neo-conservatism, as it does through US foreign policy as a whole. It is grounded in a nationalist identity of adherence to a set of universal liberal democratic ideals and an obligation to support the spread of those ideals abroad. Where different schools of thought diverge is on what that exceptionalism means and how it should be acted upon. Jonathan Monten divides the idea of US exceptionalism into 'exemplarism' and 'vindicationism'. Exemplarism emphasises the perfection of US liberal democratic institutions and values at home. It is the power of this example that has a transformative effect abroad. An activist foreign policy is considered a liability and a potential threat to US liberal democratic values at home. Vindicationism argues that the United States must move beyond mere example and take active measures to spread the liberal democratic values and institutions it considers universal. Monten argues that neo-conservatism is a contemporary manifestation of vindicationist currents that pervade US foreign-policy history and have always coexisted alongside exemplarist tendencies.[52] The neo-conservative vindicationist view therefore maintains that democratic change abroad can be achieved through purposeful action.

Traditional political realism rejects this approach. It is pessimistic about America's capacity to force progressive change, arguing that international relations are governed by national self-interest and the pursuit of power from which the United States is not exempt, even if considers itself exceptional. By pursuing primacist goals the United States will fall into the trap of previous empires and overreach itself by unilaterally attempting to achieve goals for which it does not have the resources – fatally weakening itself in the process. Realism advocates balance of power and rejects strategies aimed at transcending that balance through overt pursuit of enduring primacy. Realists contend that the neo-conservative primacy strategy overestimates the nature of US power and dangerously conflates pre-eminence and omnipotence.[53]

Military power

The maintenance and use of military power is considered the very essence of America's hegemony and a vital instrument of policy. Like realists, neo-conservatives argue that military power and national security play the pivotal role in international politics and assert that US hegemony must be grounded in total military dominance of other states or possible coalitions of states – allies and adversaries alike. Military power should, according to neo-conservatives, be returned to the centre of US foreign policy and used to 'champion its ideals as well as its interests', including the spread of liberal democracy and the downfall of dictatorial regimes hostile to the United States.[54] The utility of military power is based on the belief that democracy will flourish in areas of repression once the obstacles to democracy are knocked down, and the United States has the economic, political and above all military power to remove such obstacles in some situations, for example in Iraq. It is legitimised through a belief in the benign and virtuous nature of US power.

From this perspective threats to the US-led international order should be dealt with through overwhelming force and preferably before they fully materialise. This can only be achieved by increasing the defence budget by tens of billions of dollars so that resources are provided to fulfil the neo-conservative strategy of confronting, undermining and democratising tyrannical and dictatorial regimes, rather than shaping strategy to fit available military resources. In their view, reducing US military capabilities and investment will directly undermine America's global leadership and the current global security order so conducive to US interests and values.[55]

The Middle East and East Asia

The primary focus of neo-conservative discourse is the Middle East and the rise of China as a potential threat to US hegemony and military power. Unquestioned support is lent to Israel as a functioning democracy in the Middle East with significant commonality between the hard-line policies of Israel's Likud Party and the US neo-conservative agenda. Pressure to remove Saddam Hussein from power and undermine the regime in Iran are enduring themes of the neo-conservative focus on the Middle East.[56] In East Asia, America's allies must be protected and China contained and influenced sufficiently over the longer term to enable regime change in Beijing.[57] China is considered a potential rival whilst Iran and North Korea (and formerly Iraq under Saddam Hussein) are clearly identified as adversaries.[58] Neo-conservatives argue that such regimes cannot be engaged with in pursuit of regional stability because they will never adhere to acceptable international norms of behaviour and cannot be trusted to abide by international agreements, for example those to limit or terminate WMD programmes. Instead the 'moral and strategic challenge presented by these evil regimes' must be confronted to bring about the demise of the regimes themselves.[59]

Neo-conservatism's view of strategic security is dominated by the threat from other states. Little or no mention is made of the great challenges the world faces such as enduring poverty exacerbated by a growing rich–poor divide and widespread curable disease. Nor is there any reference to the effects of human activity on a planetary scale, specifically climate change and environmental degradation, that the world must collectively address before these issues comprehensively threaten international security, including America's.

1992 Defense Planning Guidance

One of the earliest formulations of what can be described as the second generation's neo-conservative worldview is found in the 1992 draft Defense Planning Guidance (DPG). This was produced for Secretary of Defense Dick Cheney by a team led by Paul Wolfowitz, then Under Secretary of Defense for Policy, that included Zalmay Khalilzad (later Senior Director for Gulf, Southwest Asia and Other Regional Issues in George W. Bush's National Security Council) and I. Lewis Libby (later Cheney's Chief of Staff under George W. Bush). The document was produced to shape US defence policy after the Cold War as the United States moved away from its Cold War strategy of Soviet containment. The draft document was circulated in February 1992 and was soon leaked to the press, causing a major controversy.[60] The report outlined many of the ideas and policies that informed the neo-conservative worldview throughout the 1990s and into the administration of George W. Bush.[61] The Wolfowitz strategy argued that:

- The overriding post-Cold War priority should be to prevent the re-emergence of a new rival that could dominate a region vital to US interests.
- US leadership should be used to establish and protect a new order dominated by the United States that would deter other powers aspiring to or actually pursuing a role that could challenge the United States either regionally or globally.
- Coalitions should be *ad hoc*, the United States should ultimately defend the new order, and no mention was made of the United Nations for addressing international security crises. Instead it was argued that the United States

should retain 'pre-eminent responsibility for addressing selectively those wrongs which threaten not only our interests, but those of our friends, or which could seriously unsettle international relations'.

- The United States should encourage the key components of the new order, particularly democratic forms of government, open economic systems and respect for international law.
- The spread of WMD and ballistic missiles and obstruction of access to Persian Gulf oil were identified as scenarios in which US interest could be threatened. Iraq and North Korea were two of seven examples of potential trouble spots explored in the draft DPG.[62]

The original Wolfowitz strategy was changed by Powell, then Chairman of the Joint Chiefs of Staff, James Baker, then Secretary of State, and Brent Scowcroft, then National Security Advisor, after it was leaked to the press. The final version reflected much of the original but exhibited far more diplomatic language that emphasised the importance of coalitions, collective responses to international security crises and the importance of the United Nations. Talk on preventing the rise of regional or global competitors was dropped.[63]

The draft strategy was one of US primacy based on military pre-eminence, unilateral action to selectively maintain and enforce the rules of a new international order favourable to the United States, and the spread of democracy to ensure peace and stability. The Project for a New American Century's in-depth report on the nature and role of US armed forces, *Rebuilding America's Defenses*, which outlined the neo-conservative vision in 2000, acknowledged the legacy of Wolfowitz's draft Defense Planning Guidance.[64]

Neo-conservatives and the Bush administration
The first eight months

The Bush administration's first eight months were characterised by what has been labelled an assertive nationalist foreign policy grounded in both the political realist and primacist worldviews. Daalder and Lindsay define 'assertive nationalists' as 'traditional hard-line conservatives willing to use American military power to defeat threats to US security but reluctant as a general rule to use American primacy to remake the world in its image'.[65] They reflect much of Walter Russell Mead's 'Jacksonian' trend in American foreign policy, a trend that has the least regard for international law and international practice, and is rooted in a political realism that sees the world as violent and anarchic. It is a view that does not favour conflict in the absence of a clearly defined threat to the national interest, such as humanitarian interventions or moral reasons for fighting, but demands that once wars begin they are fought with the full force of the US military.[66] These Jacksonian themes of US foreign policy took root in the Pentagon under George W. Bush.[67] This assertive nationalist strain of political realism differed markedly from the liberal internationalism of the Clinton administration and the more pragmatic, internationalist realism of George H. W. Bush. But it also differed in important ways from the neo-conservative worldview.

The Vulcans

During the 2000 election campaign a number of hawkish conservative Republicans who had served on previous administrations advised and developed Bush's foreign policy perspective. The group called themselves the Vulcans, and chief among them was Condoleezza Rice, former Senior Director of Soviet and East European Affairs in George H. W. Bush's National Security Council.[68] Rice, together with Paul Wolfowitz, brought the group together in early 1999. They included Richard Armitage, Richard Perle, Stephen Hadley, Robert Blackwill, Robert Zoellick and Dov Zackheim. Two other figures, Cheney and Rumsfeld, were heavily involved in the Bush campaign. Missing from this team were the pragmatic conservative realists and moderate Republicans of the George H. W. Bush administration, the exception being Colin Powell, who remained on the periphery throughout the campaign period (see Chapter 4).[69]

Most of the Vulcans, including Rice, were not neo-conservatives but assertive nationalists. Only Perle and Wolfowitz wholly fitted the neo-conservative bill. However, the Vulcans were, according to Mann, 'the military generation' with a common experience forged in the Pentagon. This arguably played a major part in the administration's emphasis on military power and power politics. 'The top levels of the foreign policy team that took office in 2001', Mann writes, 'included two former secretaries of defense (Cheney and Rumsfeld), one former chairman of the Joint Chiefs of Staff (Powell), one former undersecretary of defence (Wolfowitz) and one former assistant secretary of defense (Armitage). Even Rice had started her career in Washington with a stint at the Pentagon, working for the Joint Chiefs of Staff.'[70] Although there were differences of opinion, all believed that US power and ideals were a force for good in the world and disagreed with liberal internationalists that American power needed tying down in international regimes and treaties.

The Bush administration's early foreign policy

A good understanding of Bush's initial approach to foreign policy can be gleaned from two pre-election foreign-policy speeches Bush made in September and November 1999, Condoleezza Rice's February 2000 article in *Foreign Affairs*, 'Promoting the National Interest', from the appointments Bush made to fill the most senior foreign-policy positions in his administration, and from the major foreign-policy actions of his first eight months in office.

Bush's two speeches and Rice's article suggested that the new Bush administration's foreign policy would be ordered around four key themes. The first of these was a strong military and rebuilding the armed forces. Bush argued in his speeches that US military forces and American defence must be the president's first priority and that his foreign policy would reflect a 'tough realism' based on 'the foundation of our peace – a strong, capable and modern military' whose budget matched the strategic vision, not vice versa.[71] Rice argued that US foreign policy should be conducted according to a clear understanding of the national interest based on a strong defence that would enable US military forces to deter war or fight and win if deterrence failed and emphasised that US military power was 'the only guarantor of global peace and stability'.

The second theme was the promotion of American values abroad. Bush argued that the promotion of US values must have its place in the realist world-view, insisting that American values and principles were universal and that any policy choice between American values and American interests was a false one. Instead, US foreign policy must have the guiding purpose of promoting democracy because the spread of American values created the conditions for peace. American foreign policy, Bush argued, 'must have a great and guiding goal: to turn this time of American influence into generations of democratic peace'. Here Bush also emphasised the formula of liberal and realist internationalism that 'economic freedom creates habits of liberty'. Rice concurred that US national interest was based on the promotion of economic growth and political openness through free trade.

The third theme centred on strategic security issues and highlighted four issues: first, the importance of cementing existing alliances to extend a democratic peace; second, the necessity of building comprehensive relationships with the major powers, particularly Russia and China. Bush argued that a new relationship should be forged with Russia based on cooperation rather than a long-dead ideological confrontation. He asserted that China should be addressed as a strategic competitor with both resolve and respect, and rejected Clinton's view of China as a 'strategic partner'.[72] Rice also insisted that China should be contained as a strategic competitor while internal change was promoted through economic interaction. However, the foundation of the Bush foreign policy towards major powers was that the United States must prevent the rise of a single or coalition of great powers that could threaten the country. In this way the United States could encourage stability from a position of strength. The third strategic security issue was the importance of dealing decisively with rogue regimes and hostile powers that threaten terrorism or WMD. Rice singled out the three states that would later constitute the 'axis of evil'– Iraq, Iran and North Korea – as regimes that needed to be dealt with 'resolutely and decisively', while insisting that there need be 'no sense of panic' since deterrence still served as a first line of defence. It is also worth noting that in 1999 the 'troubled frontiers of technology and terror' were part of Bush's foreign-policy framework. At this stage, however, Bush focused on missile defence and strengthening intelligence to halt 'the contagious spread of missile technology and weapons of mass destruction', while making passing reference to the risks of WMD terrorism.[73] Daalder and Lindsay assert that Cheney too 'shared this dark vision of the world. The perils that the United States faced abroad – from China, Russia, Iraq, North Korea, terrorists – were a staple of his conversations.'[74] The fourth important strategic issue was defence of American interests in the Persian Gulf and advancing peace in the Middle East.

The fourth broad theme was the exercise of US power; this focused on two issues. The first was a determination to use US military forces sparingly. It was stated that the humanitarian interventions of the Clinton administration would largely pass into history under Bush. Using US military power for humanitarian interventions or nation-building as Clinton had done was not in the national interest, argued Rice. Instead, foreign-policy actions should put US national interests first and if these actions benefited all humanity, then that was a positive 'second order effect'. Bush said that he would replace 'diffuse commitments with focused ones', insisting that US forces would not be permanent peacekeepers. Second, US power should not be constrained by multilateral norms, rules and treaties that inhibited pursuit of America's national interests. The United States should not, Rice proclaimed, pursue 'largely symbolic international agreements' in pursuit of 'illusory "norms"', a process that had reached 'epidemic' proportions under Clinton. The United States, she went on, 'has a special role in the world and should not adhere to every international convention and agreement that someone thinks to propose.' Bush agreed, insisting that a president must be 'a clear-eyed realist' and deal with threats not through multilateral norms, institutions and regimes, but through military strength and resolve.

These four themes: building a strong military; using US power to spread a democratic peace by exporting American values; a focus on state-to-state international security issues, particularly China and the Middle East's 'rogue' regimes; and a determination to rise above multilateralism and use military forces for fighting wars rather than humanitarian interventions and peacekeeping, together comprised the assertive nationalist worldview, described by Ikenberry as 'starkly realist'.[75] They reflected the political realist approach in their emphasis on strong military power, dealing decisively with threats, great-power relationships and a narrowly defined national interest. They also emulated the primacist goal of extending the zone of democratic capitalist societies and maintaining predominance, particularly military superiority.[76] They therefore reflected important components of the neo-conservative perspective but remained some distance from the neo-conservative worldview that emerged in the late 1990s.[77]

In his inaugural address Bush reiterated that the United States would remain engaged in the world, that allies and interests would be vigorously defended against aggression, and that the US would seek 'a balance of power that favours freedom'.[78] This would be achieved through a foreign policy that both secured US interests and promoted its highest ideals – a 'distinctly American internationalism'.[79]

Convergence and divergence with neo-conservatism

Appointments

Bush had little direct experience of foreign affairs and did not come into office with a specific foreign-policy agenda beyond the themes outlined above. Instead he declared that he would use powerful and experienced foreign- and defence-policy-makers by encouraging debate and dissenting views on foreign-policy issues on which he would then make the final decision.[80] Those he appointed to head the foreign and defence bureaucracies, however, were not neo-conservatives. The appointment of Rice as National Security Advisor and Powell as Secretary of State, both protégés of George H. W. Bush's National Security Advisor Brent Scowcroft, suggested that the cautious realist pragmatic foreign policy of the elder Bush's White House would have a major influence on the new Bush administration. The appointment of Cheney and Rumsfeld reflected a more assertive nationalist influence. None of these four could be classed as neo-conservative because they did not share the ideological zeal to aggressively export US values, particularly democracy, characteristic of their hard-line Wilsonian brethren such as Paul Wolfowitz and Richard Perle. It looked as if the neo-conservative worldview would only have a limited impact.[81]

However, Cheney and Rumsfeld had strong views on US exceptionalism, the utility of unilateralism and need for a strong defence against the nation's enemies that reflected a significant part of the neo-conservative primacist perspective.[82] Cheney was particularly influential from the outset and, as Mann writes, 'played a central role both internally, in the campaign's discussions about what positions to take on foreign policy, and externally, as the vice presidential nominee'.[83] On entering office Cheney soon established a large foreign-policy team, unusual for a vice president, populated by experienced advisers who allowed Cheney to wield a powerful influence over policy-making in the White House that was enhanced by Bush's initial lack of foreign policy experience.[84] Nevertheless, according to White House speechwriter David Frum, Cheney's rise to become one of the most powerful vice presidents, if not *the* most powerful, in history depended on 'subordinating himself entirely to Bush' to earn and retain the President's trust.[85]

The pairing of Cheney and Rumsfeld proved particularly powerful. The two had a rich history of working together from the Nixon administration onwards. They shared similarly tough views on foreign and defence policy, and Cheney played a major role in appointing Rumsfeld as Defense Secretary. Powell's cautious, pragmatic approach to foreign policy and the use of military force, on the other hand, appeared closer to that of the first Bush presidency and out of step with the assertive nationalist view that came to dominate the administration, leaving Powell's perspective relatively isolated.[86]

Not only were Cheney and Rumsfeld's views on foreign and defence policy close to those of neo-conservatives, but Cheney played a key role in bringing neo-conservatives such as Wolfowitz and Libby into the administration's foreign-

and defence-policy bureaucracies.[87] As Clarke and Halper contend, without the support of Cheney and Rumsfeld, the neo-conservative agenda would have had little influence.[88] Other neo-conservatives appointed to senior positions at the second and third levels of these bureaucracies included Elliot Abrams, Special Advisor to the President in the National Security Council, John Bolton, Under Secretary of State for Arms Control and International Security; Douglas Feith, Under Secretary of Defense for Policy; and several members of the Defense Policy Board, including James Woolsey, Elliot Cohen and its Chair, Richard Perle. In addition, a number of neo-conservative sympathisers were brought into the Defense Department such as Peter Rodman, Assistant Secretary of Defense for International Security Affairs, and Dov Zakheim, Comptroller and Under Secretary of Defense.[89]

Foreign- and defence-policy actions

The Bush administration's early foreign-policy actions reflected much of the neo-conservative agenda. The White House signalled its intentions to remove what it considered unnecessary multilateral constraints on its freedom of action by rejecting international agreements, leading to charges of unilateralism. These included the International Criminal Court, the Kyoto Protocol, the Verification Protocol of the Biological and Toxin Weapons Convention, and the Anti-Ballistic Missile (ABM) Treaty.[90] Neo-conservative officials such as Wolfowitz and Bolton were centrally involved in defeating these agreements. Bush also reined in Clinton's efforts to mediate a solution to the Israeli–Palestinian conflict and lent full support to Israel. He dismissed any further negotiations with North Korea over its nuclear weapons and ballistic missile programmes, undermining South Korean President Kim Dae Jung's 'sunshine policy' in the process, and accelerated the US missile defence programme. This confrontational approach alarmed a number of constituencies but pleased the neo-conservatives.[91]

The neo-conservative primacist position arguably had a significant influence during the administration's first eight months, but there were just as many disappointments. In April 2001 Bush faced the first major foreign-policy crisis of his presidency when a Chinese fighter jet collided in mid-air with a US EP-3 reconnaissance plane, forcing the US aircraft to land on China's Hainan Island. After an initial uncompromising response, Bush resorted to pragmatic realism in his dealings with Beijing and the crisis was resolved peacefully through Powell's diplomacy. Neo-conservatives were furious with this climb-down, described by Kagan and Kristol as a national humiliation.[92] By June 2001 neo-conservatives were expressing their dissatisfaction at the administration's reluctance to increase the defence budget on entering office, the drawn-out consultative process of withdrawing from the ABM treaty, its unwillingness to take concrete steps to remove Saddam Hussein from power (a key neo-conservative objective) and the weakness of Powell's smart sanctions policy on Iraq. Despite regular reference to Reagan's early foreign policy by the administration, within six months neo-conservatives were concerned that Bush's foreign policy would 'amount to nothing more than a variation of old-world *realpolitik*'.[93]

Worldviews

The neo-conservative worldview and the Bush administration's assertive nationalist outlook differed on a number of issues, in particular whether the United States should actively use all the means at its disposal to spread its values abroad as a key component of foreign policy. The neo-conservative concept of the national interest was much broader than that of the Bush administration. Neo-conservatives argued that the world could and should be made safer through 'vigorous application of American power and ideals' to confront the threats facing the United States and spread democratic institutions. This was deemed to be in America's national interest. Here the assertive nationalist worldview parted company since it saw the use of military force as limited to deterring and if necessary defeating aggressors, rather than remaking the world.[94] Spreading US values abroad was certainly important to Bush, but the use of military force to achieve this objective was questioned.[95] The notion that the aggressive promotion of democracy could resolve international conflict and that the United States had the ability to successfully transplant democratic ideals and institutions and shape the internal dynamics of states at will was treated with scepticism. Nation-building was not part of this administration's agenda.[96]

Despite this difference on the nature of the US national interest, neo-conservatives and assertive nationalists held a number of important values and viewpoints in common. Both views asserted the primacy of the state, military power and national security in international affairs. They shared a deep scepticism of commitments to the international rule of law and the relevance of international institutions, rejecting multilateralism and placing their faith in power rather than treaties. They firmly believed that America could and should retain its dominant position in international affairs and that only US hegemony could secure international peace and stability through an unchallengeable military. They expressed strong resolve to deal with 'rogue states' and WMD proliferation decisively, particularly through deployment of missile defences and credible threats of force. Finally, they agreed that the export of US values and ideals was a key goal of foreign policy, although they differed on the means.[97] These common positions allowed a discernible alliance, or a marriage of convenience, between the assertive nationalist worldview and the neo-conservative worldview in the Bush administration.[98]

A 9/11 transformation?

The foreign and defence policies of the Bush administration changed after the attacks of 9/11. It has been argued that the White House worldview underwent a wholesale transformation after the attacks; that it was in some sense hijacked by neo-conservatives.[99] But in fact the attacks reaffirmed many aspects of the administration's assertive nationalist worldview while shifting other aspects and appropriate policy responses.[100] The extent to which the political realist perspective informed Bush's foreign policy and the President's personal conviction that US power be exercised with humility were certainly revised, but the attacks did not cause the entire edifice of the Bush administration's pre-9/11 worldview to be jettisoned and replaced with an entirely different neo-conservative perspective.[101]

These shifts drew the White House worldview much closer to the neo-conservative perspective with which it already shared a great deal. One can imagine the assertive nationalist worldview and the neo-conservative worldview as parallel tracks that run close on some issues and objectives and further apart on others. From a broader perspective the former is much closer to the latter than it is to, say, Clinton's liberal internationalism or George H. W. Bush's pragmatic realism. The events of 9/11 brought these two tracks much closer together and on some issues created significant overlap in rhetoric and actions.[102] In particular, what may have been considered a risky neo-conservative strategy of attempting to transform the troublesome Middle East before 9/11 became politically possible after the attacks.[103]

The very presence of a robust neo-conservative worldview within the senior ranks of the administration, particularly the Pentagon, complete with a ready-made package of solutions for just such a 'war on terror', exerted a significant pull on the White House's policy choices in the days and months after the attacks. The fact that military power was going to be a crucial aspect of the 'war on terror', given the acute threat international terrorism now represented, was another important part of neo-conservative influence after the attacks. Many in the administration held a common view about the utility of military force as an instrument of policy and many of the administration's neo-conservative cohort that favoured exercising US military power to demonstrate and restore US strength were based in the Pentagon.[104] Neo-conservatives could therefore have considerable influence on how and for what purpose military forces might be used in the war on terrorism.

The role of Cheney and Rumsfeld in shifting the administration's foreign and defence policy towards that of the neo-conservatives cannot be overestimated. White House activity before 9/11 had been dominated by domestic issues such as the $1.6 trillion tax cut, education reform, energy policy and Social Security privatization. After 9/11 foreign and defence policy took precedence, areas where Bush still had little experience.[105] After the attacks Cheney and Rumsfeld came to accept much of the neo-conservative perspective and the actions it advocated as the appropriate long-term response to the attacks and strove to put it into practical effect over Iraq, even if they did not accept this worldview in its entirety. Without their support the relatively small group of neo-conservatives in the Pentagon and the White House would have had far less influence on the President's post-9/11 views and actions.

The Bush doctrine

After the attacks any president would have pursued Osama bin Laden and al-Qaida in Afghanistan and attacked the Taliban regime if it had refused to surrender the wanted men and verifiably dismantled al-Qaida's training camps and infrastructure. However, the new post-9/11 national security paradigm outlined in the 2002 State of the Union Address, the President's June 2002 West Point speech and the September 2002 National Security Strategy, often referred to as the Bush doctrine, went further and reflected much of the neo-conservative worldview.

As discussed in previous chapters, the new paradigm took the step of equating terrorist groups and actions with state sponsors or supporters, allowing the administration's 'war on terror' to target hostile regimes. To deal with those regimes the doctrine explicitly declared a policy of pre-emptive attack should the United States consider such actions necessary, insisting that deterrence, containment and arms control were no longer relevant when dealing with international terrorist groups and 'rogue' states. The exercise of force would no longer be limited to self-defence or constrained by multilateral institutions.[106]

The Middle East underpinned much of the post-9/11 neo-conservative strategy and the Bush doctrine, which maintained that the status quo in the Middle East was no longer acceptable and that Iraq supported and contributed to that status quo more than most.[107] The time had come for a new approach that would no longer confuse stability in the Middle East 'with the longevity of anti-American dictatorships'.[108] Mann writes that this post-9/11 resolve and righteousness pervaded the administration regardless of political ideology or worldview, but it was the neo-conservatives who articulated a vision of sweeping change in the Middle East.[109] Charles Krauthammer articulated this grand project in February 2004:

> The overthrow of radicalism and the beginnings of democracy can have a decisive effect in the war against the new global threat to freedom, the new existential enemy, the Arab-Islamic totalitarianism that has threatened us in both its secular and religious forms for the quarter-century since the Khomeini revolution of 1979. Establishing civilized, decent, non-belligerent, pro-Western polities in Afghanistan and Iraq and ultimately their key neighbors would, like the flipping of Germany and Japan in the 1940s, change the strategic balance in the fight against Arab-Islamic radicalism.[110]

The Bush doctrine espoused a strong and proactive neo-conservative focus on the aggressive use of US power, including military power, to spread liberal democracy to make the world safe for the United States, with particular emphasis on the Middle East and removal of its hostile 'rogue' regimes.[111] The administration emphasised a stronger commitment to 'a distinctly American internationalism that reflects the union of our values and our national interests' and a commitment to opening up societies and exporting democracy in its National Security Strategy. No nation was exempt from the 'right and true' principles of liberty and justice, and the administration would oppose those who resisted them.[112]

Any semblance of *realpolitik* power balancing that might have informed the administration's worldview before 9/11 evaporated, any contradiction between power and principles was banished and any suggestion that multilateral institutions, norms or regimes could or would prevent the United States from pursuing its chosen strategy was dismissed.[113] The new focus on influencing the domestic political structures of hostile states, thereby sidelining state sovereignty in favour of enforcing certain norms of behaviour, represented a significant departure from the political realist perspective.[114]

Monten described the Bush doctrine as the 'operationalization of neoconservatism'[115] and George Bush as 'articulating primarily neoconservative logic and language', with the views of the President constituting a 'hybrid' of the alliance of neo-conservatives and assertive nationalists.[116] Rhodes described it as 'Wilsonianism with a vengeance', whose objective was the transformation of world politics using American power to export liberal democracy,[117] and Clarke and Halper as 'an unabashed manifestation of well-documented neo-conservative thought'.[118] Finally, Karl Meyer noted that after 9/11 Bush 'metamorphosed into an avenging warrior ... as high pontiff of an ideological campaign to democratize Islamic lands'.[119]

Transforming the Middle East

As the war in Iraq came ever closer, senior members of the administration seemed to adopt the neo-conservative vision in its entirety by enunciating a broader rationale for liberating Iraq: the transformation of the Middle East. In February 2003 Bush declared that 'a liberated Iraq can show the power of freedom to transform that vital region, by bringing hope and progress into the lives of millions. America's interests in security, and America's belief in liberty, both lead in the same direction: to a free and peaceful Iraq.' A liberated Iraq would have a transformative effect in the region since 'Success in Iraq could also begin a new stage for Middle Eastern peace, and set in motion progress towards a truly democratic Palestinian state.'[120] Cheney, Rice and Wolfowitz all concurred. Cheney had stated in August 2002 that regime change in Iraq would bring about a number of benefits to the region. In particular it would cause extremists to rethink their jihadi strategies, allow moderate politics to rise and the Israeli–Palestinian peace process to move forward.[121] Rice maintained that regime change would 'open new opportunities for peace in the Middle East and new opportunities for Arab countries to give greater liberty and greater awareness to their own people'.[122] Bush continued to make this case after the war, stating in June 2005 that victory in Iraq would inspire democratic change across the Middle East and make the United States more secure.[123]

Wolfowitz was resolute that removing Saddam Hussein would be a significant step towards liberating the wider Middle East and would facilitate progress in the Israel–Palestine conflict, insisting that 'Success in Iraq would demoralize those who preach doctrines of hatred and oppression and subjugation. It would encourage those who dream the ancient dream, the ageless desire for freedom.'[124] It is worth noting, however, that in 2000 Wolfowitz did not buy into this approach. He wrote that 'both because of what the United States is, and because of what is possible, we cannot engage in promoting democracy or in nation-building as an exercise of will'. He went on to declare that

> experiences with Germany and Japan offer misleading guides to what is possible now, even in a period of American primacy. What was possible following total victory and prolonged occupation – in societies that were economically advanced but, at the same time, had lost faith in their own institutions – does not offer a model that applies in other circumstance.[125]

The events of 9/11 and the opportunity to bring down Saddam had evidently changed his mind.

This view was supported by Washington's conservative think-tanks. In March 2003 AEI's Reuel Marc Gerecht, for example, argued that removing Saddam Hussein and installing a democratic system would encourage similar change in Iran.[126] AEI's outspoken neo-conservative Michael Ledeen, reportedly an adviser to the President's political guru Karl Rove,[127] agreed that Iraq would spur a revolution in Iran. He also went much further and argued that an invasion of Iraq should serve as a springboard for removing the regimes in Syria and Saudi Arabia: 'The common denominator of our enemies in the Middle East is tyranny. The terror masters are all tyrants. So Saudi Arabia, Syria, Iran, and Iraq are all tyrannies. And I believe until these tyrannies are brought down we will continue to have terrorism.'[128] In *An End to Evil* Richard Perle and David Frum set out a manifesto for remaking the Middle East through US actions against Iran, Syria, Hamas, Hezbollah and Saudi Arabia.[129]

This vision of a Middle East transformed by importing and institutionalising democracy in Iraq led to the view that US forces would be greeted as liberators when they overthrew Saddam's regime and that this gratitude would lead to a swift, efficient and productive transfer of power to a new democratic Iraqi government. Cheney, for example, argued that the Iraqis would greet regime change with joy,[130] Wolfowitz insisted that 'we will be greeted as liberators'[131] and that 'we received such a welcome from the Afghan people. I think it's nothing compared to what the Iraqi people will say and do when they're rid of Saddam Hussein.'[132] Members of Congress were not immune to such rhetoric, with Republican Representative Dana Rohrabacher extolling the virtues of liberation, and proclaiming that Iraqis 'will be dancing in the streets, waving American flags, just as the people of Afghanistan still are grateful to us for freeing them and helping them free themselves'.[133]

This mindset that regime change in Iraq would transform the Middle East and that the United States would enjoy widespread gratitude for its actions was a crucial self-legitimising aspect of the administration's determination to depose Saddam, and was built on neo-conservative foundations. It is succinctly summed up by the respected author and journalist William Pfaff:

> Victory over Saddam, Mr. Bush's supporters say, will unlock everything. Other Arabs will see that nothing can be gained from supporting terrorism. They will turn against al-Qaida, and will tell the Palestinians to put away the bombs, arrest the bombers and take whatever settlement Israel offers ... A new pro-American government in Iraq will demonstrate the virtues of democracy and the advantages of cooperation with the United States. People elsewhere in the Arab world will demand democratic, free-market, pro-American governments, When they get them, the misery, injustice and resentment that nourish extremism and terrorism will dry up.[134]

Continuity

Nevertheless, there was also considerable continuity with the administration's pre-9/11 worldview. Good relations between the major powers and strong alliances with friends were still highlighted as a strategic priority, and democratisation through trade remained a strong theme in the NSS. The three states that comprised the 'axis of evil' – Iraq, Iran and North Korea – had long been the focus of the Bush administration before 9/11 and the Clinton White House before that. A number of geo-political, as opposed to ideological, rationales were put forward for dealing with Iraq, such as unimpeded access to oil, removal of a WMD threat, removing provocative US forces from Saudi Arabia, containing Iran and defending Israel (see Chapter 1). The administration has not, at the time of writing, taken further action to remove the Syrian or Iranian regimes from power as recommended by neo-conservatives, and has made progress in the six-party talks negotiating process with North Korea. Finally, it seems that the White House does not share the neo-conservative zeal for building democratic institutions in formerly hostile states, witnessed by the almost total absence of post-war planning in Afghanistan and Iraq.[135]

An important post-9/11 distinction remains between assertive nationalists who 'want to make the world safe for democracy' and neo-conservatives who 'want to make the world democratic'.[136] The Bush doctrine proceeded from principles evident in the administration's pre-9/11 foreign policy, a doctrine that was adopted because of 9/11 rather than neo-conservative influence, insists neo-conservative Max Boot. And whilst the September 2002 National Security Strategy was a 'quintessentially neoconservative document', Boot maintains that 'the triumph of neoconservatism was hardly permanent or complete'.[137]

An opportunity taken by neo-conservatives

Ideas play a crucial role in foreign policy. Neo-conservative ideas, i.e. their causal and normative beliefs, were persuasive after 9/11, assisted by the emphasis on military power in the new war on terrorism, the presence of neo-conservatives in the administration, the coherence of their position, and the closeness of that position to the assertive nationalist views of Cheney, Rumsfeld and to a certain extent Rice.

Dueck argues that policy-makers rely on policy ideas, or sets of beliefs and assumptions, to guide them in times of crisis, change and uncertainty. During such times alternative strategic ideas can infiltrate the highest echelons of policy-making and have a major impact through agenda-setting and defining the terms of the debate if they are advocated by senior policy-makers. The election of George W. Bush in 2000 saw a new set of strategic ideas and their advocates sweep into the White House. Similarly, the attacks of 9/11 opened a window of opportunity for new strategic ideas to permeate and embed themselves, but only those that garnered the support of senior officials. A number of ideas about how to respond to the attacks were articulated, from isolationism to multilateral cooperation and engagement, but these had little support within the administration. What did have support, in the form of Cheney and Rumsfeld, was the neo-conservative approach.[138]

The neo-conservatives in the Bush administration seized the unprecedented opportunity presented by 9/11 to push their agenda by offering a coherent and proactive solution to the difficult issues confronting the White House in the aftermath of the attacks. This 'preexisting ideological agenda', Halper and Clarke argue, 'was taken off the shelf, dusted off, and relabeled as *the* response to terror'.[139] This blueprint for dealing with international terrorism focused not on a global military counter-terrorist and politico-judicial hunt for and prosecution of al-Qaida cells, but on remaking the Middle East as the most appropriate means of eliminating the threat from international terrorism, beginning with regime change in Iraq. Neo-conservatives Richard Perle and David Frum argued that terror was being defined too narrowly and that the United States had to go after 'the governments that give terrorists aid and sanctuary' as well as the 'larger culture of incitement and hatred that justifies and supports terror'. Perle and Frum concede that their vision was adopted by the administration because 'we have offered concrete recommendations equal to the seriousness of the threat, and the soft-liners have not'.[140]

With a tailor-made solution to the 9/11 attacks, replete with 'concrete recommendations', neo-conservatives and their sympathisers in the administration moved quickly to stifle wider debate on America's possible range of responses.[141] The discourse of the administration's post-9/11 strategy was quickly fashioned to link 9/11, al-Qaida, Iraq and the possibility (if not imminence) of a WMD terrorist strike on America. By linking their focus on the Middle East and Iraq to the attacks of 9/11, the neo-conservatives successfully 'created an entirely new reality' using the power of their positions both in and out of government.[142] In order to gain necessary political acceptability, the administration had to convince Congress and the US public of the validity of this strategy, beginning with regime change in Iraq, and they worked extremely hard to do so.[143]

Conclusion

Understanding the neo-conservative worldview and its impact on the White House before and after 9/11 provides important insights into the administration's determination to confront and attack Iraq. The contemporary neo-conservative worldview emerged in the 1990s. It emphasised the necessity and legitimacy of American hegemony and unilateralism, the democratisation of tyrannical and dictatorial regimes through force if necessary as part of the US national interest, military predominance, and threats from the Middle East and East Asia. Determination to change the regime in Baghdad was an important part of this perspective.

The new Bush administration had a similar, but not identical, worldview. Instead it was an amalgamation of the neo-conservative primacist position and a tough political realist position, referred to here as an assertive nationalist worldview. Despite some important differences between the neo-conservative and assertive nationalist worldviews, they had much more in common with each other than they had with George H. W. Bush's pragmatic international realism or Clinton's liberal internationalism. This was reflected in the appointment of neo-conservatives to the Bush administration and some of the administration's foreign- and defence-policy actions in its first eight months. Nevertheless, the leaders of the administration's foreign and defence bureaucracies were not neo-conservatives.

The attacks of 11 September 2001 offered an unprecedented opportunity for neo-conservatives inside and outside the administration to push their agenda, particularly the case for regime change in Iraq. They were very successful, not least because Rumsfeld and Cheney appeared to accept that the neo-conservative worldview and the actions advocated therein offered the most appropriate solution to post-9/11 threats faced by the United States, particularly the perceived threat from Iraq. This allowed neo-conservative ideas to become embedded in the White House, as shown in the development of the new national security paradigm and the burgeoning perception that deposing Saddam would spark the transformation of the Middle East.

Before 9/11 the administration's Iraq policy review was likely to produce a more confrontational strategy for dealing with Saddam Hussein. After 9/11 the White House became increasingly determined to change the regime in Baghdad as an urgent priority. The neo-conservative worldview and its advocates within the administration played a crucial role in fuelling that determination, reinforcing and supplementing the administration's assertive nationalist worldview, and constructing the case for a pre-emptive attack to depose Saddam.

However, the transformation was not wholesale. The neo-conservative and assertive nationalist worldviews melded on the issue of regime change in Baghdad, but the neo-conservative strategy has not been taken further in the Middle East, notably because of the failure of Saddam's fall to lead to a peaceful Iraq. If Iraq had gone as the neo-conservatives predicted and it had been shown that Baghdad really did have extensive WMD programmes, then perhaps the neo-conservative plan to change the regimes in Syria, Iran and even Saudi Arabia would have been implemented.

11

CONCLUSION – AN ENDLESS ROAD?

Introduction

Writing with the benefit of hindsight, more than four years after the 9/11 attacks and three years after the start of the Iraq War, it is easy to forget the views expressed on the probability of war in the period between 9/11 and March 2003. The issue of Iraq did rise up the political agenda in the immediate aftermath of the termination of the Taliban regime at the end of 2001 and the State of the Union Address in January 2002, but the majority opinion among international relations analysts, right up to the end of 2002, was that a war with Iraq was unlikely. With the taking of the issue to the United Nations there was a presumption that a diplomatic solution was probable and that the UNMOVIC inspection process would provide sufficient assurance to make war unnecessary. This was a view maintained by many analysts, and stressed by politicians such as UK Prime Minister Tony Blair, even as the military forces were being put in place in the region. Indeed there was a strong view that the very preparations for war would make it more likely that the Saddam Hussein regime would acquiesce to the demands being made by the Bush administration.

During this period there were indications that the war itself might carry some risks for the coalition being assembled. There was little doubt that the military forces available to the United States and its major coalition partners were formidable and were easily sufficient to terminate the regime, but there were questions concerning the risk that the regime might resort to CBW if it was facing destruction. There were also many issues raised concerning the problems of occupation, both in terms of the extent to which an internal insurgency might develop and also whether the occupation of Iraq would be advantageous to the al-Qaida movement and its wider jihadist associates.[1]

Nevertheless, the war went ahead, and the regime was terminated with apparent ease. At that time, April 2003, it was confidently expected that US forces would be scaled down to around 70,000 troops or less within six months, dropping eventually to perhaps 20,000 personnel concentrated primarily in four large military bases. It was expected that a vigorous free market economy would be established by the Coalition Provisional Authority and then embraced by a new pro-American government, and that US influence in the Gulf would be much enhanced. In particular, success in Iraq with a subsequent US military presence in a country transiting to a Western market economy would send a particularly powerful message both to Iran and to the al-Qaida movement.

The Iranian government, of whatever future complexion, would recognise that the United States had demonstrated its ability and willingness to terminate antagonistic regimes to the east and west of Iran, and would therefore be cautious and conciliatory in its dealings with Washington. The al-Qaida movement would also face difficulties, not only declining in influence by losing the presumed connections with the old regime in Iraq, but also facing up to a process of democratisation in the region.

Three years later, the picture is remarkably different, with many of the early fears of some of the more cautious analysts being fulfilled. Although the regime was terminated within three weeks of the start of military operations, there were already signs, even within those three weeks, of an unconventional response, including the first suicide bombings and attacks on supply lines. Even when President Bush gave his 'mission accomplished' address on the deck of the aircraft carrier USS *Abraham Lincoln* on 1 May 2003, the insurgency was already developing. Since then, the war has cost at least 30,000 civilian lives[2] in Iraq, and US forces have lost over 2,000 killed and more than 14,000 injured.[3] Iraq remains mired in insurgency and the contrast between US expectations and actual experience is remarkable.

Numerous events that were expected to curtail the insurgency have failed to do so. These include the killing of Uday and Qusay Hussein in July 2003, the detention of Saddam Hussein six months later and the ending of the Coalition Provisional Authority in June 2004 with the appointment of an Iraqi administration. In November 2004 the assault on Fallujah was expected to greatly damage the insurgency but had little effect. There were also expectations that further political developments, including the election of a provisional government in January 2005 and the subsequent referendum in August, would undermine support for the insurgency. None of these developments had much effect and, by December 2005, the US troop levels in Iraq stood at 160,000, the highest since the termination of the regime. Furthermore, by the end of 2005, Iraq as a political issue had intruded into US domestic politics and there were indications that the Bush administration, facing mid-term Congressional elections within a year, was beginning to consider troop withdrawals.

This represented a remarkable change from the determination shown by the administration in the run-up to the war and raises the question of whether the Iraq experience is likely to lead to a major change in the security orientation in Washington. After 9/11 and the termination of the Taliban regime, this orientation had as its basis the identification of an 'axis of evil' of regimes that were unacceptable to Washington, and the evolution of a posture that allowed for pre-emptive military action against such regimes. That policy remains in force at the time of writing, and there is, even now, the possibility of a crisis developing over relations with Iran. We are therefore left with two key questions – is this forceful security posture that includes a policy of pre-emptive regime termination likely to survive, and will this be because of the strength of neo-conservative thinking in the United States? In seeking to answer these questions, it is appropriate first to summarise the main elements of the analysis presented in earlier chapters concerning the political road to war.

Clinton and Bush before 9/11

Throughout the eight years of the Clinton administration, the fundamentals of the Iraq policy were containment through a combination of sanctions, UN inspections and the use of air power to enforce northern and southern no-fly zones. The former were intended to weaken the regime, but there were strong arguments that the main effects were on Iraqi civilians. The latter provided a degree of security for northern Kurdish communities and southern Shi'a communities. The northern no-fly zone was effective in helping ensure that a semi-autonomous Kurdish economic and political entity evolved, even though deep political divisions remained. The southern no-fly zone inhibited regime actions against Shi'a communities but not to the same extent. At the same time, since the southern zone was far more extensive, it did have a considerable impact on the overall viability of the Iraqi Air Force.

At times the implementation of the no-fly zones extended to sustained military action, the most notable example being the four-day Operation Desert Fox in late 1998, but this was an exception to the rule and the essence of the policy remained one of regime containment throughout both of Clinton's periods in office. During his second term, however, an alternative view developed rapidly, centred on the Republican right and especially among those known as neo-conservatives. Think-tank critics, senior members of Congress and a number of people heavily involved in the 2000 Republican presidential campaign took the view that containment was failing. They argued persistently and persuasively that the regime was not being limited, was probably developing WMD in spite of the activities of the UN inspectors, and that the Saddam Hussein regime remained a serious threat to the United States. When George W. Bush won the November 2000 election, albeit by the narrowest of Electoral College votes and the decision of the Supreme Court, there was little doubt that Clinton's Iraq policy would be replaced with a more aggressive and confrontational stance.

On entering the White House, the Bush administration initiated a review of Iraq policy as a priority. A serious division emerged between senior members of the new administration. On the one hand, the new Secretary of State, Colin Powell, argued for the development of a tougher containment policy, with a much-strengthened sanctions programme that was specifically targeted at the Iraqi leadership. The other view, argued particularly by Paul Wolfowitz and backed to an important degree by Dick Cheney and Donald Rumsfeld, was that regime change was essential, based on full support for the opposition Iraqi

National Congress. There were variations within this, not least whether it involved support for an INC-led overthrowing of the regime or whether it required direct US military involvement, but the essential basis was that regime change was the only option to ensure US regional interests.

President Bush and his National Security Advisor, Condoleezza Rice, seemed undecided as the review proceeded through 2001, but both made it clear that Iraq was seen as a serious threat, not least because of its programmes to develop WMD and that Clinton-style containment could not continue. On balance, it seems likely that the review would have come down in favour of Cheney and Rumsfeld, meaning that a confrontation with Iraq would have been probable within Bush's first term. This might not have involved a full-scale invasion but it would also have been the case that any substantive action to terminate the Saddam Hussein regime would have had substantial support within both houses of Congress.

The impact of 9/11 on Iraq policy

The 9/11 attacks on the World Trade Center and the Pentagon halted the review process and also cast the threat from Iraq in a new light, presenting hard-line supporters of regime change with an opportunity to push hard for Saddam Hussein's removal as part of the new 'war on terrorism'. The immediate priority after 9/11 was the termination of the Taliban regime in Afghanistan, the disruption of the al-Qaida movement and the killing or detaining of leaders such as Mullah Omar and Osama bin Laden. By the end of 2001 the regime had fallen with apparent ease, demonstrating unequivocally the US determination to use military force as a core feature of the global war on terror.

President Bush's 2002 State of the Union Address to Congress at the end of January was notable for extending regime change in Afghanistan to the wider policy of confronting an 'axis of evil', with Iraq, Iran and North Korea as the primary members of the axis. This was defined by two characteristics – an intention to develop WMD and support for terrorism. Furthermore, this was in the context of other countries being 'either for us or against us', and a very clear exposition that the global war on terror extended well beyond countering the al-Qaida movement.

In effect, a new national security paradigm had been constructed that encompassed 'rogue' states that had WMD or WMD programmes, connections to terrorism and hostile attitudes towards the United States. That paradigm further embraced the belief that it was a necessary part of the US security posture to be able to terminate regimes in such states by military force if other means could not be utilised. Bush and Rice now seemed convinced that Saddam Hussein had to go, joining Rumsfeld and Cheney in this view.

From the State of the Union Address through the West Point speech and on to Bush's seminal speech at the UN in September 2002, the administration forcefully pushed the case for war, indicating its determination to depose Saddam Hussein. Iraq was repeatedly placed at the heart of the war on terror and military plans for an invasion gathered speed, if delayed by the need to restock on a wide range of specialised munitions that had been severely depleted by the actions in Afghanistan.

In Afghanistan itself, there were already indications that the first phase of the war on terror was not taking the expected course. Military activity at Tora Bora and elsewhere demonstrated a resilience among Taliban and al-Qaida elements that was surprising in view of the regime's rapid demise the previous year, and neither Osama bin Laden nor Mullah Omar had been killed or detained. Even so, these early complications in the war on terror had no discernible effect on the road to war with Iraq. Although Bush took the issue to the United Nations, this was more due to the views of Colin Powell, Tony Blair and moderate Republicans, all of whom thought that a coalition was necessary and that it would be more easily built on the basis of UN approval.

Bush's UN speech set out explicit demands and conditions for Iraq to avoid war, but there was little expectation that these could or would be met and war was now virtually inevitable. Indeed, in the months that followed the UN speech, the rhetoric escalated still further. The threat from Iraq was described in terms of a nuclear terrorist attack sponsored by the Saddam Hussein regime; it was an urgent and unique threat; Iraq had a clear relationship with al-Qaida and UN inspections were frankly useless.

The road to war

It is clear from the evidence presented in this book that the Bush administration was overwhelmingly determined to confront and terminate the Saddam Hussein regime, particularly after the 9/11 attacks. This is clear from four perspectives. First, statements from senior members of the administration before 9/11 and even before the 2000 presidential election were consistent in emphasising the dangers from the regime. Second, the construction of the post-9/11 national security paradigm left the Saddam Hussein regime very little room for manoeuvre, given what is now known about the nature of Iraq's WMD programme. Third, there was substantial manipulation of intelligence about Iraq's WMD capabilities and, finally, the administration categorically refused to compromise on its position after the UN speech.

It follows that it is appropriate to explore why the Bush administration was so determined to bring down the Saddam Hussein regime, and it makes sense to consider this in relation to strategic and ideological factors. Three motivations can be considered strategic. One was a fundamental conviction that Clinton's containment was not working. This may have interwoven with a palpable contempt for the Clinton administration that was a notable feature of the Republican right in the wake of the Lewinsky affair, but it transcended this in that it was a view that would have been very significant whatever the attitude to Clinton himself.

A second motivation was that it was simply not acceptable to have a deeply oppositional regime in power in such a crucially important region, bearing in mind that Iran, too, was viewed as antagonistic to US interests. The combination of the importance of Gulf oil reserves with the possibility that the Saddam Hussein regime might soon develop nuclear weapons was simply not acceptable. Finally, the administration was able to rely on widespread Congressional support for action against Iraq. Without this it would have found it far more difficult to conduct an aggressive pre-emptive attack in order to terminate the Baghdad regime.

In relation to ideological factors, it is the combination of the perceived threat from Iraq with the 9/11 attacks and the increasing influence of neo-conservatism that is of significance. The neo-conservative political outlook was already strong within the Bush administration before the 9/11 attacks and gained far more influence in the immediate aftermath. This outlook was greatly strengthened by the vigour and commitment of a number of key Washington think-tanks and their associated publications and links to Congress. Although the immediate response to 9/11 was the termination of the Taliban regime in Afghanistan, even by the early months of 2002 the war on terror had stretched to embrace an 'axis of evil' of rogue states, whether or not they were connected with those individuals responsible for 9/11.

Regime change in Iraq, in particular, was presented by neo-conservative analysts not just as an essential short-term component of the 'war on terror' but as the lynchpin of a greater Middle East initiative that would remake the political map of the Middle East in a manner deeply conducive to US security interests. Much as the 'domino theory' of Soviet-inspired regime change in 1960s Asia involved the risk of a succession of regime changes that would be damaging to US interests, so regime change in Iraq would have a singularly positive effect, setting in motion a domino pattern of positive political evolution in the Middle East towards an emancipated and pro-American polity. While there was no immediate expectation of regime change in Iran, there was also the belief that a success in Iraq would be a clear marker for Tehran that US influence was dominant in the region and that it was in Iran's interest to recognise this.

The end of the road?

It is in the broad context of the post-9/11 US political environment that we can now question whether, three years after the fall of the Saddam Hussein regime, the new security paradigm will survive the problems encountered in Iraq and, to a lesser extent, in Afghanistan. By the end of 2005 there was already an assumption that neo-conservative influence in Washington was declining. Paul Wolfowitz had moved on to the World Bank, Douglas Feith was returning to private practice, I. Lewis Libby was facing court action, John Bolton had moved from the State Department to the US mission to the United Nations, and there was increasing speculation over the future of Donald Rumsfeld at the Pentagon. Not all of these figures could be described as neo-conservative, and it is also possible to argue that the relocation of Wolfowitz and Bolton to the World Bank and the UN were actually examples of an extension of influence to new quarters. The New American Century might be experiencing temporary problems in Iraq but that was no reason to avoid enhancing the dream in multinational forums.

Even so, the consensus among most analysts was of a dream in retreat, yet there are three broad reasons for questioning this conclusion – the geopolitical significance of the Persian Gulf region, the development of the al-Qaida movement in the past four years and the relatively limited role that neo-conservatism has actually played in the recent evolution of the American political system.

As argued in Chapter 1, the Persian Gulf region has been one of steadily increasing importance for well over forty years, receiving particular emphasis at the time of the 1973/4 oil price rises and the further supply problems in the wake of the Iranian Revolution in 1979/80. US military force planning identified the Persian Gulf oil reserves as essential for US security during the last fifteen years of the Cold War, leading to the establishment of the Rapid Deployment Force at the end of the 1970s and its subsequent elevation to US Central Command in the early 1980s. In the past twenty years, the Soviet issue has disappeared altogether but regional security has been seen to be at risk from countries such as Iraq and Iran. This is against a background of the steadily increasing significance of Gulf oil reserves, made more relevant by the increasing import dependence of the United States followed, since 1993, by China.

Although reserves in South America, Alaska, Canada, Africa and Central Asia will be exploited with alacrity, the Gulf retains nearly two-thirds of known world oil reserves and a substantial minority of world gas reserves. Moreover, the oil reserves are generally of a high quality and are relatively easy to extract, certainly when compared to Alaska, the Canadian tar sands or offshore reserves in West Africa or elsewhere. For the United States, the consequence of these trends is that it is particularly important to retain a sympathetic and secure administration in power in Baghdad. Iran is still regarded as a rogue state and there is a deep unwillingness on the part of the House of Saud to have US forces based in the Kingdom. While the lesser Sheikdoms and Emirates remain welcoming to the United States, to fail to have substantial influence in Iran, Saudi Arabia and Iraq in the coming two to three decades would be most unfortunate, especially as competition with China grows. It therefore follows that there are powerful reasons to retain military forces in Iraq, even if there is a desire to avoid involvement in the continuing insurgency, preferably retaining a few major bases with a long-term military presence.

What is highly unlikely is any complete US withdrawal. To that extent, an apparent decline in neo-conservatism will have little effect on the US posture in the region since that posture is dictated more by the political economy of oil. Where the neo-conservative influence may have been most significant is in ensuring that violent externally imposed regime change was the chosen way to deal with the Saddam Hussein regime. Once that was done, the result was a very large US presence within Iraq and the development of a potent insurgency. Disengagement in such circumstances is implausible.

If the oil factor is an important underlying feature of US motivations, then the US presence in Iraq is of long-term value to the al-Qaida movement. While the use of that term does not imply a highly structured trans-national paramilitary entity, the al-Qaida phenomenon is certainly one that is greatly aided by developments in Iraq. This is ironic in that one of the neo-conservative arguments for enforced regime change was that the Saddam Hussein regime was supportive of al-Qaida. There remains very little evidence of this and it is post-Saddam Iraq that is, instead, turning out to be of real value to the wider jihadist movement.

Claims that external jihadists are at the root of the insurgency should be treated with great caution as the indications are that, at the very most, perhaps one in ten of the insurgents are coming from abroad. Nevertheless, the Iraq insurgency is very useful to the wider movement for three reasons. One is that the intensive reporting of development in Iraq by independent regionally based news outlets means that knowledge of the civilian casualties and wider collateral damage is widespread, particularly in Islamic communities across the world. Moreover, Al-Jazeera, Al-Arabiya and other mainstream and generally accurate networks are supplemented by substantial propagandistic material in the form of web-casts, DVDs and videos. These parallel processes serve to increase support for anti-American actions, and while these may result primarily in an oppositional mood, they will also encourage, to a more limited extent, the recruitment of young people prepared to take more extreme action.

The second value of Iraq to the jihadist movement is that it is starting to constitute a training ground in urban guerrilla warfare techniques for a new generation of radical paramilitaries. Afghanistan served this function in two different ways over two decades, first against the Soviet occupiers in the 1980s and then alongside the Taliban against the Northern Alliance in the civil war of the 1990s. What is remarkable in retrospect is that the United States terminated the Taliban regime, thereby limiting the status of Afghanistan as a training zone, only to create a new zone in Iraq. Moreover, Iraq is a far more relevant training environment for al-Qaida in the coming decades as it involves largely urban combat against the world's best-equipped military forces.

Finally, Iraq serves as a remarkable symbol for al-Qaida and related movements, given the indirect Israeli involvement in the training and equipping of US forces and in the direct Israeli involvement in the Kurdish areas of North-East Iraq. Although this is not substantial, it is hugely valuable in terms of propaganda. In short, jihadist propagandists can point to Iraq as being part of the heartland of the Islamic world that is currently under occupation by neo-Christian crusader forces supported by their Zionist allies. It can further be claimed that this occupation is dedicated partly to ensuring control over Arab oil. Even more ironic, given that a long-term al-Qaida aim is the re-establishment of an Islamic Caliphate, is that these neo-Christian/Zionist forces are occupying Baghdad, the centre of the most notable historic Islamic Caliphate, the Abbasids.

These two forces, the US need to maintain security in the Persian Gulf and the jihadist aim of opposing this as part of its longer-term strategy, together mean that the war in Iraq is likely to be a long-term affair. In this context, the neo-conservative influence may have been crucial along the political road to war, but any demise of this influence may not have any effect on ensuring a change in the security paradigm. Beyond the neo-conservative vision lies the assertive nationalism that is even more deeply embedded in US politics and has been for many decades.

That remains, and in combination with the core importance of Gulf oil security it means that a full withdrawal from Iraq would only happen in the event of a quite extraordinary change in the political environment in the United States. It is for these reasons that the road to peace may be very much longer than the road to war.

NOTES

1 OIL AND PERSIAN GULF SECURITY – THE CONTEXT OF REGIME TERMINATION

1 The early history of oil is discussed in full in Yergin, D., *The Prize*, New York: Simon & Schuster, 1993.
2 For a detailed discussion of the early US concerns about oil security, see Klare, M., *Blood and Oil*, London: Hamish Hamilton, 2004.
3 The founding and early history of OPEC is discussed in Sampson, A., *The Seven Sisters*, New York: Bantam Books, 1991.
4 Shelley, T., *Oil: Politics, Poverty and the Planet*, London: Zed Books, 2005.
5 *Oil Fields as Military Objectives: A Feasibility Study*, Report to the Special Subcommittee on Investigations of the House Committee on International Relations, Congressional Research Service, Washington, DC, August 1975.
6 Ibid.
7 The establishment of the Rapid Deployment Force is discussed in Rogers, P. and Dando, M., *A Violent Peace: Global Security After the Cold War*, London: Brasseys, 1992.
8 Record, J., *The Rapid Deployment Force and U.S. Military Intervention in the Persian Gulf*, Institute for Foreign Policy Analysis, Washington, DC, 1981.
9 The Organization of the Joint Chiefs of Staff, *US Military Posture for FY 1982*, US Government Printing Office, 1981.
10 Rogers and Dando, *A Violent Peace*.
11 Tirpal, J., 'The Secret Squirrels', *Air Force Magazine*, US Air Force Association, April 1994.
12 Watson, Bruce W., George, Bruce, Tsouras, Peter and Cyr, B.L., *Military Lessons of the Gulf War*, New York: Greenhill Books, 1991.
13 Gresham, J. D., 'Navy Area Ballistic Missile Defense Coming on Fast', *Proceedings of the US Naval Institute*, Washington, DC, January 1999.
14 Ibid.
15 Rogers, P., 'Towards an Ideal Weapon: Political and Military Implications of Directed Energy Weapons', *Defense Analysis*, Vol. 17 (2001) No. 1, pp. 73–88.
16 The main sources for material on this issue are a series of reports from the UN Special Commission (UNSCOM) on Iraq, especially: *Report of the Secretary-General on the status of the implementation of the Special Commission's plan for ongoing monitoring and verification of Iraq's compliance with relevant parts of Section C of Security Council resolution 687 (1991)*, UN Security Council Report S/1995/864, New York, 11 October 1995.
17 Ibid.

18 Ibid.
19 In 1996, the US Department of Defense made available on the Internet a large number of reports and studies relating to the Gulf War of 1991. These included, by mistake, a classified report relating to a National Intelligence Estimate of November 1990. The report was quickly removed from the website but not before it had been read by a number of analysts.
20 UNSCOM *Report*.

2 CONTAINMENT-PLUS: CLINTON AND IRAQ AT THE END OF THE 1990s

1 *Chronology of Main Events*, Iraq Nuclear Verification Office, IAEA, December 2002. Available at <http://www.iaea.org/worldatom/Programmes/ActionTeam/chronology.html> (accessed on 26 October 2005).
2 *Chronology of Main Events*, United Nations, December 1999. Available at <http://www.un.org/Depts/unscom/Chronology/chronologyframe.htm> (accessed on 26 October 2005).
3 Specifically, by March 1998 UNSCOM had supervised the destruction of 48 operational long-range missiles, 14 conventional missile warheads, 6 operational mobile launchers, 28 operational fixed-launch pads, 32 fixed launch pads (under construction), 30 missile chemical warheads, and other missile support equipment and materials, 38,537 filled and empty chemical munitions, 690 tonnes of chemical weapons agent, more than 3,000 tonnes of precursor chemicals, 426 pieces of chemical weapons production equipment, 91 pieces of related analytical instruments, the entire Al-Hakam, the main biological weapons production facility and a variety of biological weapons production equipment and materials. *UNSCOM Main Achievements*, United Nations, March 1998. Available at <http://www.un.org/Depts/unscom/Achievements/achievements.html> (accessed on 19 October 2005).
4 White House transcript, *The President's Radio Address*, The White House, 7 February 1998. Available at <http://frwebgate5.access.gpo.gov/cgi-bin/waisgate.cgi?WAISdocID=990016193354+35+0+0&WAISaction=retrieve> (accessed on 23 June 2005).
5 *Iraq Weapons of Mass Destruction Programs*, US State Department, 13 February 1998. Available at <http://www.state.gov/www/regions/nea/iraq_white_paper.html> (accessed on 27 August 2005).
6 Quoted in Kagan, R., 'How to Attack Iraq', *The Weekly Standard*, 16 November 1998, p. 34.
7 Cohen, W. S., *DoD News Briefing*, US Department of Defense, 7 December 1999. Available at <http://www.defenselink.mil/transcripts/1999/t12071999_t207afri.html> (accessed on 4 December 2004).
8 Tenet, G., *Testimony Before the Senate Foreign Relations Committee, The Worldwide Threat in 2000: Global Realities of Our National Security*, US Senate Foreign Relations Committee, 21 March 2000. Available at <http://www.state.gov/www/global/terrorism/000321_tenet_terrorism.html> (accessed on 2 June 2005).
9 *Saddam Hussein's Iraq*, US State Department, September 1999.
10 Butler, R., *The Greatest Threat*, New York: Public Affairs, 2000, p. xvii.
11 Amorim, C., *Amorim Report*, United Nations, March 1999. Available at <http://www.un.org/Depts/unmovic/documents/Amorim%20Report.htm> (accessed on 26 October 2005).

12 Blix, H., *Disarming Iraq: The Search for Weapons of Mass Destruction*, London: Bloomsbury, 2004, p. 33.

13 US Government Printing Office, 'Address to the Nation Announcing Military Strikes on Iraq', *Public Papers of the Presidents, William J. Clinton – 1998*, Vol. 2, pp. 2182–2185.

14 Albright, M., *Remarks on State of the Union and Visit to Europe, the Gulf, and the Middle East*, US State Department, 28 January 1998. Available at <http://secretary.state.gov/www/statements/1998/980128.html> (accessed on 23 June 2005).

15 Office of the Coordinator for Counterterrorism, *Patterns of Global Terrorism 2000*, US State Department, 2000. Available at <http://www.state.gov/s/ct/rls/pgtrpt/2000/2441.htm> (accessed on 27 June 2005). Interestingly, the report also states 'the regime has not attempted an anti-Western terrorist attack since its failed plot to assassinate former President Bush in 1993 in Kuwait'.

16 *Extremist Movements And Their Threat To The United States, Hearing Before The Subcommittee On Near Eastern And South Asian Affairs Of The Committee On Foreign Relations United States Senate*, US Senate Committee On Foreign Relations, 2 November 1999. Available at <http://frwebgate.access.gpo.gov/cgi-bin/getdoc.cgi?dbname=106_senate_hearings&docid=f:61869.wais> (accessed on 2 July 2005).

17 Cohen, W. S., *Annual Report to the President and Congress 1998*, US Department of Defense, 1998. Available at <http://www.defenselink.mil/execsec/adr98/toc.html> (accessed on 25 March 2005). See Ch. 1: the Defense Strategy of the United States. This strategy remained the same in 1999 and 2000 Department of Defense Annual Reports.

18 Albright, M., *Press Remarks At The State Pavilion – Barajas Airport, Madrid*, US State Department, 30 January 1998. Available at <http://secretary.state.gov/www/statements/1998/980130.html> (accessed on 4 December 2004).

19 Walker, E., *Testimony Before Senate Committee on Foreign Relations*, US Senate Committee on Foreign Relations, 22 March 2000. Available at <http://www.state.gov/www/policy_remarks/2000/000322_walker_iraq.html> (accessed on 23 June 2005).

20 Clinton declared, 'I know I speak for everyone in this chamber, Republicans and Democrats, when I say to Saddam Hussein, "You cannot defy the will of the world," and when I say to him, "You have used weapons of mass destruction before; we are determined to deny you the capacity to use them again".' Clinton, W. J., *State of the Union Address*, The White House, 1998.

21 *Resolution 1134*, United Nations Security Council, 23 October 1997. Available at <http://daccessdds.un.org/doc/UNDOC/GEN/N97/283/87/PDF/N9728387.pdf?OpenElement> (accessed on 22 August 2005). This was enforced through UNSC Resolution 1137 on 12 November 1997.

22 Pollack K., *The Threatening Storm*, New York: Random House for the Council on Foreign Relations, 2002, pp. 88–89.

23 Annan, K., *Letter Dated 25 February 1998 from the Secretary-General Addressed to the President of the Security Council*, United Nations Security Council, 27 February 1998. Available at <http://daccessdds.un.org/doc/UNDOC/GEN/N98/047/97/PDF/N9804797.pdf?OpenElement> (accessed on 7 July 2005).

24 Annan, K., *Kofi Annan's Conference in New York*, 24 February 1998. Available at <http://www.pbs.org/newshour/bb/middle_east/jan-june98/annan_2-24.html> (accessed on 19 October 2005).

25 Albright, M., *Statement before the Subcommittee on Foreign Operations*, Export Financing and Related Programs, House Appropriations Committee, US State

Department, 4 March 1998. Available at <http://secretary.state.gov/www/statements/1998/980304.html> (accessed on 5 July 2005).

26 Joffe, J., 'Clinton's World: Purpose, Policy and *Weltanshauung*', *The Washington Quarterly*. Vol. 24 (2001), no. 1, p. 141.

27 Slocombe, W., *Defense Aspects of United States Policy Towards Iraq*, US Senate Armed Services Committee, 28 January 1999. Available at <http://armed-services.senate.gov/statemnt/1999/990128ws.pdf> (accessed on 8 January 2004).

28 Romanowski, A., *Testimony of Alina Romanowsk*, US House of Representatives International Relations Committee, 23 March 2000. Available at <http://www.state.gov/www/regions/nea/000323_romanowski_iraq.html> (accessed on 30 July 2005).

29 Clinton, W. J., *The President's Radio Address*, The White House, 7 February 1998. Available at <http://frwebgate5.access.gpo.gov/cgi-bin/waisgate.cgi?WAISdocID=990016193354+35+0+0&WAISaction=retrieve> (accessed on 15 June 2005).

30 Clinton, W. J., *Address to the Nation Announcing Military Strikes on Iraq*, The White House, 16 December 1998. Available at <http://frwebgate5.access.gpo.gov/cgi-bin/waisgate.cgi?WAISdocID=990016193354+7+0+0&WAISaction=retrieve> (accessed on 7 July 2005).

31 Cohen, W. S., *DoD News Briefing*, US Department of Defense, 8 December 1999. Available at <http://www.defenselink.mil/transcripts/1999/t12101999_t208flor.html> (accessed on 2 July 2005).

32 Cohen, W. S., *DoD News Briefing*, US Department of Defense, 31 January 1998. Available at <http://www.defenselink.mil/transcripts/1998/t02041998_t31bcast.html> (accessed on 7 July 2005).

33 Cohen, W. S., *DoD News Briefing*, US Department of Defense, 18 April 1998. Available at <http://www.globalsecurity.org/wmd/library/news/iraq/1998/ t04231998_t418incr.html> (accessed on 20 March 2005).

34 See Butler, *Greatest Threat*, for a full account of UNSCOM's last few years.

35 Secretary of State Madeleine Albright stated in September 1998 that 'There's been no question that the toll of having a sanctions regime for this long is that there is a fraying, and that we [members of the UN Security Council] don't all have exactly the same approach.' Albright, M., *Remarks at the Carnegie Endowment for International Peace, Washington, D.C.*, US State Department, 17 September 1998. Available at <http://secretary.state.gov/www/statements/1998/980917.html> (accessed on 2 March 2005).

36 Simons, G., *The Scourging of Iraq*, Basingstoke: Macmillan, 1998.

37 *Saddam Hussein's Iraq*, US State Department.

38 See <http://www.globalsecurity.org/wmd/library/news/iraq/2000/iraq-001005.htm>, (accessed on 20 October 2005).

39 *Radio Free Europe Newsline*, Vol. 4, No. 221, Part I, 14 November 2000. Available at <http://www.globalsecurity.org/wmd/library/news/iraq/2000/iraq-001114.htm> (accessed on 12 August 2005).

40 'Speech by France's Permanent Representative to the United Nations Security Council', 24 March 2000. Available at <http://www.globalsecurity.org/wmd/library/news/iraq/2000/000324-iraq30.gb.htm> (accessed on 12 August 2005).

41 Katzman, K., 'Iraq: U.S. Policy Options', *CRS Report for Congress*, Washington, DC: Congressional Research Service, 23 December 1998.

42 See Ed Warner, 'Rethinking Iraq', *Voice of America*, 12 April 2000. Available at <http://www.globalsecurity.org/wmd/library/news/iraq/2000/000412-iraq2.htm> (accessed on 12 August 2005); John Tkach, 'US–Iraq Sanctions', *Voice of America*, 16 February 2000. Available at <http://www.globalsecurity.org/wmd/library/news/iraq/2000/000216-iraq1.htm>, accessed on 20 October 2005; and Lisa Bryant, 'Iraq Sanctions', Voice of America, 16 February 2000. Available at <http://www.

globalsecurity.org/wmd/library/news/iraq/2000/000216-iraq2.htm> (accessed on 20 October 2005).

43 Katzman, K. and Prados, A., 'Iraq: Erosion of International Isolation?' *CRS Report for Congress*, Washington, DC: Congressional Research Service, October 1999.

44 For example, in 1997 a Russian consortium of Lukoil, Zarubezhneft and Mashinoimport signed a $3.5 billion deal to develop Iraq's Al Qurna oilfield, China signed a $1.2 billion contract for the Chinese National Petroleum Corporation to develop Iraq's Al Ahdab oilfield and French–Belgian firm Total Fina and French firm Elf Aquitaine negotiated agreements to develop other oil fields in Iraq. In addition, Katzman reports, several US energy firms have had discussions with Iraq about future investments in Iraq's petroleum industry. Ibid.

45 *Saddam Hussein's Iraq*, US State Department; Pollack, *Threatening Storm*, p. 216.

46 See *Civilian Flights to Iraq*, Global Policy Forum. Available at <http://www.global policy.org/security/sanction/iraq1/civflight/cvflyidx.htm> (accessed on 2 November 2005).

47 Gause, F. G., 'Getting it Backward on Iraq', *Foreign Affairs*, Vol. 78, (1999) No. 3.

48 Clinton, W. J., *Remarks at the Pentagon in Arlington, Virginia*, The White House, 17 February 1998. Available at <http://frwebgate5.access.gpo.gov/cgi-bin/waisgate. cgi?WAISdocID=990016193354+10+0+0&WAISaction=retrieve> (accessed on 19 July 2005).

49 Cohen, W. S., *DoD News Briefing*, US Department of Defense, 8 December 1999. Available at <http://www.defenselink.mil/transcripts/1999/t12101999_t208flor. html> (accessed on 19 July 2005).

50 Albright, M., *Statement before the House International Relations Committee*, US State Department, 16 February 2000. Available at <http://secretary.state.gov/www/ statements/2000/000216.html> (accessed on 18 July 2005).

51 Walker, E., *Testimony Before Senate Committee on Foreign Relations*.

52 Clinton, W. J., *The President's Radio Address*, The White House, 19 December 1998. Available at <http://frwebgate5.access.gpo.gov/cgi-bin/waisgate.cgi?WAISdocID= 990016193354+37+0+0&WAISaction=retrieve> (accessed on 24 August 2005).

53 Foley, J., *Excerpt from the Daily Press Briefing*, US State Department, 17 July 1999. Available at <http://www.state.gov/www/regions/nea/990617_foley_excerpt.html> (accessed on 6 March 2005).

54 Cohen argued in January 2000 that 'We have tried to find ways in which we could alleviate the suffering of the Iraqi people, but we will continue to point out that that suffering has been caused by Saddam Hussein and – who continues to try to exploit their suffering for his own political advantage.' Cohen, W. S., *DoD News Briefing*, US Department of Defense, 27 January 2000. Available at <http://www.defenselink. mil/transcripts/2000/t01272000_t0027uk_.html> (accessed on 9 July 2005).

55 Cohen, W. S., *DoD News Briefing*, US Department of Defense, 15 July 1999. Available at <http://www.defenselink.mil/transcripts/1999/t07151999_t0715ank. html> (accessed on 14 July 1005).

56 State Department transcript, *Interview on NBC–TV's 'Meet The Press' With Tim Russert*, US State Department, 9 August 1998. Available at <http://secretary. state.gov/www/statements/1998/980809.html> (accessed on 2 March 2005).

57 Rubin, J., *Excerpt from the Daily Press Briefing*, US State Department, 6 October 1999. Available at <http://www.state.gov/www/regions/nea/991006_rubin _excerpt. html> (accessed on 6 March 2005).

58 Clinton, W. J., *Address to the Nation Announcing Military Strikes on Iraq*, The White House, 16 December 1998. Available at <http://frwebgate5.access.gpo.gov/cgi-bin/ waisgate.cgi?WAISdocID=990016193354+7+0+0&WAISaction=retrieve> (accessed on 23 August 2005).

59 Clinton, W. J., *Remarks Prior to Discussions With Prime Minister Tony Blair of the United Kingdom and an Exchange With Reporters*, The White House, 5 February 1998. Available at <http://frwebgate5.access.gpo.gov/cgi-bin/waisgate.cgi?WAISdocID=990016193354+28+0+0&WAISaction=retrieve> (accessed on 23 July 2005).

60 Cohen, W. S., *Print Media Year End Interview*, US Department of Defense, 31 January 1998. Available at <http://www.defenselink.mil/transcripts/1998/ t02171998 _t131prnt.html> (accessed on 23 July 2005).

61 Clinton, W. J., *Remarks on the Situation in Iraq and an Exchange With Reporters*, The White House, 15 November 1998. Available at <http://frwebgate5.access. gpo.gov/cgi-bin/waisgate.cgi?WAISdocID=990016193354+8+0+0&WAISaction= retrieve> (accessed on 9 July 2005).

62 Cohen, W. S., *DoD News Briefing*, 31 January 1998.

63 Joffe, 'Clinton's World: Purpose, Policy and *Weltanshauung*', p. 147.

64 Albright M., *Madam Secretary: a Memoir*, London: Macmillan, 2003, p. 277.

65 Clinton, *Address to the Nation Announcing Military Strikes on Iraq*. Albright again articulated these 'red lines' in August 2000: 'he cannot threaten his neighbors or our forces, or reconstitute his weapons of mass destruction, or move against the Kurds in the North. We have a force in region, and we have made our position very clear.' State Department transcript, Interview on CNN's Late Edition, US State Department, 10 August 2000. Available at <http://secretary.state.gov/www/statements/2000/ 001008a.html> (accessed on 18 July 2005).

66 Clinton, *The President's Radio Address*, The White House, 19 December 1998.

67 Cohen, W. S., *DoD Budget Briefing*, US Department of Defense, 2 February 1998. Available at <http://www.defenselink.mil/transcripts/1998/t02021998_t202bdgt. html> (accessed on 23 July 2005).

68 Cohen, *DoD News Briefing*, 31 January 1998.

69 Joffe, 'Clinton's World: Purpose, Policy and *Weltanshauung*', p. 147.

70 The determination of success was based on the bombing campaign's degradation of 'Iraq's capability to use weapons of mass destruction in two important ways. First, we estimate that we delayed Iraq's development of ballistic missiles by at least a year. This is going to make it more difficult for Iraq to use deadly chemical and biological weapons against its neighbors. Second, we diminished Iraq's overall capability to direct and protect its weapons of mass destruction program. And we also diminished Iraq's ability to attack its neighbors by severely damaging the Iraqi military command and control system.' Cohen, W. S., *DoD News Briefing*, US Department of Defense, 21 December 1998. Available at <http://www. defenselink.mil/transcripts/1998/t12211998_t1221fox.html> (accessed on 9 July 2005).

71 Slocombe, W., *Statement of the Honorable Walter B. Slocombe: Defense Aspects of United States Policy toward Iraq*, US Senate Armed Service Committee, 19 September 2000. Available at <http://armed-services.senate.gov/statemnt/ 2000/000919ws.pdf> (accessed on 17 January 2004).

72 Gause argues that after Desert Fox the rules of engagement for US and British pilots patrolling the no-fly zones were expanded to the extent that Iraqi provocations and coalition reprisals were occurring almost daily in order to increase pressure on Saddam Hussein. Gause, 'Getting it Backward on Iraq', p. 1.

73 Albright, *Madam Secretary: a Memoir*, p. 287.

74 Pollack, *Threatening Storm*, pp. 95–99.

75 Clinton, *The President's Radio Address*.

76 Clinton, W. J., *Letter to Congressional Leaders Reporting on Iraq's Compliance With United Nations Security Council Resolutions*, The White House, 3 March 1999.

Available at <http://frwebgate5.access.gpo.gov/cgi-bin/waisgate.cgi?WAISdocID =979478141531+0+0+0&WAISaction=retrieve> (accessed on 23 June 2005).

77 Ibid.

78 Cohen, W. S., *DoD News Briefing*, US Department of Defense, 2 June 1999. Available at <http://www.defenselink.mil/transcripts/1999/t06021999_t0602kuw. html> (accessed on 18 July 2005); Cohen, W. S., *DoD News Briefing*, US Department of Defense, 19 October 1999. Available at <http://www.defenselink.mil/ transcripts/1999/t10191999_t1019qat.html> (accessed on 18 July 2005).

79 Walker, E., *Testimony Before Senate Committee on Foreign Relations*. See also Defense Department transcript, Interview with Abu Dhabi Television, Abu Dhabi, United Arab Emirates, US Department of Defense, 10 April 2000. Available at <http://www.defenselink.mil/transcripts/2000/t04112000_t410abud.html> (accessed on 18 July 2005).

80 *Saddam Hussein's Iraq*, US State Department.

81 Pollack, *Threatening Storm*, p. 102.

82 Indyk, M., *Remarks at the Council on Foreign Relations, New York City*, US State Department, 22 April 1999. Available at <http://www.state.gov/www/policy_ remarks/1999/990422_indyk_mepolicy.html> (accessed on 12 May 2005).

83 Riedel, B., *Middle East Forum*, National Security Council, 26 April 1999. Available at <http://www.state.gov/www/regions/nea/990426_riedel_iraq.html> (accessed on 6 March 2005).

84 Walker, E., *Testimony Before Senate Committee on Foreign Relations*.

85 Clinton, *Address to the Nation Announcing Military Strikes on Iraq*.

86 Bacon, K., *DoD News Briefing*, US Department of Defense, 1 August 2000. Available at <http://www.defenselink.mil/transcripts/2000/t08012000_t0801asd. html> (accessed on 9 July 2005).

87 Albright, M., *Remarks on State of the Union and visit to Europe, the Gulf, and the Middle East*, US State Department, 28 January 1998. Available at <http://secretary. state.gov/www/statements/1998/980128.html> (accessed on 20 July 2005). Albright regularly articulated the concept of Saddam Hussein trapped in a box by US/UN policy and actions. Also see State Department transcript, *Interview on NBC's 'Meet The Press' With Tim Russert and Andrea Mitchell*, US State Department, 2 January 2000. Available at <http://secretary.state.gov/www/statements/2000/000102. html> (accessed on 18 July 2000).

88 Tenet, G., *The Worldwide Threat in 2000: Global Realities of Our National Security*, US Senate Foreign Relations Committee, 21 March 2000. Available at <http://www.state.gov/www/global/terrorism/000321_tenet_terrorism.html> (accessed on 2 June 2005).

89 Cohen, W. S., *DoD News Briefing*, US Department of Defense, 2 April 2000. Available at <http://www.defenselink.mil/transcripts/2000/t04042000_t402isra. html> (accessed on 18 July 2005).

90 State Department transcript, *Interview on 'The Charlie Rose Show' with Charlie Rose*, US State Department, 11 November 1998. Available at <http://secretary. state.gov/www/statements/1998/981111.html> (accessed on 2 March 2005).

91 *United Nations Security Council Omnibus Resolution on Iraq fact sheet*, US State Department, 17 December 2000. Available at <http://usinfo.state.gov/dhr/ Archive_Index/unsc_resolution.html> (accessed on 26 October 2005).

92 Butler, *Greatest Threat*, p. 225.

93 Ricciardone, F. J., *Press Briefing after Meetings at Ministry of Foreign Affairs, Ankara, Turkey*, US State Department, 14 April 2000. Available at <http://www. state.gov/www/policy_remarks/2000/000414_ricciardone_iraq.html> (accessed on 18 July 2005).

94 Pickering, T., *Press Briefing, Aftermath of Airstrikes on Iraq*, US State Department, 22 December 1998. Available at <http://www.state.gov/www/policy_remarks/1998/981222_pickering_iraq.html> (accessed on 2 June 2005).

95 Cohen, W. S., *DoD News Briefing*, US Department of Defense, 2 November 1999. Available at <http://www.defenselink.mil/transcripts/1999/t11021999_t1102azi.html> (accessed on 3 August 2005).

96 Guardia, A. L., 'Oil price new weapon for warlike Saddam', *The Daily Telegraph*, 19 September 2000.

97 Myers, S. L., 'Flight Tests By Iraq Show Progress Of Missile Program', *New York Times*, 1 July 2000; Simeone, N., *Iraq/Weapons*, Voice of America, 1 February 2000. Available at <http://www.globalsecurity.org/wmd/library/news/iraq/2000/000201-iraq1.htm> (accessed on 3 November 2000).

98 Kampfner, J., *Blair's Wars*, London: Free Press, 2003, p. 155.

99 Quoted in *Current Situation in Iraq*, Congressional Record Online (Senate), 10 February 1998. Available at <http://frwebgate5.access.gpo.gov/cgi-bin/waisgate.cgi?WAISdocID=496628129290+44+0+0&WAISaction=retrieve> (accessed on 6 March 2005).

100 Pickering, *Press Briefing, Aftermath of Airstrikes on Iraq*.

101 *Saddam Hussein's Iraq*, US State Department, September 1999.

102 *Bush/Gore/Iraq*, Voice of America, 6 July 2000. Available at <http://www.globalsecurity.org/wmd/library/news/iraq/2000/000706-iraq1.htm> (accessed on 7 August 2005). See also Gore's statement in support of the INC available at the same website: Gore, A., *Joint Statement by Vice President Al Gore and Leaders of the Iraqi National Congress*, The White House, 26 July 2000.

103 Indyk, *Remarks at the Council on Foreign Relations*.

104 Albright, *Madam Secretary: a Memoir*, p. 276.

3 CONTAINMENT UNDER PRESSURE: OPPOSITION FROM CONGRESS AND CONSERVATIVE THINK-TANKS

1 For example, Senator Helms argued in September 1999 that 'it would be utterly foolish to assume that he is not taking the opportunity of that absence to reconstitute these weapons of mass destruction programs'. *Facing Saddam's Iraq: Disarray in the International Community, Hearing before the Senate Committee on Foreign Relations*, US Senate Committee on Foreign Relations, 28 September 1999. Available at <http://www.iraqwatch.org/government/US/HearingsPreparedstatements/SFRC-hearing-9-28-99.htm> (accessed on 6 March 2005). In October 1999 Senator Brownback maintained that Saddam Hussein 'is developing weapons of mass destruction, and I have no doubt he is willing to use those weapons. Saddam Hussein is evil, and it is your [the Iraqi National Congress] mission and ours to rid the world of this man.' Brownback, S., *Statement of Senator Sam Brownback to The National Assembly Of The Iraqi National Congress*, 29 October 1999. Available at <http://www.iraqwatch.org/government/US/Letters,%20reports%20and%20statements/brownbacke-INC.htm> (accessed on 9 August 2005).

2 See resolution P. L. 105–2335 (S. J. Res. 54) in Sharp, J., 'Congressional Action on Iraq 1990–2002: A Compilation of Legislation', *CRS Report for Congress*, Washington, DC: Congressional Research Service, 2002.

3 The letter read: 'we urge you, after consulting with Congress, and consistent with the U.S. Constitution and laws, to take necessary actions (including, if appropriate, air and missile strikes on suspect Iraq sites) to respond effectively to the threat posed by Iraq's refusal to end its weapons of mass destruction programs'. The letter was signed by Senators Carl Levin, Joe Lieberman, Frank R. Lautenberg, Dick Lugar, Kit

Bond, Jon Kyl, Chris Dodd, John McCain, Kay Bailey Hutchison, Alfonse D'Amato, Bob Kerrey, Pete V. Domenici, Dianne Feinstein, Barbara A. Mikulski, Thomas Daschle, John Breaux, Tim Johnson, Daniel K. Inouye, Arlen Specter, James Inhofe, Strom Thurmond, Mary L. Landrieu, Wendell Ford, John F. Kerry, Chuck Grassley, Jesse Helms and Rick Santorum. *Concern over Recent Developments in Iraq*, Congressional Record Online (Senate), 9 October 1998, pp. S12239–S12240. Available at <http://frwebgate4.access.gpo.gov/cgi-bin/waisgate.cgi?WAISdocID= 996299125+10+0+0&WAISaction=retrieve> (accessed on 9 August 2005).

4 See Senator Trent Lott, *IRAQ*, Congressional Record Online (Senate), 12 February 1998, p. S709. Available at <http://frwebgate4.access.gpo.gov/cgi-bin/waisgate.cgi? WAISdocID=996299125+4+0+0&WAISaction=retrieve> (accessed on 9 August 2005).

5 For example Senator Chuck Hagel argued in February 1998 that 'there is a growing chorus which suggests that perhaps our short-term objective should be more than Saddam Hussein's full compliance with U.N. Resolution 687, that our immediate short-term objective should be to expel Saddam Hussein from Iraq, to sweep him from the world stage. This kind of talk is very dangerous...', and more presciently, 'We must guard against the short-term objective turning into a long-term unexpected problem. After our lightning success in Desert Storm, I fear that we, as Americans, may have been lulled into a false sense of believing that modern wars can be fought relatively quickly and painlessly, with high-tech weapons and very limited casualties. This is not the case, nor will it ever be the case in warfare ... With the current tensions in this region and the grim prospects for peace in the Middle East, this area of the world could erupt like a tinder box. Whatever military action might be taken against Saddam Hussein, it must be surgical, it must be precise, and it must be focused and, above all, well thought out.' *Establishing a Clear Objective in Iraq*, Congressional Record Online (Senate), 1998, p. S466. Available at <http:// frwebgate3.access. gpo.gov/ cgi-bin/waisgate.cgi?WAISdocID=49327829023+22+0+0&WAISaction=retrieve> (accessed on 9 August 2005).

6 *Iraq*, Congressional Record Online (Senate), 2 March 1998, p. S1178. Available at <http://frwebgate3.access.gpo.gov/cgi-bin/waisgate.cgi?WAISdocID=49327829023 +16+0+0&WAISaction=retrieve> (accessed on 6 March 2005).

7 *US Policy Toward Iraq*, Congressional Record Online (Senate), 31 August 1998, S9676. Available at <http://www.iraqwatch.org/government/US/Letters,%20reports %20and%20statements/kyl-8-31-98.html> (accessed on 20 March 2005).

8 *IRAQ LIBERATION ACT OF 1998*, Congressional Record Online (House), 5 October 1998, p. H9488. Available at <http://frwebgate4.access.gpo.gov/cgi-bin/ waisgate.cgi?WAISdocID=996299125+8+0+0&WAISaction=retrieve> (accessed on 6 March 2005).

9 *Failed Policy on Iraq*, Congressional Record Online (Senate), 25 February 1999, p. S1996. Available at <http://frwebgate1.access.gpo.gov/cgi-bin/waisgate.cgi? WAISdocID=779311305181+0+0+0&WAISaction=retrieve> (accessed on 6 March 2005).

10 Murkowski, F., 'Our Toothless Policy on Iraq', *Washington Post*, 25 January 1999.

11 *The Liberation of Iraq: A Progress Report, Hearing Before the Subcommittee on Near Eastern and South Asian Affairs*, US Senate Committee on Foreign Relations, 28 June 2000. Available at <http://frwebgate.access.gpo.gov/cgi-bin/getdoc.cgi? dbname=106_senate_hearings&docid=f:68120.wais> (accessed on 20 January 2004).

12 Gregg, J., *Addressing Iraq in Context*, Congressional Record Online (Senate), 12 February 1998, p. S686. Available at <http://www.iraqwatch.org/government/US/ Letters,%20reports%20and%20statements/gregg-2-12-98.html> (accessed on 20 March 2005).

13 *US Policy Toward Iraq*, Congressional Record Online (Senate), 31 August 1998, p. S9676.

14 Spence, F., 'Background and Perspective on Important National Security and Defense Policy Issues', *National Security Report*, Vol. 2, (1998) No. 5.

15 Hamilton, L., *US Policy Toward the Persian Gulf*, Congressional Record Online (Extensions), 3 February 1998, p. E66. Available at <http://www.iraqwatch.org/government/US/Letters,%20reports%20and%20statements/hamilton-2-3-98.html> (accessed on 20 March 2005).

16 *Facing Saddam's Iraq: Disarray in the International Community*, US Senate Committee on Foreign Relations, 28 September 1999, pp. 2–3. Available at <http://www.iraqwatch.org/government/US/HearingsPreparedstatements/SFRC-hearing-9-28-99.htm> (accessed on 6 March 2005).

17 *US Policy Toward Iraq*, Congressional Record Online (Senate), 31 August 1998.

18 The Iraqi Crisis, Congressional Record Online (Senate), 27 February 1998, p. S1151. Available at <http://frwebgate1.access.gpo.gov/cgi-bin/waisgate.cgi?WAISdocID=39552360082+24+0+0&WAISaction=retrieve> (accessed on 6 March 2005).

19 Spence, F., *Chairman Spence on Statement on Military Action Against Iraq*, US House of Representatives, 7 December 1998. Available at <http://www.iraqwatch.org/government/US/Letters,%20reports%20and%20statements/hnsc-pressrelease-12-17-98.htm> (accessed on 20 March 2005).

20 Cox, C., *Leader of Iraqi Resistance to Meet With House Leaders*, US House of Representatives Republican Policy Committee, 25 February 1998. Available at <http://www.policy.house.gov/subcommittees/107/html/news_release.cfm.770.html > (accessed on 2 June 2005).

21 *US Policy Toward Iraq*, Congressional Record Online (Senate), 31 August 1998.

22 *IRAQ LIBERATION ACT OF 1998*, Congressional Record Online (House), 5 October 1998, p. H9488.

23 LaRocque, S., *Congress First Voted to Back Regime Change in Iraq in 1998*, US State Department, International Information Programs, 19 September 2002. Available at <http://www.usembassy.it/file2002_09/alia/a2091905.htm> (accessed on 3 January 2004).

24 Cited in *Kerry, Kerry, Quite Contrary Part I*, Conservativetruth.org, 4 October 2004. Available at <http://www.conservativetruth.org/article.php?id=2528> (accessed on 12 June 2005).

25 See Kyl, John, *Saddam's Iraq: Sanctions and U.S. Policy*, US Senate Committee on Foreign Relations, 22 March 2000. Available at <http://frwebgate.access.gpo.gov/cgi-bin/getdoc.cgi?dbname=106_senate_hearings&docid=f:67659.wais> (accessed on 6 March 2005).

26 See Senator Joseph Biden, *IRAQ*, Congressional Record Online (Senate), 12 February 1998, p. S10290. Available at <http://frwebgate4.access.gpo.gov/cgi-bin/waisgate.cgi?WAISdocID=996299125+4+0+0&WAISaction=retrieve> (accessed on 12 August 2005).

27 See Katzman, K. 'Iraq's Opposition Movement', *CRS Report for Congress*, Washington, DC: Congressional Research Service, March 1998. Available at <http://www.fas.org/irp/crs/crs-iraq-op.htm> (accessed on 21 October 2005).

28 For example, when addressing the National Assembly of the Iraqi National Congress in October 1999 Representative Gilman declared, 'We in the Congress stand ready to support you. If, as a product of this meeting, you bring to us a credible plan for escalating the challenge to Saddam Hussein, we will do everything we can to help you carry it out. If new tools are required, we will try to get them to you... I commend you, I support you, and I urge you to persevere.' Gilman, B., *Statement of Congressman Benjamin A. Gilman, Chairman, House Committee on*

International Relations to the National Assembly of the Iraqi National Congress, 31 October 1999. Available at <http://www.iraqwatch.org/government/US/Letters,%20reports%20and%20statements/gilman-INC.html> (accessed on 6 March 2005).

29 Lott, T., Lieberman, J., Helms, J., Kerrey, R., Shelby, R., Brownback, S., Gilman, B., and Berman, H., *Letter to the President*, US Congress, 11 August 1999. Available at <http://www.iraqwatch.org/government/US/Letters,%20reports%20and%20statements/letterfromcongr-8-1-99.htm> (accessed on 20 March 2005).

30 See Lott, T., *Establishing a Program to Support a Transition to Democracy in Iraq*, Congressional Record Online (Senate), 7 October 1998, p. S11811. Available at <http://frwebgate5.access.gpo.gov/cgi-bin/waisgate.cgi?WAISdocID=496628129290+25+0+0&WAISaction=retrieve> (accessed on 6 March 2005).

31 *United States Policy Toward Iraq, Hearing Before The Subcommittee on Near Eastern and South Asian Affairs*, US Senate Committee On Foreign Relations, 1 March 2001. Available at <http://frwebgate.access.gpo.gov/cgi-bin/getdoc.cgi?dbname=107_senate_hearings&docid=f:71541.wais> (accessed on 6 March 2005).

32 *Iraq*, Congressional Record Online (Senate), 2 March 2000, p. S1150.

33 *Extremist Movements And Their Threat To The United States, Hearing Before the Subcommittee on Near Eastern and South Asian Affairs*, US Senate Committee On Foreign Relations, 2 November 1999.

34 *The Liberation of Iraq: A Progress Report*.

35 Lott, T. *et al.*, *Letter to the President*.

36 See, for example, a *New York Times* article by Robert Kagan and William Kristol forcefully advocating regime change. Kristol, W. and Kagan, R., 'Bombing Iraq Isn't Enough', *New York Times*, 30 January 1998. Available at <http://www.newamericancentury.org/iraq-013098.htm> (accessed on 17 December 2003).

37 Phillips, J. and Holmes, K., *The Anatomy of Clinton's Failure in Iraq (Backgrounder #1161)*, Heritage Foundation, 27 February 1998. Available at <http://www.heritage.org/Research/MiddleEast/BG1161.cfm> (accessed on 4 April 2005).

38 Bolton, J., 'Surrendering to Saddam', *Weekly Standard*, 7 September 1998.

39 Bolton, J., 'Who Really Won the Gulf War?', *Weekly Standard*, 27 December 1999.

40 Kristol, W. and Kagan. R., 'A "Great Victory" for Iraq', *Washington Post*, 26 February 1998.

41 Bolton, J., *Statement to the House International Relations Committee*, US House of Representatives International Relations Committee, 8 October 1998. Available at <http://www.aei.org/publications/pubID.18123,filter.all/pub_detail.asp> (accessed on 4 April 2005).

42 Kagan, R., 'Saddam Wins – Again', *Weekly Standard*, 4–11 January 1999, p. 34.

43 Clawson, P., *Testimony before the Subcommittee on Near Eastern and South Asian Affairs*, US Senate Foreign Relations Committee, 23 June 1999. Available at <http://www.washingtoninstitute.org/templateC07.php?CID=6> (accessed on 4 April 2005).

44 *The Liberation of Iraq: A Progress Report*.

45 Bolton, J., 'Our Pitiful Iraq Policy', *Weekly Standard*, 21 December 1998.

46 Gerecht, R. M., 'Liberate Iraq', *Weekly Standard*, 14 May 2001, p. 34.

47 Kagan, 'Saddam Wins – Again', p. 34.

48 Phillips and Holmes, *The Anatomy of Clinton's Failure in Iraq*.

49 *Clinton on Iraq: Wrong Question, Wrong Answer: It's Not the Weapons — It's the Regime, Stupid*, Center for Security Policy, 6 February 1998. Available at <http://www.centerforsecuritypolicy.org/index.jsp?section=papers&code=98-D_25> (accessed on 3 February 2005).

50 Schmitt, G., *Memorandum to Opinion Leaders: Iraq*, Project for a New American Century, 17 June 1998. Available at <http://www.newamericancentury.org/iraqjun1798.htm> (accessed on 13 December 2003).

51 Clawson, P., 'Show of Farce: Why Our Iraq Policy Won't Work'.

52 Kristol and Kagan, 'A "Great Victory" for Iraq'.

53 Kagan, 'Saddam Wins – Again', p. 34.

54 Bolton, 'Who Really Won the Gulf War?'

55 Kagan and Kristol, 'Bombing Iraq Isn't Enough'.

56 Kristol and Kagan, 'A "Great Victory" for Iraq'.

57 Kagan argued that the risks and difficulties of removing Saddam now were considerably less than 'allowing Saddam to get out of his box and wield weapons of mass destruction – as he is sure to do in a matter of months if we remain on the present course'. Kagan, R., 'Saddam's Impending Victory'.

58 Anderson, J., *Downplaying the Iraqi Crisis Is Doomed to Failure (Executive Memorandum #547)*, Heritage Foundation, 19 August 1998. Available at <http://www.heritage.org/Research/MiddleEast/em547.cfm> (accessed on 4 April 2005).

59 Satloff, R., *Blueprint: Ideas for a New Century*, Washington Institute for Near East Policy, Winter 2000. Available at <http://www.washingtoninstitute.org/template C06.php?CID=631> (accessed on 4 April 2005).

60 Lagon, M., *Memorandum to Opinion Leaders: Iraq*.

61 Perle, R., *Statement of Richard Perle*, US Senate Armed Services Committee, 28 September 2000. Available at <http://armed-services.senate.gov/statemnt/2000/000928rp.pdf> (accessed on 23 January 2004).

62 Wolfowitz, P., *Statement before the House National Security Committee*, US House of Representatives, 18 September 1998. Available at <http://www.newamerican century.org/iraqsep1898.htm> (accessed on 20 March 2005).

63 Lagon, *Memorandum to Opinion Leaders: Iraq*.

64 See Kagan, R., 'How to Attack Iraq'; Wolfowitz, *Statement before the House National Security Committee*. The plan was also fully endorsed by the Center for Security Policy; see *Clinton on Iraq: Wrong Question, Wrong Answer*, Center for Security Policy.

65 Solarz, S. and Wolfowitz, P., 'Letters to the Editor', *Foreign Affairs*, Vol. 78, 1999, No. 2.

66 Perle, R., 'A Clean Break: A New Strategy for Securing the Realm', *The Institute for Advanced Strategic and Political Studies*, 1996.

67 Perle, *Statement of Richard Perle*.

68 Phillips, J., *Why the United States should help the Iraqi opposition (Executive Memorandum #563)*, Heritage Foundation, 14 December 1998. Available at <http://www.heritage.org/Research/MiddleEast/em563.cfm> (accessed on 4 April 2005). See also Phillips J. and Anderson, J., *Air Strikes Are Necessary To Weaken, Discredit, and Punish Saddam Hussein (Executive Memorandum #508)*, Heritage Foundation, 5 February 1998. Available at <http://www.heritage.org/Research/MiddleEast/em508.cfm> (accessed on 4 March 2005).

69 Feith, D., 'Before the next Iraqi crisis: Support Saddam's opposition', *Jerusalem Post*, 20 March 1998, p. 9.

70 Satloff, *Blueprint: Ideas for a New Century*.

71 Wolfowitz, *Statement before the House National Security Committee*.

72 *PolicyWatch #306: U.S. Objectives in Iraq: Rollback vs. Containment*, Washington Institute for Near East Policy, 6 March 1998. Available at <http://www.washington institute.org/templateC05.php?CID=1184> (accessed on 2 June 2005).

73 *Clinton on Iraq: Wrong Question, Wrong Answer*, Center for Security Policy.

74 *PolicyWatch #475: The Iraqi Opposition and U.S. Policy: An Update*, Washington Institute for Near East Policy, 7 July 2000. Available at <http://www.washington institute.org/templateC05.php?CID=1353> (accessed on 4 April 2005).

75 Burgess, L., '"Smart Sanctions" Policy Will Make U.S. Look Weak, Policy Experts Claim', *Stars and Stripes*, 3 March 2001. Available at <http://ww2.pstripes.osd.mil/01/mar01/ed030301e.html> (accessed on 2 July 2005).

76 Albright, M., *Statement before the Subcommittee on Foreign Operations, Export Financing and Related Programs, House Appropriations Committee*, US State Department, 4 March 1998.

77 Indyk, *Remarks at the Council on Foreign Relations*, US State Department, 22 April 1998.

78 Katzman, K., 'Iraq's Opposition Movements', *CRS Report for Congress*, Washington, DC: Congressional Research Service, 2000.

79 Noyes, J., 'Fallacies, Smoke and Pipe Dreams: Forcing Change in Iran and Iraq', *Middle East Policy*, Vol. VII, 2000, No. 3, p. 45.

80 Pollack, K., Byman D., and Gideon R., 'The Rollback Fantasy', *Foreign Affairs*, Vol. 78, Jan/Feb 1999, No. 1.

81 Abrams, E., Armitage, R., Bennett, W., Bergner, J., Bolton, J., Dobriansky, P., Fukuyama, F., Kagan, R., Khalilzad, Z., Kristol, W., Perle, R., Rodman, P., Rumsfeld, D., Schneider, W., Weber, V., Wolfowitz, P., Woolsey, J. and Zoellick, R., 26 January 1998. Available at <http://www.newamericancentury.org/iraqclintonletter.htm> (accessed on 3 January 2004).

82 Solarz, S., Perle, R., Abrams, E., Allen, R., Armitage, R., Bergner, J., Bolton, J., Bryen, S., Burt, R., Carlucci, F., Clark, W., Feith, D., Gaffney, F., Gedmin, J., Ikle, F., Kagan, R., Khalilzad, Z., Kraemer, S., Kristol, W., Ledeen, M., Lewis, B., Lewis, F., Lynch, J., McFarlane, R., Muravchik, J., Pastor, R., Peretz, M., Robinson, R., Rodman, P., Rosenblatt, P., Rumsfeld, D., Schmitt, G., Singer, M., Sonnenfeldt, H., Weinberger, C., Wienseltier, L., Wolfowitz, P., Wurmser, D. and Zakheim, D., 19 February 1998. Available at <http://www.casi.org.uk/discuss/2001/msg00103.html> (accessed on 17 December 2003).

83 Abrams, E., Bennett, W., Bergner, J., Bolton, J., Dobriansky, P., Fukuyama, F., Kagan, R., Khalilzad, Z., Kristol, W., Perle, R., Rodman, P., Rumsfeld, D., Schneider, W., Weber, V., Wolfowitz, P., Woolsey, J., and Zoellick, R., 1998. Available at <http://www.newamericancentury.org/iraqletter1998.htm> (accessed on 18 December 2003).

84 Ibid.

85 Lott, T., *Military Action Against Iraq Averted*, US Senate, 25 February 1998. Available at <http://www.iraqwatch.org/government/US/Letters,%20reports%20and %20statements/lott-2-25-98.html> (accessed on 20 March 2005).

86 Noyes, 'Fallacies, Smoke and Pipe Dreams: Forcing Change in Iran and Iraq', p. 45.

4 RETHINKING IRAQ: A NEW PRESIDENT AND NEW FOREIGN POLICY

1 Dao, J. and Schmitt, E., 'Iraq Is Focal Point as Bush Meets With Joint Chiefs', *New York Times*, 11 January 2001.

2 Daalder, I. H. and Lindsay J. M., *America Unbound*, Washington, DC: The Brookings Institution, 2003, p. 22.

3 Powell, C., *Remarks at the National Newspaper Association's 40th Annual Government Affairs Conference*, US State Department, 23 March 2001. Available at

<http://www.state.gov/secretary/former/powell/remarks/2001/1666.htm> (accessed on 14 August 2005). The policy review process was referred to on a number of occasions. On 20 February Powell stated that 'we are reviewing with the Pentagon and all other parts of the US Government the full range of options available to us'. See Powell, C., *Press Availability with German Minister of Foreign Affairs Joschka Fischer and Secretary Colin L. Powell*, US State Department, 20 February 2001. Available at <http://www.state.gov/secretary/former/powell/remarks/2001/613.htm> (accessed on 6 August 2005).

4 Rumsfeld, D., *Secretary Rumsfeld Interview with the New York Times*, US Department of Defense, 16 May 2001. Available at <http://www.defenselink.mil/transcripts/2001/t05242001_t0516sdc.html> (accessed on 20 July 2005).

5 Suskind, R., *The Price of Loyalty: George W. Bush, the White House and the Education of Paul O'Neill*, New York: Simon & Schuster, 2004, pp. 72–75; Bamford J., *A Pretext for War*, New York: Anchor Books, 2005, p. 261.

6 Suskind, *Price of Loyalty*, p. 83.

7 Ibid., p. 160.

8 Rumsfeld D., *Media Availability with Secretary Rumsfeld*, US Department of Defense, 3 August 2001. Available at <http://www.defenselink.mil/transcripts/2001/t08032001_t0803asd.html> (accessed on 20 July 2005).

9 *CATO Daily Dispatch*, 6 October 2000. Available at <http://www.cato.org/dispatch/10-06-00d.html#two> (accessed on 2 September 2005).

10 Powell, C., *Confirmation Hearing by Secretary-Designate Colin L. Powell*, US Senate, 17 January 2001. Available at <http://www.state.gov/secretary/former/powell/remarks/2001/443.htm> (accessed on 5 August 2005).

11 State Department transcript, *Interview on CNN's 'Late Edition' Secretary Colin L. Powell*, US State Department, 11 February 2001. Available at <http://www.state.gov/secretary/former/powell/remarks/2001/548.htm> (accessed on 6 August 2005).

12 State Department transcript, *Press Briefing Abroad Aircraft En Route to Cairo, Egypt, Secretary Colin L. Powell*, US State Department, 23 February 2001. Available at <http://www.state.gov/secretary/former/powell/remarks/2001/931.htm> (accessed on 6 August 2005). See also statements made during Powell's press conference with Ariel Sharon in February 2001, State Department transcript, *Press Availability with Prime Minister-elect Ariel Sharon with Secretary Colin L. Powell, Jerusalem*, US State Department, 25 February 2001. Available at <http://www.state.gov/secretary/former/powell/remarks/2001/935.htm> (accessed on 14 August 2005). Powell employed the 'box' metaphor on several occasions, mimicking Madeleine Albright on 27 February in saying 'If they [weapons inspectors] don't come back in, then the conditions set by the United Nations will not be met, and he will consider himself still trapped in the box that he has constructed for himself'; see State Department transcript, *Press Availability with Commissioner Christopher Patten at European Commission and Secretary Colin L. Powell, Brussels, Belgium*, US State Department, 27 February 2001. Available at <http://www.state.gov/secretary/former/powell/remarks/2001/962.htm> (accessed on 14 August 2005).

13 State Department transcript, *Press Availability with German Minister of Foreign Affairs Joschka Fischer and Secretary Colin L. Powell*.

14 Powell, C., *Press Remarks with Foreign Minister of Egypt Amre Moussa and Secretary Colin L. Powell, Cairo*, US State Department, 24 February 2001. Available at <http://www.state.gov/secretary/former/powell/remarks/2001/933.htm> (accessed on 6 August 2005).

15 State Department transcript, *Interview on CBS's 'Face the Nation' Secretary*, US State Department, 11 February 2001. Available at <http://www.state.gov/secretary/former/powell/remarks/2001/549.htm> (accessed on 6 August 2005).

16 Powell, C., *Testimony at Budget Hearing before the Senate Foreign Relations Committee*, US State Department, 8 March 2001. Available at <http://www.state.gov/ secretary/former/powell/remarks/2001/1164.htm> (accessed on 14 August 2005).

17 Powell, *Press Remarks with Foreign Minister of Egypt Amre Moussa and Secretary Colin L. Powell*.

18 Powell, C., *Press Briefing Secretary Colin L. Powell*, US State Department, 1 February 2001. Available at <http://www.state.gov/secretary/former/powell/ remarks/2001/73.htm> (accessed on 30 July 2005). See also State Department transcript, *Interview on ABC's 'This Week'*, US State Department, 4 February 2001. Available at <http://www.state.gov/secretary/former/powell/remarks/2001/516.htm> (accessed on 17 August 2005) in which Powell says the 'UN has to remain steadfast and demand that he [Saddam Hussein] do what he said he was going to do'.

19 White House transcript, *Exchange With Reporters in Waco, Texas*, The White House, 7 August 2001. Available at <http://frwebgate1.access.gpo.gov/cgi-bin/waisgate. cgi?WAISdocID=390939174014+13+0+0&WAISaction=retrieve> (accessed on 17 August 2005).

20 President Bush stated in February 2001 that the sanctions policy was being reviewed: 'I have said that the sanction regime is like Swiss cheese. That meant that they weren't very effective. And we're going to review current sanction policy and review options as to how to make the sanctions work.' Bush, G. W., *The President's News Conference*, The White House, 22 February 2001. Available at <http://frweb-gate1.access.gpo.gov/cgi-bin/waisgate.cgi?WAISdocID= 390939174014+0+0+0&WAISaction=retrieve> (accessed on 5 August 2005).

21 State Department transcript, *Press Availability with Commissioner Christopher Patten at European Commission and Secretary Colin L. Powell*.

22 *Powell calls for stiff sanctions against Iraq*, CNN, 16 December 2000. Available at <http://archives.cnn.com/2000/WORLD/meast/12/16/powell.iraq.reut/> (accessed on 6 August 2005). See also Powell, C., *Confirmation Hearing by Secretary-Designate Colin L. Powell*, US Senate, 17 January 2001. Available at <http://www.state. gov/secretary/former/powell/remarks/2001/443.htm> (accessed on 5 August 2005).

23 Powell, C., *Testimony before the Foreign Operations, Export Financing and Related Programs Subcommittee of the Senate Appropriations Committee*, US State Department, 15 May 2001. Available at <http://www.state.gov/secretary/former/ powell/remarks/2001/1164.htm> (accessed on 14 August 2005).

24 'When we took over on the 20th of January, I discovered that we had an Iraq policy that was in disarray, and the sanctions part of that policy was not just in disarray; it was falling apart.' Powell, *Testimony at Budget Hearing before the Senate Foreign Relations Committee*.

25 State Department transcript, *Interview on CBS's 'Face the Nation' Secretary Colin L. Powell*.

26 State Department transcript, *Press Briefing Abroad Aircraft En Route to Cairo*, US State Department, 23 February 2001.

27 State Department transcript, *Remarks to the Press, En route to Shannon Airport*, US Senate, 13 April 2001. Available at <http://www.state.gov/secretary/former/ powell/remarks/2001/2169.htm> (accessed on 14 August 2005).

28 Guardia, A. L., 'Bush determined to finish the job', *The Daily Telegraph*, 17 February 2001.

29 State Department transcript, *Interview by Tim Russert, NBC's 'Meet The Press'*, US State Department, 3 June 2001. Available at <http://www.state.gov/secretary/former/ powell/remarks/2001/3255.htm> (accessed on 14 August 2005).

30 Powell said 'it is kind of astonishing to me that countries – some countries in the P-5 that were arguing for years that we ought to simplify the list, sell more, make it

easier, don't hurt civilians, now are frustrating that effort for reasons that are not entirely clear to me'. State Department transcript, *Interview at Associated Press Roundtable*, US State Department, 22 June 2001. Available at <http://www.state.gov/secretary/former/powell/remarks/2001/3760.htm> (accessed on 20 July 2005).

31 Guardia, A. L., 'Iraq smart sanctions derailed by Russia', *The Daily Telegraph*, 4 July 2001.

32 Powell, C., *Remarks With British Secretary of State Of Foreign and Commonwealth Affairs Jack Straw*, US State Department, 11 July 2001. Available at <http://www.state.gov/secretary/former/powell/remarks/2001/4055.htm> (accessed on 20 July 2005). Powell was clearly at a loss, saying that 'I wish they [sanctions] had been modified but they have not been ... It is just interesting to me that, trying to do what the Russians had said for a couple of years we should do; and that is to get relief from some of the more onerous aspects of the sanctions and let civilian goods go in, they could not sign up to that at the end of the day and to give relief to the Iraqi civilians. It was the Iraqi government and the Russians who fought that the most...' Powell, C., *Remarks on Trip to G-8 Foreign Ministers Meeting, En Route To Rome, Italy*, US State Department, 17 July 2001. Available at <http://www.state.gov/secretary/former/powell/remarks/2001/4135.htm> (accessed on 20 July 2005).

33 Quoted in Guardia, 'Iraq smart sanctions derailed by Russia'.

34 Yaphe, J., 'Iraq: The Exception to the Rule', *The Washington Quarterly*, Vol. 24, 2001, No. 1, p. 128.

35 Bush, *Exchange With Reporters in Waco, Texas*.

36 State Department transcript, *Press Availability with UN Secretary General Kofi Annan and Secretary Colin L. Powell*, US State Department, 14 February 2001. Available at <http://www.state.gov/secretary/former/powell/remarks/2001/584.htm> (accessed on 14 August 2005).

37 Powell, *Testimony at Budget Hearing before the Senate Foreign Relations Committee*.

38 *Rice Vows 'Resolute' Action Against Iraq*, CNN, 30 July 2001. Available at <http://archives.cnn.com/2001/US/07/29/rice.iraq/> (accessed on 17 December 2003).

39 State Department transcript, *Press Briefing Secretary Colin L. Powell*, US State Department, 9 February 2001. Available at <http://www.state.gov/secretary/former/powell/remarks/2001/542.htm> (accessed on 6 August 2005).

40 Powell, *Testimony at Budget Hearing before the Senate Foreign Relations Committee*.

41 State Department transcript, *Press Briefing Secretary Colin L. Powell*, 9 February 2001.

42 *Rice Vows 'Resolute' Action Against Iraq*, CNN.

43 Defense Department transcript, *Secretary of Defense Donald Rumsfeld Interview on ABC News Sunday*, US Department of Defense, 11 February 2001. Available at <http://www.defenselink.mil/transcripts/2001/t02122001_t0211abc.html> (accessed on 20 July 2005).

44 See the *Report of the Commission to Assess the Ballistic Missile Threat to the United States*, 15 July 1998. The commission was chaired by Rumsfeld and is often referred to as the Rumsfeld Commission. The Commission found US intelligence agency analysis of the ballistic missile threat from countries such as Iraq, Iran and North Korea too optimistic and argued that those agencies could not provide the US government sufficient, timely warning of the development and deployment of new ballistic missile threats. Paul Wolfowitz also served on the Commission. The Executive Summary is available at <http://www.fas.org/irp/threat/bm-threat.htm> (accessed on 25 October 2005).

45 Reinckens, W., 'Saddam Still Pursuing Nuclear Weapons, Says Iraqi Scientist', *Washington File*, Office of International Information Programs, US Department of State, 2 November 2000. Available at <http://www.globalsecurity.org/wmd/library/news/iraq/2000/iraq-001102.htm> (accessed on 15 December 2003).

46 Berry, J., 'Saddam has made two atomic bombs, says Iraqi defector', *The Daily Telegraph*, 28 January 2001.

47 State Department transcript, *Interview on ABC's 'This Week' Secretary Colin L. Powell*.

48 Powell, *Testimony at Budget Hearing before the Senate Foreign Relations Committee*.

49 Powell, C., *Testimony before the Foreign Operations, Export Financing and Related Programs Subcommittee of the Senate Appropriations Committee*, US State Department, 15 May 2001. Available at <http://www.state.gov/secretary/former/powell/remarks/2001/1164.htm> (accessed on 14 August 2005).

50 Cited in State Department transcript, *Interview on ABC's 'This Week' Secretary Colin L. Powell*.

51 Rice, C., 'Promoting the National Interest', *Foreign Affairs*, Vol. 79, 2000, No. 1.

52 Response to a question posed at a forum organised the Council of Foreign Relations and the Republican National Convention. See <http://www.sourcewatch.org/index.php?title=Condoleezza_Rice> (accessed on 25 October 2005).

53 *PBS News hour with Jim Lehrer*, PBS, 11 March 2001. Available at <http://www.pbs.org/newshour/bb/white_house/jan-june02/rice_3-11.html> (accessed on 20 July 2005).

54 *Rice Vows 'Resolute' Action Against Iraq*, CNN.

55 President Bush, cited in State Department transcript, *Interview on ABC's 'This Week' Secretary Colin L. Powell*.

56 Suskind, *Price of Loyalty*, p. 85.

57 Defense Department transcript, *Deputy Secretary Wolfowitz Interview with CNN*, US Department of Defense, 8 July 2001. Available at <http://www.defenselink.mil/transcripts/2001/t07302001_t0728cnn.html> (accessed on 20 July 2005).

58 Myers, S. L. and Schmitt, E., 'Bush Administration Warns Iraq on Weapons Programs', *The New York Times*, 23 January 2001.

59 *United States Policy toward Iraq, Hearing Before the Subcommittee on Near Eastern and South Asian Affairs*, US Senate Committee on Foreign Relations, 1 March 2001.

60 Burgess, L., 'Smart Sanctions Policy Will Make U.S. Look Weak, Policy Experts Claim', *Stars and Stripes*, 3 March 2001.

61 Suskind, *Price of Loyalty*, p.86.

62 *U.S. Considers Iraqi Coup*, NewsMax.com, 2001. Available at <http://www.newsmax.com/cgi-bin/printer_friendly.pl?page> (accessed on 18 December 2003).

63 Belida, A., *US/Iraq*, Voice of America, 27 July 2001. Available at <http://www.globalsecurity.org/wmd/library/news/iraq/2001/iraq-010727-37609da5.htm> (accessed on 12 December 2004).

64 Fenton, B., 'US launches air strikes on Baghdad', *The Daily Telegraph*, 17 February 2001. Richard Perle was quoted as saying that 'The air strikes are just the beginning of a more robust response . . . the Bush administration recognises that this is the only way to resolve the problem'. 'Saddam's removal "is not British policy"', *The Daily Telegraph*, 26 February 2001.

65 Quoted in Guardia, A. L., 'Britain and US ready to raid Iraq again', *The Daily Telegraph*, 26 February 2001.

66 Guardia, A. L., 'Germans attack bombing as rift on Iraq deepens', *The Daily Telegraph*, 20 February 2001. At this stage then British Defence Secretary Geoff Hoon stated on the record that 'It has always been US policy that they worked for the removal of Saddam Hussein. Regime change has not been part of UK policy so

far.' Quoted in 'Saddam's removal "is not British policy"', *The Daily Telegraph*, 26 February 2001.

67 *The Liberation of Iraq: A Progress Report.*

68 *Ten Years after Saddam Survived Desert Storm, It's Time to adopt 'Bush Team' Blueprint for Ending His Dangerous Misrule*, Center for Security Policy, 17 January 2001. Available at <http://www.centerforsecuritypolicy.org/index.jsp?section =papers&code=01-D_07> (accessed on 7 March 2005).

69 Donnelly, T., *Memorandum To: Opinion Leaders*, Project for a New American Century, 6 July 2001. Available at <http://www.newamericancentury.org/iraq-070601.htm> (accessed on 20 January 2004).

70 *The Bush Doctrine, Decision Brief*, Center for Security Policy, 3 December 2001. Available at <http://www.centerforsecuritypolicy.org/index.jsp?section=papers& code=01-D_19> (accessed on 7 March 2005).

71 Gerecht, R. M., 'Liberate Iraq', *Weekly Standard*, 14 May 2001, p. 34.

72 Rubin, M., 'U.S. Should Intensify Pressure on Hussein', *Baltimore Sun*, 9 August 2001.

73 Clawson, P., *PolicyWatch #518: Powell to the Middle East: Assessing the Key Elements of Iraq Policy*, Washington Institute for Near East Policy, 20 February 2001. Available at <http://www.washingtoninstitute.org/templateC05.php?CID=1396> (accessed on 2 December 2004).

74 Byman, D., 'A farewell to arms inspections', *Foreign Affairs*, Vol. 79, 2000, No. 1.

75 Ledeen, M., 'Powell's Great Adventure', *National Review*, 5 March 2001. Available at <http://www.aei.org/publications/pubID.14813,filter.all/pub_detail.asp> (accessed on 20 January 2004).

76 Ledeen, M., 'So You Wanna Be a Superpower?', *National Review*, 30 August 2001. Available at <http://www.aei.org/publications/pubID.13118,filter.all/pub_detail.asp> (accessed on 20 January 2004).

77 Cited in Burgess, 'Smart Sanctions Policy Will Make U.S. Look Weak, Policy Experts Claim'.

78 Ibid.

79 Helms, J., *Towards a Compassionate Conservative Foreign Policy*, American Enterprise Institute, 2001. Available at <http://www.aei.org/publications/ pubID.17927, filter.all/pub_detail.asp> (accessed on 17 July 2005).

80 Hyde, H., Remarks delivered at AIPAC, 19 March 2001.

81 'Time to Establish a War Crimes Tribunal Regarding Saddam Hussein's Crimes', *Congressional Record*, 30 July 2001, p. H4785.

5 9/11 AND IRAQ

1 Halper and Clarke describe an 'echo chamber' built into the US media debate on Iraq underpinned by 'a sustained bombardment of aggressive rhetoric forging a national consensus around the need for broad military action' from conservative TV and radio stations. Clarke, J. and Halper, S., *America Alone*, Cambridge: Cambridge University Press, 2004, pp. 192–195.

2 Bush, G. W., *Address to a Joint Session of Congress and the American People*, White House, 20 September 2001. Available at <http://www.whitehouse.gov/news/releases/ 2001/09/20010920-8.html> (accessed on 22 September 2005).

3 Mann, J., *Rise of the Vulcans*, New York: Viking, 2004, p. 297.

4 Department of Defense transcript, *Secretary Rumsfeld Interview with the Washington Post*, 9 January 2002. Available at <http://www.defenselink.mil/transcripts/2002/ t02052002_t0109wp.html> (accessed on 22 July 2005); Woodward, B., *Bush at War*, London: Simon & Schuster, 2002, p. 49.

5 *Plans For Iraq Attack Began On 9/11*, CBS News, 4 September 2002. Available at <http://www.cbsnews.com/stories/2002/09/04/september11/main520830.shtml> (accessed on 12 September 2005).

6 Clarke, R., *Against All Enemies: Inside America's War on Terror*, New York: Free Press, 2004, p. 30.

7 Ibid., p. 232. The theory of Iraqi involvement in the 1993 attack has been investigated and no evidence found to support it. Its chief proponent has been Laurie Mylroie, who pursued the case and presented her findings in *Study of Revenge: Saddam's Unfinished War against America* published by the American Enterprise Institute in 2000. Mylroie has some influential supporters including former CIA director James Woolsey and to a lesser degree, Paul Wolfowitz. Woolsey, J., 'Saddam may be target Americans are looking for', *The Daily Telegraph*, 17 September 2001.

8 Clarke, *Against All Enemies*, p. 32.

9 Woodward, *Bush at War*, p. 79.

10 Ibid., p. 83; Suskind, *Price of Loyalty*, p. 187.

11 Woodward, *Plan of Attack*, p. 25.

12 State Department transcript, *Interview by Richard Wolffe of Newsweek*, US State Department, 13 March 2003. Available at <http://www.state.gov/secretary/former/powell/remarks/2003/18766.htm> (accessed on 25 July 2005).

13 State Department transcript, *Interview on ABC's This Week*, US State Department, 23 September 2001. Available at <http://www.state.gov/secretary/former/powell/remarks/2001/5011.htm> (accessed on 25 July 2005). Powell clarified this further in October stating that 'the first focus of this campaign is on al-Qaida and Usama bin Laden in Afghanistan and in the other places where al-Qaida is located throughout the world' while recognising that 'there are other regimes that give haven and harbor to terrorist activity, and we will turn our attention to them in due course'. See State Department transcript, *Interview on CNN with Paula Zahn*, US State Department, 10 October 2001. Available at <http://www.state.gov/secretary/former/powell/remarks/2001/5295.htm> (accessed on 25 July 2005), and State Department transcript, *Interview on CNN's Late Edition with Wolf Blitzer*, US State Department, 21 October 2001. Available at <http://www.state.gov/secretary/former/powell/remarks/2001/5470.htm> (accessed on 25 July 2005).

14 Defense Department transcript, *Deputy Secretary Wolfowitz Interview with Sam Tannenhaus*, Vanity Fair, US Department of Defense, 9 May 2003. Available at <http://www.defenselink.mil/transcripts/2003/tr20030509-depsecdef0223.html> (accessed on 12 December 2003).

15 Woodward, *Plan of Attack*, p. 21.

16 Sciolino, E. and Tyler, P., 'Some Pentagon officials and advisors seek to oust Iraq's leader in war's next phase', *New York Times*, 12 October 2001.

17 Borger, J., 'Washington's Hawk Trains Sights on Iraq', *The Guardian*, 26 September 2001; Bamford, J., *A Pretext for War*, New York: Anchor Books, 2005, p. 287.

18 Woodward, *Bush at War*, p. 61.

19 Wright, R. and McManus, D., *Bush Camp Split on Anti-Terror Policy*, 21 September 2001.

20 Bush, G. W., *Statement by the President in His Address to the Nation*, The White House, 11 September 2001. Available at <http://www.whitehouse.gov/news/releases/2001/09/20010911-16.html> (accessed on 3 August 2005).

21 Ross, W. S., *Bush Says Iraq Must Permit Weapons Inspections*, US Embassy, Italy, 26 November 2001. Available at <http://www.usembassy.it/file2001_11/alia/a1112602.htm> (accessed on 12 December 2003).

22 Bush, G. W., *Remarks by the President in Welcoming to the White House the Aid Workers Rescued From Afghanistan*, The White House, 26 November 2001.

Available at <http://www.whitehouse.gov/news/releases/2001/11/20011126-1.html> (accessed on 12 August 2003).

23 Harnden, T., 'Bush Points to Iraq as His Next Target', *The Daily Telegraph*, 12 December 2001.

24 In April 2001 the US State Department's *Patterns of Global Terrorism 2000* report named Iran, Iraq, Syria, Libya, Cuba, North Korea and Sudan as state sponsors of terrorism. Overview available at <http://www.state.gov/s/ct/rls/pgtrpt/2000/2441. htm> (accessed on 20 November 2005).

25 Ross, *Bush Says Iraq Must Permit Weapons Inspections*.

26 Harnden, 'Bush Points to Iraq as His Next Target'.

27 State Department transcript, *Interview on CNN's Late Edition*, US State Department, 2 December 2001. Available at <http://www.state.gov/secretary/former/powell/ remarks/2001/dec/6613.htm> (accessed on 25 July 2005).

28 From speech writer David Frum's perspective inside the White House 'it suddenly seemed that American power could do *anything*' following the swift defeat of the Taliban in Afghanistan and begged the question 'what precisely *did* it wish to do?' Frum D., *The Right Man: An Inside Account of the Bush White House*, New York: Random House, 2005, p. 195.

29 Ross, *Bush Says Iraq Must Permit Weapons Inspections*.

30 Bush, *Remarks by the President in Welcoming to the White House the Aid Workers Rescued From Afghanistan*.

31 Bush, G. W., *Remarks by the President and Prime Minister Bulent Ecevit of Turkey*, The White House, 16 January 2002. Available at <www.whitehouse.gov/news/ releases/2002/01/20020116-5.html> (accessed on 12 August 2005).

32 For example the President was quizzed by reporters in October on whether there was a definite link between the anthrax letters and Iraq or al-Qaida. See *Remarks by President Bush and President Jiang Zemin*, White House, 19 October 2002. Available at <http://www.whitehouse.gov/news/releases/2002/01/iraq/20020129-11. html> (accessed on 5 July 2005). In October Wolf Blitzer, host of CNN's Late Edition, stated in an interview with Secretary of State Colin Powell that former CIA Director Jim Woolsey and some Members of Congress were 'pointing a finger at Iraq in looking at the anthrax-laced letters.' *Interview on CNN's Late Edition with Wolf Blitzer*, US State Department, 21 October 2001. Available at <http://www.state.gov/ secretary/former/powell/remarks/2001/5470.htm> (accessed on 25 July 2005).

33 Suskind, *The Price of Loyalty*, p. 187, p. 204.

34 See Harnden, T., 'President Plots Path Between Powell and Rumsfeld', *The Daily Telegraph*, 9 October 2001, and Defense Department transcript, *DoD News Briefing – Secretary Rumsfeld and Gen. Myers*, 9 October 2001. Available at <http://www. defenselink.mil/transcripts/2001/t10092001_t1009sd.html> (accessed on 22 July 2005).

35 Defense Department transcript, *Secretary Rumsfeld Editorial Board with the New York Times*, 14 November 2001. Available at <http://www.defenselink.mil/transcripts/ 2001/t11202001_t1114nyt.html> (accessed on 22 July 2005).

36 Defense Department transcript, *Secretary Rumsfeld Interview with CNN Novak and Hunt*, 30 November 2001. Available at <http://www.defenselink.mil/transcripts/ 2001/t11302001_t1130cnn.html> (accessed on 22 July 2005).

37 In contrast with Iran, Rumsfeld said that the possibility of Iran reforming itself was remote, but 'considerably above zero.' Ibid.

38 Wolfowitz, P., *'Building a Military for the 21st Century' Statement before the Senate Armed Services Committee*, 4 October 2001. Available at <http://armed-services. senate.gov/statemnt/2001/011004wolf.pdf> (accessed on 17 December 2003).

39 Beaumont, P., Vulliamy, E. and Beaver, P., 'Secret US Plan for Iraq War', *The Observer*, 2 December 2001.

40 Usher, A., 'Former CIA chief: "Iraq was involved in terror attacks"', *The Independent*, 23 October 2001.

41 Woolsey, 'Saddam may be target Americans are looking for', *The Daily Telegraph*, 17 September 2001.

42 American Enterprise Institute transcript, *The Battle for Ideas in the U.S. War on Terrorism*, American Enterprise Institute, 29 October 2001. Available at <http://www.aei.org/events/filter.,eventID.364/transcript.asp> (accessed on 18 August 2005).

43 'Gunning for Saddam, James Woolsey', *PBS Frontline*, 8 November 2001.

44 Defense Department transcript, *Deputy Secretary Wolfowitz Roundtable with European Journalists*, US Department of Defense, 27 November 2001. Available at <http://www.defenselink.mil/transcripts/2001/t12032001_t1127dsd.html> (accessed on 15 December 2003).

45 Slavin B., 'Pentagon Builds Case to Bomb Iraq', *USA Today*, 19 November 2001.

46 'Gunning for Saddam, Richard Perle', *PBS Frontline*, 8 November 2001. Available at <http://www.pbs.org/wgbh/pages/frontline/shows/gunning/interviews/perle.html> (accessed on 24 January 2004).

47 NewsMax.com, *Top Bush Adviser: 'Get Saddam Out Violently'*, 21 November 2001. Available at <http://www.newsmax.com/archives/articles/2001/11/20/202218.shtml> (accessed on 18 December 2004).

48 Perle, R., 'Should Iraq be Next?', *San Diego Union-Tribune*, 16 December 2001. Available at <http://www.aei.org/publications/pubID.13478,filter.all/pub_detail.asp> (accessed on 18 August 2005).

49 Mann, *Rise of the Vulcans*, p. 302; Pfaff, W., *Fear, Anger and Failure*, New York: Algora Publishing, 2004, p. 14. Pfaff, writing in the *International Herald Tribune* on 18 October 2001, described this as 'a notorious debate going on between the State Department, skeptical about wars, and some leaders in the Defense department and the neo-conservative intellectual community who want to attack Saddam Hussein in Iraq, and possibly other rogue states'.

50 Frum, *The Right Man*, pp. 196–200.

51 Kristol, W., Bauer, G., Bell, J., Bennett, W., Bergner, J., Cohen, E., Cropsey, S., Decter, M., Donnelly, T., Friedberg, A., Fradkin, H., Fukuyama, F., Gaffney, F., Gedmin, J., Gerecht, R. M., Hill, C., Jackson, B., Jacons, E., Joyce, M., Kagan, D., Kagan, R., Kirkpatrick, J., Krauthammer, C., Lehman, J., May, C., Perle, R., Peretz, M., Podhoretz, N., Scheunemann, R., Schmitt, G., William Schneider, J., Shultz, R., Sokolski, H., Weber, V., Wieseltier, L. and Wittmann, M., 'Open Letter to the President', *The Weekly Standard*, 20 September 2001. Available at <http://www.newamericancentury.org/Bushletter.htm> (accessed on 4 November 2005).

52 American Enterprise Institute transcript, *The Battle for Ideas in the U.S. War on Terrorism*.

53 Gedmin, J., *Collecting the Anti-Terror Coalition*, American Enterprise Institute, 1 October 2001. Available at <http://www.aei.org/publications/pubID.13212,filter.all/pub_detail.asp> (accessed on 18 August 2005).

54 Phillips, J., *Target Iraq's Terrorist Regime, not just Osama bin Laden, to win War on Terrorism*, Heritage Foundation, 2 October 2001. Available at <http://www.heritage.org/Research/MiddleEast/EM780.cfm> (accessed on 18 August 2005).

55 Kagan, R. and Kristol, W., 'What to Do about Iraq', *Weekly Standard*, 21 January 2001.

56 State Department transcript, *Interview by BBC*, US State Department, 21 September 2001. Available at <http://www.state.gov/secretary/former/powell/remarks/2001/5004.htm> (accessed on 25 July 2005).

57 Rice, C., *National Security Advisor Interview with AL Jazeera TV*, White House, 16 October 2001. Available at <http://www.whitehouse.gov/news/releases/2001/10/20011016-3.html> (accessed on 12 August 2005).

58 White House transcript, *Interview of Vice President Cheney with Diane Sawyer of ABC*, White House Office of the Press Secretary, 29 November 2001. Available at <http://www.whitehouse.gov/vicepresident/news-speeches/speeches/vp20011129.html> (accessed on 6 September 2005).

59 El Deeb, S., 'Arabs warn U.S. not to target fellow Arab in anti-terror campaign', *Associated Press Worldstream* (subscription only), 11 November 2001.

60 Powell, C., *Press Briefing on Board Plane En Route Pakistan*, US State Department, 15 October 2001. Available at <http://www.state.gov/secretary/former/powell/remarks/2001/5383.htm> (accessed on 25 July 2005).

61 Diamond, J., Keen, J., Moniz, D., Page, S. and Slavin, B., 'Iraq course set from tight White House circle', *USA Today*, 11 September 2002.

62 Beaumont, P. *et al.*, 'Secret US Plan for Iraq War'.

63 Woodward, *Plan of Attack*, p. 2, p. 38.

64 Frum, *The Right Man*, p. 224.

65 Kaplan, L. F., 'Why the Bush administration will go after Iraq', *The New Republic*, 10 December 2001.

66 Harnden, 'Bush Points to Iraq as His Next Target', *The Daily Telegraph*, 12 December 2001.

67 White House transcript, *The Vice President Appears on NBC's Meet the Press*, White House Office of the Press Secretary, 9 December 2001. Available at <http://www.whitehouse.gov/vicepresident/news-speeches/speeches/vp20011209.html> (accessed on 6 September 2005).

68 White House transcript, *Interview of the Vice President by Jim Angle of Fox TV News*, White House Office of the Press Secretary, 11 December 2001. Available at <http://www.whitehouse.gov/vicepresident/news-speeches/speeches/vp20011211.html> (accessed on 6 September 2005).

69 Lahoud, L., 'Rice calls America "Israel's best friend"', *Jerusalem Post*, 18 December 2001.

70 Bush, G. W., *President Delivers State of the Union Address*, White House, 29 January 2002. Available at <http://www.whitehouse.gov/news/releases/2002/01/iraq/20020129-11.html> (accessed on 27 January 2004).

71 On 7 January 2002 *Newsweek* cited a 'senior American envoy in the Middle East' who stated 'The question is not if the United States is going to hit Iraq; the question is when.' Dickey, C. and Barry, J., 'After September 11, Washington sees Iraq's weapons capabilities as a direct and intolerable threat to American national security. So what will be done?' *Newsweek*, 7 January 2002. In February 2002 a Bush administration official stated: 'This is not an argument about whether to get rid of Saddam Hussein. That debate is over.' 'Bush Administration Decides to Oust Iraq's Saddam Hussein from Power', *Knight–Ridder Washington Bureau*, 13 February 2002.

72 Defense Department transcript, *Deputy Secretary Wolfowitz Interview with Sam Tannenhaus, Vanity Fair*.

73 Beaumont, *et al.*, 'Secret US Plan for Iraq War'.

74 *Newsweek* reported that a 'general consensus' had emerged at the highest levels of the Bush administration for regime change in Iraq and a framework strategy developed. The report, based on discussions with a 'senior administration official', said, 'The United States will step up pressure on Saddam to admit U.N. arms inspectors to look for Iraq's weapons of mass destruction. No one expects Saddam to fully comply, but the process will buy time: to show Saddam's intransigence, get America's allies on board, find and support freedom fighters in Iraq, and prepare for an inva-

sion, if necessary. The time line could take anywhere from six to 18 months'. Evan Thomas, 'Chemistry in the War Cabinet: Reports of rivalry are overblown. Bush's team works via consensus-and cutting up. Exhibit A: The new plan for Iraq', *Newsweek*, 28 January 2001.

6 CONSTRUCTING THE CASE: FROM THE 'AXIS OF EVIL' TO THE UNITED NATIONS

1 Woodward, *Plan of Attack*, p. 72.
2 Mann, *Rise of the Vulcans*, p. 333.
3 Condoleezza Rice was quoted as saying in February 2002 that 'Iraq comes up in this office whenever somebody walks in'. Ron Fournier, '*Rice: Al-Qaida Could be Regrouping*', Associated Press Online (subscription only), 14 February 2001.
4 Schieffer, B. and Borger, G., 'Face the Nation', *CBS*, 17 February 2002.
5 'Iraq status quo not acceptable: Rice', *Agence France Presse*, 5 May 2002.
6 Powell, C., *Interview on ABC's Nightline With Ted Koppel*, US State Department, 15 July 2002. Available at <http://www.state.gov/secretary/former/powell/remarks/2002/11866.htm> (accessed on 25 July 2005).
7 State Department transcript, *Interview on the Diane Rehm Show*, US State Department, 18 July 2002. Available at <http://www.state.gov/secretary/former/powell/remarks/2002/11919.htm> (accessed on 25 July 2005).
8 Woodward notes that 'Cheney's biggest concern was still the possibility that bin Laden or other terrorists would acquire and use weapons of mass destruction.' Woodward, *Bush at War*, p. 137.
9 White House transcript, *Remarks by the Vice President to the Council on Foreign Relations*, White House Office of the Press Secretary, 15 February 2001. Available at <http://www.whitehouse.gov/vicepresident/news-speeches/speeches/vp20020215.html> (accessed on 6 September 2005).
10 Bush, G. W., *Remarks by the President and Prime Minister Sharon of Israel in Photo Opportunity*, White House, 7 February 2002. Available at <http://www.whitehouse.gov/news/releases/2002/02/20020207-15.html> (accessed on 12 August 2005).
11 Cornwell, R., 'The Message from Bush is Clear: War against Saddam is inevitable', *The Independent*, 12 March 2002.
12 Woodward, *Plan of Attack*, p. 111.
13 White House transcript, *Remarks by the President and the Vice President upon Conclusion of Breakfast*, White House, 21 March 2002. Available at <http://www.whitehouse.gov/news/releases/2002/03/20020321-6.html> (accessed on 29 June 2002).
14 See Raum, T., 'Cheney ends Mideast tour with scant support for strikes on Iraq', *Associated Press Worldstream* (subscription only), 20 March 2002, and 'Arab leaders "concerned" by Saddam Hussein: Cheney', Agence France Presse, 21 March 2002.
15 White House transcript, *The Vice President Appears on Late Edition (CNN)*, White House, 24 March 2002. Available at <http://www.whitehouse.gov/vicepresident/news-speeches/speeches/vp20020324-2.html> (accessed on 6 September 2005).
16 Cheney insisted this was 'a top priority for us, and that we'll spend whatever time we need to seeing to it that this threat is, in fact, dealt with'. White House transcript, *The Vice President Appears on Meet the Press (NBC)*, White House Office of the Press Secretary, 24 March 2002. Available at <http://www.whitehouse.gov/vicepresident/news-speeches/speeches/vp20020324.html> (accessed on 6 September 2005).
17 Eisenberg, D., 'We're Taking Him Out', *Time Magazine Online*, 5 May 2002. Available at <http://www.time.com/time/world/article/0,8599,235395,00.html> (accessed on 26 September 2005).

18 Bush, *Remarks by the President and the Vice President upon Conclusion of Breakfast*, White House, 21 March 2002). Available at <http://www.whitehouse.gov/news/releases/2002/03/20020321-6.html> (accessed on 12 August 2005).

19 Bush, G. W., *Remarks by President Bush and Prime Minister Tony Blair in Joint Press Availability*, White House, 6 April 2002. Available at <http://www.whitehouse.gov/news/releases/2002/04/20020406-3.html> (accessed on 12 August 2005).

20 Bush, G. W., *Remarks by President Bush and President Musharraf of Pakistan in Press Availability*, White House, 13 February 2002. Available at <http://www.whitehouse.gov/news/releases/2002/02/20020213-3.html> (accessed on 12 August 2005).

21 Bush, G. W., *Remarks by the President to South Carolina First Responders Wyche Pavilion, Greenville, South Carolina*, White House, 27 March 2002. Available at <http://www.whitehouse.gov/news/releases/2002/03/20020327-6.html> (accessed on 12 August 2005).

22 Bush, *Remarks by President Bush and Prime Minister Tony Blair in Joint Press Availability*.

23 Transcript available at <http://www.downingstreetmemo.com/docs/04-APR-2002-Interview.pdf> (accessed 16 November 2005).

24 Rice, C., *Remarks by National Security Advisor Condoleezza Rice on Terrorism and Foreign Policy*, White House, 29 April 2002. Available at <http://www.whitehouse.gov/news/releases/2002/04/20020429-9.html> (accessed on 12 August 2005).

25 Bush, *Remarks by President Bush and President Musharraf of Pakistan in Press Availability*.

26 Bush, *Remarks by the President and the Vice President upon Conclusion of Breakfast*.

27 Bush, *Remarks by President Bush and Prime Minister Tony Blair in Joint Press Availability*.

28 Bush, *Remarks by the President to South Carolina First Responders*.

29 White House transcript, *Press Conference by the President*, White House, 13 March 2002. Available at <http://www.whitehouse.gov/news/releases/2002/03/20020313-8.html> (accessed on 12 August 2005).

30 Bush, *Remarks by the President to South Carolina First Responders*.

31 George W. Bush, *Remarks by President Bush and Chancellor Schroeder of Germany in Press Availability, Kanzlerant, Berlin*, White House, 23 May 2002. Available at <http://www.whitehouse.gov/news/releases/2002/05/20020523-1.html> (accessed on 24 August 2005).

32 In April Bush said 'I can't imagine people not seeing the threat and not holding Saddam Hussein accountable for what he said he would do, and we're going to do that.' Bush, *Remarks by President Bush and Prime Minister Tony Blair in Joint Press Availability*.

33 Seymour Hersh reported in the *New Yorker* on 27 October 2003 that in March 2002 'it was understood by many in the White House that the President had decided, in his own mind, to go to war' citing a 'former White House official'. Available at <http://www.newyorker.com/fact/content/?031027fa_fact> (accessed on 12 August 2005). In addition a leaked Downing Street memo of a British government cabinet meeting in July 2002 cited British Foreign Secretary Jack Straw saying 'Bush had made up his mind to take military action'. Daniszewski, J., 'Indignation Grows in U.S. Over British Prewar Documents', *Los Angeles Times*, 12 May 2005; 'Downing Street Memo', *The Times Online*, 1 May 2005. Available at <http://www.timesonline.co.uk/article/0,,2087-1593607,00.html> (accessed on 2 November 2004).

34 White House transcript, President Bush Delivers Graduation Speech at West Point, White House, 1 June 2002. Available at <http://www.whitehouse.gov/news/releases/2002/06/20020601-3.html> (accessed on 19 February 2004).

35 McCall, W., 'Cheney's Message: Iraq's A Threat', *The Colombian*, 25 June 2002.

36 Richard Haass, Director of Policy Planning at the State Department, found this out in July 2002: 'I raised this issue about were we really sure that we wanted to put Iraq front and center at this point, given the war on terrorism and other issues,' he later recalled in an interview with the *New Yorker*. 'And she [Condoleezza Rice] said, essentially, that that decision's been made, don't waste your breath.' Lemann, N., How it Came to War, *The New Yorker*, 31 March 2003. Available at <http://www.newyorker.com/printables/fact/030331fa_fact> (accessed on 2 November 2005). In addition after Paul Wolfowitz's trip to Turkey in July 2002 Turkish Prime Minister Bulent Ecevit is reported to have stated on Turkish television that 'The American administration is not hiding that it is determined on a military intervention against Iraq'. Hayes, S., 'The coming war with Saddam', *The Weekly Standard*, 29 July 2002. Available at <http://www.newamericancentury.org/iraq-072202.pdf> (accessed on 18 August 2005).

37 Defense Department transcript, *Secretary Rumsfeld Media Availability at Kuwait City International Airport*, 10 June 2002. Available at <http://www.defenselink.mil/transcripts/2002/t06102002_t0610kc.html> (accessed on 22 July 2005).

38 Pincus, W., 'Rumsfeld Disputes Value of Iraq Arms Inspections', *Washington Post*, 16 April 2002.

39 Defense Department transcript, *Secretary Rumsfeld Interview with the Washington Times*, 27 June 2002. Available at <http://www.defenselink.mil/transcripts/2002/t07012002_t0627wt.html> (accessed on 22 July 2005).

40 Defense Department transcript, *Secretary Rumsfeld Interview with CBS Face the Nation*, 24 February 2002. Available at <http://www.defenselink.mil/transcripts/2002/t02242002_t0224cbs.html> (accessed on 22 July 2005).

41 Defense Department transcript, *Secretary Rumsfeld Media Availability at Kuwait City International Airport*, 10 June 2002.

42 Defense Department transcript, *Secretary Rumsfeld Interview with CBS Face the Nation*, 24 February 2002.

43 Defense Department transcript, *Secretary Rumsfeld Interview with the Washington Times*, 27 June 2002. Available at <http://www.defenselink.mil/transcripts/2002/t07012002_t0627wt.html> (accessed on 22 July 2005).

44 Ibid.

45 Of the three 'axis of evil' states Iran, Iraq and North Korea, Rumsfeld placed Iraq at the bottom of the list of where internal change was most likely. Defense Department transcript, *Secretary Rumsfeld Interview with Bloomberg News*, 24 June 2002. Available at <http://www.defenselink.mil/transcripts/2002/t06262002_t0624sd.html> (accessed on 22 July 2005).

46 Defense Department transcript, *Secretary Rumsfeld Media Availability at Kuwait City International Airport*, 10 June 2002.

47 Wolfowitz declared that dealing with the likes of Iraq, Iran and North Korea had been put off under Clinton, 'sort of pushed off into the future and now it is the future'. Defense Department transcript, *Deputy Secretary Wolfowitz Interview with Baltimore Sun*, 12 April 2002. Available at <http://www.defenselink.mil/transcripts/2002/t05132002_t0412dsd.html> (accessed on 26 July 2005).

48 Defense Department transcript, *Deputy Secretary Wolfowitz Interview with Greta Van Susteren, Fox News Channel*, 9 July 2002. Available at <http://www.defenselink.mil/transcripts/2002/t07102002_t0709fox.html> (accessed on 26 July 2005).

49 'Saddam's Ultimate Solution', *PBS Wideangle*, 7 November 2002.

50 State Department transcript, *Interview on Fox News Sunday with Tony Snow*, US State Department, 16 December 2001. Available at <http://www.state.gov/secretary/former/powell/remarks/2001/dec/6864.htm> (accessed on 25 July 2005).

51 State Department transcript, *Interview on NBC's 'Meet the Press'*, Department of State, 17 February 2002. Available at <http://www.state.gov/secretary/former/powell/remarks/2002/8071.htm> (accessed on 25 July 2005).

52 Ibid.

53 Did September 11 'change the prism through which we viewed Iraq? Yes, definitely', was Powell's answer to his rhetorical question shortly before the outbreak of war in March 2003. State Department transcript, *Interview by Richard Wolffe of Newsweek*, Department of State, 13 March 2003. Available at <http://www.state.gov/secretary/former/powell/remarks/2003/18766.htm> (accessed on 25 July 2005).

54 Ricks, T. E., Military Bids to Postpone Iraq Invasion', *Washington Post*, 24 May 2002. Available at <http://www.washingtonpost.com/wp-dyn/articles/A1822-2002May23.html> (accessed on 12 November 2005).

55 Woodward, *Plan of Attack*, p. 59.

56 Ibid., p. 80.

57 *The Guardian* reported on 26 March 2004 that 'The fact that the Pentagon pulled the fighting force most equipped for hunting down Osama bin Laden from Afghanistan in March 2002 in order to pre-position it for Iraq cannot be denied.' James, P., 'Running Scared'.

58 Harnden, 'Bush has blueprint to oust Saddam', *The Daily Telegraph*, 29 April 2002; Woodward, *Plan of Attack*, pp. 113–114.

59 Lutwak, E., 'Why President Bush has given the go ahead for Iraq attack', *The Daily Telegraph*, 23 June 2002; Schmitt, E., 'US Plan for Iraq Is Said to Include Attack on Three Sides', *New York Times*, 4 July 2002.

60 Rogers, P., *War by February*, OpenDemocracy, 18 September 2002. Available at <http://www.opendemocracy.net/themes/article-2-164.jsp> (accessed on 19 February 2004).

61 Beaumont, P., Hinsliff, G. and Beaver, P., 'Bush ready to declare war', *The Observer*, 4 August 2002.

62 *Attacking Iraq – Countdown Timeline*, GlobalSecurity.org, 2003. Available at <http://www.globalsecurity.org/military/ops/iraq-timeline.htm> (accessed on 19 February 2004).

63 Clare Short, the British Secretary for International Development who later resigned in protest of the impending invasion of Iraq, said in June 2003 that three senior British Intelligence officials told her before the war that Bush and Blair's decision to attack Iraq had been made sometime during the summer of 2002 and that it would likely begin in mid-February 2003. 'Three extremely senior people in the Whitehall system said to me very clearly and specifically that the target date was mid-February.' Wintour, P., 'Short: I was Briefed on Blair's Secret War Pact', *The Guardian*, 18 June 2003.

64 Winnett, R., 'Key No 10 Aides Were Split Over War', *Sunday Times*, 31 July 2005. In November 2002 the British newspaper *The Independent* reported that 'British and American warplanes are attacking Iraq's air defences almost daily, and making practice runs on other targets. US special forces are reported to be on the ground in western and northern Iraq, and military engineers are preparing and upgrading airfields in the Kurdish zone. In many ways, the war on Iraq has already begun.' Whitaker, R., 'U.S., U.K. Launch Secret Gulf War', *The Independent*, 25 November 2002.

65 Smith, M., '100 Jets Join Attack on Iraq', *The Daily Telegraph*, 6 September 2002.

66 State Department transcript, Interview on CNN's Larry King Live, Department of State, 26 November 2001. Available at <http://www.state.gov/secretary/former/powell/remarks/2001/6336.htm> (accessed on 25 July 2005).

67 State Department transcript, *Remarks with Russian Foreign Minister Igor Ivanov*, Department of State, 14 May 2002. Available at <http://www.state.gov/secretary/former/powell/remarks/2002/10141.htm> (accessed on 25 July 2005).

68 State Department transcript, *Interview by Juan Williams on NPR's Morning Edition*, Department of State, 4 June 2002. Available at <http://www.state.gov/secretary/former/powell/remarks/2002/10850.htm> (accessed on 25 July 2005).

69 Bush, G. W., *Remarks by the President with British Prime Minister Tony Blair*, The White House, 31 January 2003). Available at <http://www.whitehouse.gov/news/releases/2003/01/20030131-23.html> (accessed on 15 August 2002).

70 State Department transcript, *Interview on CBS's Face the Nation*, Department of State, 2 December 2001. Available at <http://www.state.gov/secretary/former/powell/remarks/2001/dec/6612.htm> (accessed on 25 July 2005).

71 State Department transcript, *Interview on ABC's This Week with Sam Donaldson and Cokie Roberts*, Department of State, 5 May 2002. Available at <http://www.state.gov/secretary/former/powell/remarks/2002/9941.htm> (accessed on 25 July 2005).

72 Suskind, *The Price of Loyalty*, p. 278.

73 Bamford, *Pretext for War*, p. 318.

74 Schneider, W., 'A Question of Timing', *National Journal*, 21 September, 2002. Available at <http://www.aei.org/publications/pubID.14293,filter.all/pub_detail.asp> (accessed on 18 August 2005).

75 State Department transcript, *Interview by Richard Wolffe of Newsweek*, Department of State, 13 March 2003. Available at <http://www.state.gov/secretary/former/powell/remarks/2003/18766.htm> (accessed on 25 July 2005). See also Burrough, B., Peretz, E., Rose, D. and Wise, D., 'Special Report: The Rush to Invade Iraq – The Ultimate Inside Account', *Vanity Fair*, May 2004.

76 A CNN–*Time* poll in March found that '70 percent of Americans said they think the United States should use military action to topple Saddam, while 23 percent opposed it'. This issue of international support was important and support dropped to 55 per cent without Arab or European backing with opposition rising to 39 per cent. 'War against Iraq will take patience, resources, maybe years', *Knight–Ridder Washington Bureau*, 21 Marc 2002. The poll of 1,014 adults had a margin of error of 3 percentage points.

77 In August 2002 Scowcroft argued 'It is beyond dispute that Saddam Hussein is a menace. He terrorizes and brutalizes his own people. He has launched war on two of his neighbors. He devotes enormous effort to rebuilding his military forces and equipping them with weapons of mass destruction. We will all be better off when he is gone.' He advocated pressing the UNSC to 'insist on an effective no-notice inspection regime for Iraq – any time, anywhere, no permission required'. A refusal by Saddam 'could provide the persuasive casus belli which many claim we do not now have'. Scowcroft was concerned that a war with Iraq would divert from the war on terrorism, but he insisted that if a UN resolution was passed and Saddam Hussein refused to comply, then the US should go ahead and take unilateral action. See Scowcroft, B., 'Don't Attack Saddam – It Would Undermine our Antiterror Efforts', *Wall Street Journal*, 15 August 2002; *GOP Backing Out of Iraq Offensive?*, Fox News, 16 August 2002. Available at <http://www.foxnews.com/story/0,2933,60626,00.html> (accessed on 4 November 2005); and NBC transcript, Brent Scowcroft Interviewed by Tim Russert on NBC News: Meet the Press, NBC News, 15 September 2002. Available at <http://www.ffip.com/interviews091502.htm> (accessed on 23 September 2005). Baker also published his views in August 2002. He agreed with Scowcroft that 'Saddam Hussein ran an 'outlaw regime' in violation of UNSC resolutions, and that he had ongoing WMD programmes and was therefore a threat to peace and stability. He too insisted that the best way forward was to 'advocate the adoption by the United Nations Security Council of a simple and straightforward resolution that Iraq submit to intrusive inspections anytime, any-

where, with no exceptions, and authorizing all necessary means to enforce it'. The first time Saddam Hussein restricted inspections, Baker wrote, the United States should use whatever means necessary to change the regime including a US-led armed invasion an occupation of Iraq. Baker, J. A., 'The Right Way To Change a Regime', *New York Times*, 25 August 2002.

78 Bush, G. W., *Remarks by the President in Meeting with Central African Leaders, The Waldorf Astoria, New York*, White House, 13 September 2002. Available at <http://www.whitehouse.gov/news/releases/2002/09/20020913.html>, accessed on 26 August 2005.

79 Kampfner, J., *Blair's Wars*, London: Free Press, 2003, p. 194.

80 Bush, G. W., *Remarks by the President in Photo Opportunity with Secretary of State Colin Powell*, White House, 19 September 2002. Available at <http://www.whitehouse. gov/news/releases/2002/09/20020919-1.html> (accessed on 22 August 2005). See also Bush, G. W., *Remarks by the President and Prime Minister Berlusconi of Italy*, White House, 14 September 2002. Available at <http://www.whitehouse.gov/news/ releases/2002/09/20020914-2.html> (accessed on 26 August 2005).

81 Bush, G. W., *Remarks by the President in Meeting with Congressional Leaders*, White House, 18 September 2002). Available at <http://www.whitehouse.gov/news/ releases/2002/09/20020918-1.html> (accessed on 26 August 2005).

82 Woodward, *Bush at War*, p. 347.

83 Cheney, D., *Vice President Cheney's Speech to the Veterans of Foreign Wars*, Project for a New American Century, 26 August 2002. Available at <http://www.newamerican century.org/iraq-082602.htm> (accessed on 19 February 2004).

84 Cheney, D., *Vice President Honors Veterans of Korean War, Texas*, White House, 29 August 2002. Available at <http://www.whitehouse.gov/news/releases/2002/08/ 20020829-5.html> (accessed on 19 February 2004).

85 Bush, G. W., *Remarks by the President and Prime Minister Tony Blair in Photo Opportunity Camp David, Maryland*, White House, 7 September 2002. Available at <http://www.whitehouse.gov/news/releases/2002/09/20020907-2.html> (accessed on 12 August 2005).

86 Bush, G. W., *Remarks by the President to the Pool Before and After Golf – Crawford, Texas, Ridgewood Country Club, Waco, Texas*, White House, 10 August 2002). Available at <http://www.whitehouse.gov/news/releases/2002/08/20020810-3.html>, (accessed on 12 August 2005).

87 White House transcript, *President's Remarks at the United Nations General Assembly*, The White House, 12 September 2003. Available at <http://www.whitehouse. gov/news/releases/2002/09/print/20020912-1.html> (accessed on 22 February 2004). The full text of the demands was:
1. If the Iraqi regime wishes peace, it will immediately and unconditionally forswear, disclose, and remove or destroy all weapons of mass destruction, long-range missiles, and all related material.
2. If the Iraqi regime wishes peace, it will immediately end all support for terrorism and act to suppress it, as all states are required to do by U.N. Security Council resolutions.
3. If the Iraqi regime wishes peace, it will cease persecution of its civilian population, including Shi'a, Sunnis, Kurds, Turkomans, and others, again as required by Security Council resolutions.
4. If the Iraqi regime wishes peace, it will release or account for all Gulf War personnel whose fate is still unknown. It will return the remains of any who are deceased, return stolen property, accept liability for losses resulting from the invasion of Kuwait, and fully cooperate with international efforts to resolve these issues, as required by Security Council resolutions.

5. If the Iraqi regime wishes peace, it will immediately end all illicit trade outside the oil-for-food program. It will accept U.N. administration of funds from that program, to ensure that the money is used fairly and promptly for the benefit of the Iraqi people.

88 Woodward, *Plan of Attack*, p. 222.

89 Powell stated that main reason why the United States took its case to the UN was 'not the terrorism angle as much, although that is also part of the resolutions, as it is the weapons of mass destruction and the other elements of the resolutions'. State Department transcript, *Interview on CBS' Face the Nation*, Department of State, 15 September 2002. Available at <http://www.state.gov/secretary/former/powell/remarks/2002/13479.htm> (accessed on 25 July 2005).

90 State Department transcript, *Press Briefing*, Department of State, 4 September, 2002. Available at <http://www.state.gov/secretary/former/powell/remarks/2002/13266.htm> (accessed on 25 July 2005).

91 State Department transcript, *Interview by Tony Snow and Brit Hume on Fox News Sunday*, Department of State, 8 September 2002. Available at <http://www.state.gov/secretary/former/powell/remarks/2002/13324.htm> (accessed on 25 July 2005).

92 Clarke, R., *Against All Enemies: Inside America's War on Terror*, New York: Free Press, 2004, p. 265.

7 FROM THE UNITED NATIONS TO WAR

1 See Bush, G. W., *Remarks by the President on After Meeting with Members of Congress*, The White House, 1 October 2002. Available at <http://www.whitehouse.gov/news/releases/2002/10/20021001-1.html> (accessed on 22 August 2005).

2 Bush, G. W., *Remarks by President at Tennessee Welcome*, The White House, 8 October 2002. Available at <http://www.whitehouse.gov/news/releases/2002/10/20021008.html> (accessed on 28 August 2005).

3 Bush, G. W., *Remarks by the President at Thaddeus McCotter for Congress Dinner*, The White House, 14 October 2002). Available at <http://www.whitehouse.gov/news/releases/2002/10/20021014-3.html> (accessed on 25 July 2005).

4 Bush, G. W., *Remarks by the President on Iraq*, The White House, 7 October 2002. Available at <http://www.whitehouse.gov/news/releases/2002/10/20021007-8.html> (accessed on 28 August 2005).

5 Bush, G. W., *State of the Union Address*, The White House, 28 January 2003. Available at <http://www.whitehouse.gov/news/releases/2003/01/20030128-23.html> (accessed on 15 August 2002).

6 Defense Department transcript, *Testimony of U.S. Secretary of Defense Donald H. Rumsfeld before the House Armed Services Committee regarding Iraq (Transcript)*, US Department of Defense, 18 September 2002. Available at <http://www.defenselink.mil/speeches/2002/s20020918-secdef2.html> (accessed on 22 July 2005).

7 Defense Department transcript, *Remarks as delivered by Secretary of Defense Donald H. Rumsfeld at the Hoover Institution Board of Overseers*, US Department of Defense, 25 February 2003. Available at <http://www.defenselink.mil/speeches/2003/sp20030225-secdef0084.html> (accessed on 27 January 2004).

8 Powell, C., *The Administration's Position With Regard to Iraq*, US State Department, 26 September 2002. Available at <http://www.state.gov/secretary/former/powell/remarks/2002/13765.htm> (accessed on 25 July 2005).

9 Bush, G. W., *President Bush Calls on Congress to Act on Nation's Priorities, Army National Guard Aviation Support Facility*, The White House, 23 September 2002). Available at <http://www.whitehouse.gov/news/releases/2002/09/20020923-2.html> (accessed on 22 August 2005).

10 Bush, G. W., *Remarks by the President on Iraq*, The White House, 26 September 2002. Available at <http://www.whitehouse.gov/news/releases/2002/09/20020926-7.html> (accessed on 22 August 2005).

11 Bush, *Remarks by the President on Iraq*, 7 October 2002.

12 Bush, G. W., *Remarks by the President at Bob Ehrlich for Governor Reception*, The White House, 2 October 2002. Available at <http://www.whitehouse.gov/news/releases/2002/10/20021002-14.html> (accessed on 28 August 2005).

13 Bush G. W., *Remarks by the President at Thaddeus McCotter for Congress Dinner*.

14 Bush, G. W., *President Bush: 'World Can Rise to This Moment'*, The White House, 6 February 2003). Available at <http://www.whitehouse.gov/news/releases/2003/02/20030206-17.html> (accessed on 29 June 2002).

15 The President made his case against Iraq on 22 October at Bangor (Maine) and Downingtown (Pennsylvania); on 24 October at Columbia (South Carolina) and Charlotte (North Carolina); on 27 October at Phoenix (Arizona); on 28 October at Denver (Colorado) and Alamogordo (New Mexico); on 31 October at South Bend (Indiana), Northern State University (South Dakota), and Charleston (West Virginia); on 1 November at Louisville (Kentucky), Portsmouth (New Hampshire) and Harrisburg (Pennsylvania); on 2 November at Blountville (Tennessee), Atlanta (Georgia), Garden City (Georgia) and Tampa (Florida); on 3 November at Springfield (Illinois), St Paul (Minnesota) and Sioux Falls (South Dakota); and on 4 November at Bentonville (Arkansas), St Louis (Missouri), Cedar Rapids (Iowa) and Dallas (Texas).

16 Cheney, D., *The Vice President makes remarks at the NRCC Gala Salute to Dick Armey and J.C. Watts*, The White House, October 2, 2002). Available at <http://www.whitehouse.gov/news/releases/2002/10/20021002-15.html> (accessed on 29 June 2002).

17 Cheney, D., *Remarks by the Vice President at the Air National Guard Senior Leadership Conference*, The White House, 2 December 2002. Available at <http://www.whitehouse.gov/news/releases/2002/12/20021202-4.html> (accessed on 29 June 2002).

18 Lumpkin, J., 'Rice: Iraq providing shelter, chemical weapons help to al-Qaida', *Associated Press Worldstream*, 26 September 2002. In November she insisted 'We know one thing about bad guys – they tend to travel in packs. They do tend to help each other, they do tend to coalesce around issues. Saddam Hussein has a long ter-rorist past. Whether it is in support of Palestinian rejectionists or the Abu Nidal organization, or helping some al-Qaida operatives gain training in CBRN [chemical, biological, radiological or nuclear weapons], or having meetings with – between Iraqis and al-Qaida in various parts of the world, there's a relationship here.' Rice, C., *Press Briefing by National Security Advisor Dr. Rice on the President's Trip to NATO Summit*, The White House, 15 November 2002. Available at <http://www.whitehouse.gov/news/releases/2002/11/20021115-1.html> (accessed on 12 August 2005).

19 Defense Department transcript, *Secretary Rumsfeld Interview with Good Morning America*, US Department of Defense, 9 September 2002. Available at <http://www.defenselink.mil/transcripts/2002/t09092002_t0909sdgma.html> (accessed on 22 July 2005).

20 Defense Department transcript, *Testimony of U.S. Secretary of Defense Donald H. Rumsfeld before the House Armed Services Committee regarding Iraq (Transcript)*, 18 September 2002.

21 Rumsfeld, D., *Statement before the House Armed Services Committee*, 18 September 2002. Available at <http://www.house.gov/hasc/openingstatementsandpress releases/107thcongress/02-09-18rumsfeld.html> (accessed on 19 February 2004).

22 Defense Department transcript, *DoD News Briefing – Secretary Rumsfeld and Gen. Pace*, US Department of Defense, 20 August 2002. Available at <http://www.defenselink.mil/transcripts/2002/t08202002_t0820sd.html> (accessed on 22 July 2005).

23 Rumsfeld went on to state in the ensuing discussion with members of the Armed Service Committee that 'even if they [terrorist states] did not have terrorist connections, which indeed they do, the potential they have to use terrorist networks to dispense weapons of mass destruction is what's qualitatively different in our current [post-9/11] circumstance'. Defense Department transcript, *Testimony of U.S. Secretary of Defense Donald H. Rumsfeld before the House Armed Services Committee regarding Iraq (Transcript)*, 18 September 2002.

24 Defense Department transcript, *Testimony as delivered to the Senate Select Committee on Intelligence and the House Permanent Select Committee on Intelligence by Deputy Secretary of Defense Paul Wolfowitz*, 19 September 2002. Available at <http://www.defenselink.mil/speeches/2002/s20020919-depsecdef2. html> (accessed on 26 July 2005).

25 Defense Department transcript, *Remarks by Deputy Secretary of Defense Paul Wolfowitz, Fletcher Conference, Ronald Reagan Building and International Trade Center, Washington*, US Department of Defense, 16 October 2002. Available at <http://www.defenselink.mil/speeches/2002/s20021016-depsecdef.html> (accessed on 27 January 2004).

26 Kristol, W., *Iraq – al-Qaida connection*, Project for a New American Century, 12 December 2002. Available at <http://www.newamericancentury.org/iraq-121202. htm> (accessed on 18 August 2005).

27 *The case against Saddam (III): There is an 'Al-Qaida connection'*, Center for Security Policy, 18 September 2002. Available at <http://www.centerforsecuritypolicy. org/index.jsp?section=papers&code=02-F_34> (accessed on 18 August 2005).

28 See Gaffney, F., *Saddam Possibly Tied to Oklahoma City*, Foxnews.com, 23 October 2002. Available at <http://www.foxnews.com/story/0,2933,66505,00.html> (accessed on 18 August 2005), and *George Bush's finest hour*, Center for Security Policy, 27 January 2003. Available at <http://www.centerforsecuritypolicy.org/ index.jsp?section=papers&code=03-D_04> (accessed on 18 August 2005).

29 The letter stated

Should Saddam conclude that a U.S.-led attack could no longer be deterred, he probably would become much less constrained in adopting terrorist actions. Such terrorism might involve conventional means, as with Iraq's unsuccessful attempt at a terrorist offensive in 1991, or C.B.W. Saddam might decide that the extreme step of assisting Islamist terrorists in conducting a W.M.D. attack against the US would be his last chance to exact vengeance by taking a large number of victims with him ... Our understanding of the relationship between Iraq and al-Qaida is evolving and is based on sources of varying reliability. Some of the information we have received comes from detainees, including some of high rank. We have solid reporting of senior level contacts between Iraq and al-Qaida going back a decade. Credible information indicates that Iraq and al-Qaida have discussed safe haven and reciprocal nonaggression. Since Operation Enduring Freedom, we have solid evidence of the presence in Iraq of al-Qaida members, including some that have been in Baghdad. We have credible reporting that al-Qaida leaders sought contacts in Iraq who could help them acquire W.M.D. capabilities. The reporting also stated that Iraq has provided training to al-Qaida members in the areas of poisons and gases and making conventional bombs. Iraq's increasing support to extremist Palestinians coupled with growing indications of a relationship with al-Qaida, suggest that Baghdad's links to terrorists will increase, even absent U.S. military action.

GlobalSecurity.org, *C.I.A. Letter to Senate on Baghdad's Intentions*, 7 October 2002. Available at <http://www.globalsecurity.org/wmd/library/news/iraq/2002/iraq-021007-cia01.htm> (accessed on 2 August 2005).

30 In February 2003, Rohan Gunaratna of the Center for the Study of Terrorism and Political Violence at the University of St Andrews in Scotland stated that he 'had examined several tens of thousands of documents recovered from Al-Qaida and Taliban sources. In addition to listening to 240 tapes taken from Al-Qaida's central registry, I debriefed several Al-Qaida and Taliban detainees. I could find no evidence of links between Iraq and Al-Qaida. The documentation and interviews indicated that Al-Qaida regarded Saddam, a secular leader, as an infidel.' Gunaratna, R., 'Iraq and Al-Qaida: No evidence of alliance', *International Herald Tribune*, 19 February 2003. In January 2003 the British Defence Intelligence Staff Agency (DIS) completed a classified study which concluded that Saddam Hussein and Bin Laden's earlier attempts to collaborate had 'foundered' due to ideological differences. The report says: 'While there have been contacts between al-Qaida and the regime in the past, it is assessed that any fledgling relationship foundered due to mistrust and incompatible ideology.' *Leaked report rejects Iraqi al-Qaida link*, BBC News online, 5 February 2003. Available at <http://news.bbc.co.uk/2/hi/uk_news/2727471.stm> (accessed on 2 November 2005).

31 Bush, G. W., *Remarks by the President on Iraq*, The White House, 26 September 2002. Available at <http://www.whitehouse.gov/news/releases/2002/09/20020926-7.html> (accessed on 22 August 2005).

32 CNN transcript, *Interview with Condoleezza Rice; Pataki Talks About 9-11; Graham, Shelby Discuss War on Terrorism on Late Edition with Wolf Blitzer*, CNN, 8 September 2008. Available at <http://transcripts.cnn.com/TRANSCRIPTS/0209/08/le.00.html> (accessed on 3 November 2005).

33 Bush, G. W., *President Bush Outlines Iraqi Threat*, The White House, 7 October 2002. Available at <http://www.whitehouse.gov/news/releases/2002/10/20021007-8.html> (accessed on 25 August 2005).

34 Bush, G. W., *President, House Leadership Agree on Iraq Resolution*, The White House, 2 October 2002. Available at <http://www.whitehouse.gov/news/releases/2002/10/20021002-7.html> (accessed on 3 August 2002).

35 Edwards, B., 'Profile: Bush administration's continuing push for actions against Iraq', *Morning Edition NPR*, 3 September 2002.

36 White House transcript, *The Vice President Appears on Late Edition (CNN)*, 24 March 2002.

37 Quoted Pincus, W. and Priest, D., 'Bush, Aides Ignored CIA Caveats on Iraq', *Washington Post*, 7 February 2004.

38 Quoted in Barstow, D., Broad, W. J., and Gerth, J., 'Skewed Intelligence Data in March to War in Iraq', *New York Times*, 3 October 2004.

39 Howard Cincotta, *Cheney: End of Diplomatic Phase on Iraq is Approaching*, Washington File, US State Department, 16 March 2003. Available at <http://www.usembassy.it/file2003_03/alia/a3031604.htm> (accessed on 3 June 2005).

40 *Interview with Vice-President Dick Cheney, NBC Meet the Press*, NBC, 16 March 2003. Available at <http://www.mtholyoke.edu/acad/intrel/bush/cheneymeetthepress.htm> (accessed on 2 November 2005). IAEA director Mohamed El Baradei said a month before the war that the remaining questions could all be resolved by mid-April. Blix, H., *Disarming Iraq: The Search for Weapons of Mass Destruction*, London: Bloomsbury, 2004, p. 184.

41 Cheney, D., *Remarks by the Vice President to the Veterans of Foreign Wars 103rd National Convention*, The White House, 26 August 2002. Available at <http://www.whitehouse.gov/news/releases/2002/08/20020826.html> (accessed on 29 June 2002).

42 Knowlton, B., 'Bush's timetable: matter of "weeks"', *International Herald Tribune*, 31 January 2003.

43 Hersh, S., 'The Stovepipe', *The New Yorker*, 27 October 2003.

44 *Niamey signed an agreement to sell 500 tons of uranium a year to Baghdad*, National Military Joint Intelligence Center, Executive Highlight, Vol. 028-02, 12 February 2002. See *Report on the U.S. Intelligence Community's Prewar Intelligence Assessments on Iraq*, US Senate Select Committee on Intelligence, 7 July 2004, pp. 36–38.

45 Wilson, J., 'What I Didn't Find in Africa', *New York Times*, 6 July 2003.

46 Bamford, *A Pretext for War*, pp. 323–4.

47 *Report on the U.S. Intelligence Community's Prewar Intelligence Assessments on Iraq*, US Senate Select Committee on Intelligence, 7 July 2004, pp. 129–132.

48 Bush, *Remarks by the President on Iraq*, 26 September 2002.

49 Bush, G. W., *President, House Leadership Agree on Iraq Resolution*, The White House, 2 October 2002). Available at <http://www.whitehouse.gov/news/releases/2002/10/20021002-7.html> (accessed on 28 August 2005).

50 Bush, *Remarks by the President on Iraq*, 7 October 2002.

51 Bush, *President, House Leadership Agree on Iraq Resolution*.

52 State Department transcript, *Remarks at the World Economic Forum*, US State Department, 26 January 2003. Available at <http://www.state.gov/secretary/former/powell/remarks/2003/16869.htm> (accessed on 25 July 2005).

53 In the discussion with members of the Committee Rumsfeld said,

> Iraq is unique. No other living dictator matches Saddam Hussein's record of waging aggressive war against his neighbors, pursuing weapons of mass destruction, using them against his own people, launching missiles against his neighbors, brutalizing and torturing his own citizens, harboring terrorist networks, engaging in terrorist acts, including the attempted assassination of foreign officials, violating international commitments, lying and hiding his WMD programs from inspectors, deceiving and defying the expressed will of the United Nations over and over again.

Defense Department transcript, *Testimony of U.S. Secretary of Defense Donald H. Rumsfeld before the House Armed Services Committee regarding Iraq (Transcript)*, 18 September 2002.

54 Defense Department transcript, *Secretary Rumsfeld Interview with The Sunday Times London*, US Department of Defense, 21 September 2002. Available at <http://www.defenselink.mil/transcripts/2002/t09222002_t921londontimes.html> (accessed on 22 July 2005).

55 Defense Department transcript, *Testimony by Secretary of Defense Donald H. Rumsfeld at Defense Subcommittee of Senate Appropriations Committee*, US Department of Defense, 21 May 2002. Available at <http://www.defenselink.mil/speeches/2002/s20020521-secdef.html> (accessed on 22 July 2005).

56 Gilmore, G., 'Containing Saddam Is a Dangerous Notion, Wolfowitz Says', *American Forces Information Service*, 16 November 2002. Available at <http://www.defenselink.mil/news/Nov2002/n11162002_200211162.html> (accessed on 27 January 2004).

57 The deterrent argument was, according to Rumsfeld, 'so obviously fallacious'. Defense Department transcript, *Secretary Rumsfeld Interview with Jim Lehrer, News*

Hour, PBS WETA, US Department of Defense, 18 September 2002. Available at <http://www.defenselink.mil/transcripts/2002/t09192002_t0918sd.html> (accessed on 22 July 2005).

58 A few days later Rumsfeld claimed 'If Iraq launched a chemical or biological attack on the US it would not necessarily have an obvious return address. There are a variety of ways to conceal responsibility for such attacks. For example, they could give biological or chemical weapons to terrorist networks who could operate from within our country or against our forces or interests elsewhere in the world.' Defense Department transcript, Metro Atlanta *Chamber of Commerce Remarks by Secretary of Defense Donald H. Rumsfeld, Atlanta*, US Department of Defense, 27 September 2002. Available at <http://www.defenselink.mil/speeches/2002/s20020927-secdef.html> (accessed on 22 July 2005).

59 Defense Department transcript, *Testimony of U.S. Secretary of Defense Donald H. Rumsfeld before the House Armed Services Committee regarding Iraq (Transcript)*, 18 September 2002.

60 Defense Department transcript, *Secretary Rumsfeld Interview with Jim Lehrer, News Hour, PBS WETA*, US Department of Defense, 18 September 2002.

61 Defense Department transcript, *Deputy Secretary Wolfowitz Interview with U.S. News and World Report*, US Department of Defense, 4 October 2002. Available at <http://www.defenselink.mil/transcripts/2002/t10092002_t1004usn.html> (accessed on 26 July 2005).

62 Defense Department transcript, *Remarks by Deputy Secretary of Defense Paul Wolfowitz, Fletcher Conference, Ronald Reagan Building and International Trade Center, Washington*, US Department of Defense, 16 October 2002. Available at <http://www.defenselink.mil/speeches/2002/s20021016-depsecdef.html> (accessed on 27 January 2004).

63 *The National Security Strategy of the US of America*, The White House, September 2002, p. 14.

64 *National Strategy to Combat Weapons of Mass Destruction*, The White House, December 2002, p. 3. Available at <http://www.whitehouse.gov/news/releases/2002/12/WMDStrategy.pdf> (accessed on 3 June 2004).

65 Rice, C., *Dr. Condoleezza Rice Discusses President's National Security Strategy*, The White House, 1 October 2002. Available at <http://www.whitehouse.gov/news/releases/2002/10/20021001-6.html> (accessed on 12 August 2005).

66 Bush, G. W., *Remarks by the President in Photo Opportunity with Secretary of State Colin Powell*, The White House, 19 September 2002.

67 Bush, G. W., *President Signs National Defense Authorization Act*, The White House, 2 December 2002. Available at <http://www.whitehouse.gov/news/releases/2002/12/20021202-8.html> (accessed on 22 August 2005).

68 Defense Department transcript, *Secretary Rumsfeld Interview with The Sunday Times*.

69 Defense Department transcript, *DoD News Briefing – Secretary Rumsfeld and Gen. Myers*, US Department of Defense, 3 September 2002. Available at <http://www.defenselink.mil/transcripts/2002/t09032002_t0903sd.html> (accessed on 22 July 2005).

70 Defense Department transcript, *International Institute for Strategic Studies, Remarks by Deputy Secretary of Defense Paul Wolfowitz, London*, US Department of Defense, 2 December 2002. Available at <http://www.defenselink.mil/speeches/2002/s20021202-depsecdef.html> (accessed on 26 July 2005).

71 *Testimony of Richard Perle on U.S. Policy Toward Iraq*, House Committee on International Relations, 9 September 2002. Available at <http://commdocs.house.gov/committees/intlrel/hfa81813.000/hfa81813_0f.htm> (accessed on 20 February 2004).

72 *Statement of Richard Perle*, House Armed Services Committee, 26 September 2002. Available at <http://www.house.gov/hasc/openingstatementsandpressreleases/107thcongress/02-09-26perle.html> (accessed on 1 February 2004).

73 Bolton made the remarks in a BBC radio interview reported in the *Sunday Mail* newspaper. Mckenzie, S., 'US Plans Winter Invasion on Iraq to Oust Saddam', *Sunday Mail*, 4 July 2002.

74 Rumsfeld argued, 'The Congress' regime change legislation would still stand, and obviously when one thinks about the extent to which the people there were oppressed, and the conventional threat Saddam Hussein poses to its neighbors, those problems would still be there…' Defense Department transcript, *Secretary Rumsfeld Interview with Good Morning America*, US Department of Defense, 9 September 2002. Available at <http://www.defenselink.mil/transcripts/2002/t09092002_t0909sdgma.html> (accessed on 22 July 2005).

75 Bush, G. W., *Remarks by the President to Prague Atlantic Student Summit*, The White House, 20 November 2002). Available at <http://www.whitehouse.gov/news/releases/2002/11/20021120-4.html> (accessed on 22 August 2005).

76 Defense Department transcript, *Deputy Secretary Wolfowitz Interview with Today Programme Radio Four*, US Department of Defense, 3 December 2002. Available at <http://www.defenselink.mil/transcripts/2002/t12132002_t1203dsd.html> (accessed on 26 July 2005).

77 In January 2003 Perle warned that the inspection process was creating the impression 'that they are trying hard to find weapons of mass destruction – and because they can't find them, maybe they do not exist'. Perle R., *Why Blix has got it all wrong*, American Enterprise Institute, 26 January 2003. Available at <http://www.aei.org/publications/pubID.15827,filter.all/pub_detail.asp> (accessed on 18 August 2005).

78 State Department transcript, *Interview on The News Hour with Jim Lehrer*, US State Department, 22 January 2002. Available at <http://www.state.gov/secretary/former/powell/remarks/2003/16812.htm> (accessed on 25 July 2005).

79 On 6 December 2002 White House Press Secretary Ari Fleischer stated: 'The president of the US and the Secretary of Defense would not assert as plainly and bluntly as they have that Iraq has weapons of mass destruction if it was not true, and if they did not have a solid basis for saying it.' When pressed for details, he adds: 'President Bush has said Iraq has weapons of mass destruction. Tony Blair has said Iraq has weapons of mass destruction. Donald Rumsfeld has said Iraq has weapons of mass destruction. Richard Butler has said they do. The United Nations has said they do. The experts have said they do. Iraq says they don't. You can choose who you want to believe.' *Washington won't release evidence of Iraqi weapons*, CBC News, 6 December 2002. Available at <http://www.cbc.ca/stories/2002/12/05/iraq021205> (accessed on 2 November 2005).

80 Gaffney, F., *Too clever by half?*, Center for Security Policy, 21 October 2002. Available at <http://www.centerforsecuritypolicy.org/index.jsp?section=papers&code=02-D_53> (accessed on 18 August 2005).

81 Gaffney, F., *Accept No Substitutes: Regime Change is the Way to Disarm Iraq*, Center for Security Policy, 17 September 2002. Available at <http://www.centerforsecuritypolicy.org/index.jsp?section=papers&code=02-F_33> (accessed on 20 February 2004).

82 Phillips, J., *Disarming Iraq: The Lessons of UNSCOM*, Heritage Foundation, 28 October 2002. Available at <http://www.heritage.org/Research/MiddleEast/bg1608.cfm> (accessed on 18 August 2005).

83 Blix, H., *Disarming Iraq*, pp. 106–118, 188–190.

84 Ibid., p. 139.

85 Ibid., pp. 208–212.

86 Defense Department transcript, *Testimony of U.S. Secretary of Defense Donald H. Rumsfeld before Senate Armed Service Committee regarding Iraq (Transcript)*, 18 September 2002.

87 Defense Department transcript, *Secretary Rumsfeld Interview with Jim Lehrer, News Hour, PBS WETA*, 18 September 2002. Available at <http://www.defenselink.mil/transcripts/2002/t09192002_t0918sd.html> (accessed on 22 July 2005).

88 Defense Department transcript, *Testimony of U.S. Secretary of Defense Donald H. Rumsfeld before Senate Armed Service Committee regarding Iraq (Transcript)*, 18 September 2002.

89 Defense Department transcript, *Secretary Rumsfeld's Press Conference In Warsaw*, 25 September 2002. Available at <http://www.defenselink.mil/transcripts/2002/t09252002_t925warsaw.html> (accessed on 26 July 2005).

90 Defense Department transcript, *DoD News Briefing – Secretary Rumsfeld and Gen. Myers*, 22 October 2002. Available at <http://www.defenselink.mil/transcripts/2002/t10222002_t1022sd.html> (accessed on 26 July 2005).

91 State Department transcript, *Interview on NBC's Meet The Press with Tim Russert*, US State Department, 16 December 2001. Available at <http://www.state.gov/secretary/former/powell/remarks/2001/dec/6865.htm> (accessed on 25 July 2005).

92 Schmitt, E., and Sanger, D., 'Bush Has Received Pentagon Options on Attacking Iraq', *New York Times*, 21 September 2002.

93 Woodward, *Plan of Attack*, p. 214.

94 *Attacking Iraq – Countdown Timeline*, GlobalSecurity.org, 2003. Available at <http://www.globalsecurity.org/military/ops/iraq-timeline.htm> (accessed on 19 February 2004).

95 Gordon, C., *Quiet U.S. military buildup in gulf*, 2002. Available at <http://www.global security.org/org/news/2002/021004-iraq1.htm> (accessed on 16 December 2004); Woodward, *Plan of Attack*, p. 281.

96 Smith, M., 'Quarter of British Army sent to Gulf to confront Saddam', *The Daily Telegraph*, 21 January 2003.

97 Bowman, S., 'Iraq: Potential U.S. Military Operations', *CRS Report for Congress*, Washington, DC: Congressional Research Service, 3 March 2003.

98 Bush, G. W., *Remarks by the President on the House Vote on the Resolution Authorizing the Use of Force in Iraq*, The White House, 10 October 2002. Available at <http://www.whitehouse.gov/news/releases/2002/10/20021010-5.html> (accessed on 28 August 2005).

99 White House transcript, *Statement by the President*, The White House, 16 October 2002. Available at <http://www.whitehouse.gov/news/releases/2002/10/iraq/20021016-11.html> (accessed on 27 January 2004).

100 White House transcript, *President Pleased with U.N. Vote*, The White House, 8 November 2002. Available at <http://www.whitehouse.gov/news/releases/2002/11/iraq/20021108-1.html> (accessed on 27 January 2004).

101 Powell, C., *Iraq: Still Failing to Disarm: Secretary Colin L. Powell Remarks at the Center for Strategic and International Studies Washington, D.C.*, US State Department, 5 March 2003. Available at <http://www.state.gov/secretary/former/powell/remarks/2003/18307.htm> (accessed on 25 July 2005).

102 Bush, G. W., *Remarks by the President After Meeting with the Cabinet*, The White House, 13 November 2002. Available at <http://www.whitehouse.gov/news/releases/2002/11/2002113-1.html> (accessed on 15 August 2002).

103 Such questions posed by Powell included 'Where is the anthrax? Where is the botulinum toxin?... Where are the missiles that we know exist? The mobile biological warfare labs?' State Department transcript, *Interview on BBC's NewsNight*, US State

Department, 20 February 2003. Available at <http://www.state.gov/secretary/former/powell/remarks/2003/17837.htm> (accessed on 25 July 2005).

104 Bush, G. W., *President Signs Iraq Resolution*, The White House, 16 October 2002. Available at <http://www.whitehouse.gov/news/releases/2002/10/20021016-1.html> (accessed on 22 August 2005).

105 Blix wrote that he doubted the report was a full declaration of Iraq's WMD programmes. Blix, *Disarming Iraq*, p. 107.

106 Bush, G. W., *Excerpt from President's remarks in St. Louis*, The White House, 12 January 2003. Available at <http://www.whitehouse.gov/news/releases/2003/01/20030122-9.html> (accessed on 15 August 2002).

107 Bush, G. W., *Remarks by President Bush and Polish President Kwasniewski in Photo Opportunity*, The White House, 14 January 2003. Available at <http://www.whitehouse.gov/news/releases/2003/01/20030114-2.html> (accessed on 15 August 2002).

108 Bush, G. W., *State of the Union Address*, The White House, 28 January 2003. Available at <http://www.whitehouse.gov/news/releases/2003/01/20030128-23.html> (accessed on 15 August 2002).

109 Knowlton, B., 'Bush's timetable: matter of "weeks"', *International Herald Tribune*, 31 January 2003.

110 Holland, G., 'Rice exhorts United Nations to stand up to Saddam', *Associated Press Worldstream* (subscription only), 16 February 2003.

111 'As U.N. gathers more data, Bush ream calls Saddam "serial liar"', *Knight–Ridder Washington Bureau*, 9 February 2003.

112 *What Does Disarmament Look Like?*, The White House, January 2003. Available at <http://www.whitehouse.gov/infocus/iraq/disarmament/disarmament.pdf> (accessed on 18 November 2005).

113 Kampfner, *Blair's Wars*, p. 295.

114 White House transcript, *President Bush Meets with Prime Minister Blair*, The White House, 31 January 2003. Available at <http://www.whitehouse.gov/news/releases/2003/01/print/20030131-23.html> (accessed on 19 February 2004).

115 Bush, G. W., *President George Bush Discusses Iraq in National Press Conference*, The White House, 6 March 2003). Available at <http://www.whitehouse.gov/news/releases/2003/03/20030306-8.html> (accessed on 29 June 2002).

116 Eichler, T., 'Powell, Rice Argue For Regime Change in Iraq', *Washington File*, 9 March 2003. Available at <http://www.usembassy.it/file2003_03/alia/a3030701.htm> (accessed on 4 June 2005).

117 *CNN Late Edition with Wolf Blitzer*, 19 January 2003. Available at <http://transcripts.cnn.com/TRANSCRIPTS/0301/19/le.00.html> (accessed on 8 September 2005).

118 Woodward, *Plan of Attack*, p. 316.

119 Bush, G. W., *Remarks by the President in Address to the Nation*, The White House, 17 March 2003. Available at <http://www.whitehouse.gov/news/releases/2003/03/20030317-7.html> (accessed on 29 June 2002).

8 UNQUALIFIED SUPPORT: CONGRESS AND WAR WITH IRAQ

1 Joint Resolution S.J. Res. 23, *To authorize the use of United States Armed Forces against those responsible for the recent attacks launched against the United States*, United States Senate, 14 September 2001. The resolution was passed by Congress on 14 September 2001 and signed into law by the President four days later. The resolution authorised the President to 'use all necessary and appropriate force against those nations, organizations, or persons he determines planned, authorized, committed, or aided the terrorist attacks that occurred on 11 September 2001, or harbored such

organizations or persons, in order to prevent any future acts of international terrorism against the United States by such nations, organizations or persons'.

2 Dodd, S., 'U.S. May Target Iraq, Helms Says', *Knight Ridder/Tribune News Service*, 23 September 2001.

3 La Guardia, A., 'Saddam Could be Next Target of US Strikes', *Daily Telegraph*, 10 October 2001. Available at <http://www.telegraph.co.uk/news/main.jhtml?xml=/news/2001/10/08/wirq08.xml> (accessed on 31 August 2005).

4 'Interview with Trent Lott', *Fox News Sunday*, 9 December 2001. Lott repeated in April 2002 that the White House should lend full support to the Iraqi opposition as a first step to ousting Saddam. 'Interview with Trent Lott', *Fox News Network*, 28 April 2002.

5 Lieberman was quoted as saying that the administration should turn its attention from Afghanistan to Iraq as a nation supporting and harbouring terrorists and that 'as long as Saddam is there, Iraq is not just going to be a thorn in our side, but a threat to our lives'. 'UN-Iraq Relations Remain Stalled as Fears of New War Grow', *Disarmament Diplomacy*, No. 61, October–November 2001. Available at <http://www.acronym.org.uk/dd/dd61/61new08.htm> (accessed on 12 August 2005).

6 'Where Should Mr Bush Put His Chips Now?' *The Economist*, 30 November 2001.

7 'Interview with Joseph Lieberman', *Fox News Sunday*, 16 December 2001.

8 Hyde, H., *Regarding Monitoring of Weapons Development in Iraq*, Congressional Record Online (House), Vol. 147, No. 177, 19 December 2002, p. H10419. Available at <http://frwebgate.access.gpo.gov/cgi-bin/getpage.cgi?dbname=2001_record&page=H10419&position=all> (accessed on 25 August 2005).

9 Lantos, T., *Regarding Monitoring of Weapons Development in Iraq*, Congressional Record Online (House), Vol. 147, No. 177, 19 December 2002, p. H10420. Available at <http://frwebgate.access.gpo.gov/cgi-bin/getpage.cgi?dbname=2001_record&page=H10420&position=all> (accessed on 25 August 2005).

10 Gilman, B., *Regarding Monitoring of Weapons Development in Iraq*, Congressional Record Online (House), United States Congress, 19 December 2001, p. H10426. Available at <http://frwebgate.access.gpo.gov/cgi-bin/getpage.cgi?dbname=2001_record&page=H10426&position=all> (accessed on 12 August 2005).

11 *U.S. Policy Toward Iraq*, Transcript of Hearing by the House of Representatives Committee on International Relations, Subcommittee on the Middle East and South Asia, 4 October 2001. Available at <http://commdocs.house.gov/committees/intlrel/hfa75563.000/hfa75563_0f.htm> (accessed on 4 January 2004).

12 Rohrabacher, Dana, *Regarding Monitoring of Weapons Development in Iraq*, Congressional Record Online (House), Vol. 147, No. 177, 19 December 2002, p. H10423. Available at <http://frwebgate.access.gpo.gov/cgi-bin/getpage.cgi? dbname=2001_record&page=H10423&position=all> (accessed on 25 August 2005).

13 Graham, L., *Regarding Monitoring of Weapons Development in Iraq*, Congressional Record Online (House), vol. 147, no. 177, 19 December 2002, p. H10423. Available at <http://frwebgate.access.gpo.gov/cgi-bin/getpage.cgi?dbname=2001_record&page=H10423&position=all> (accessed on 25 August 2005).

14 Cohen, N., 'Analysis: Whether Iraq Should be Targeted in the War on Terror', *Talk of the Nation (National Public Radio)*, 26 December 2001.

15 'Congressmen: Iraq Will Have to be Dealt With', *CNN.com*, 10 January 2002. Available at <http://archives.cnn.com/2002/US/01/10/ret.iraq.terror/index.html> (accessed on 2 August 2005).

16 Wheeler, L., 'Republicans look to Iraq next', *Gannet News Service* (subscription only), 4 December 2001.

17 *Iraq's Refusal of Inspections Called 'Act of Aggression'*, 5 December 2001. Available at <http://www.usembassy.it/file2001_12/alia/a1120503.htm> (accessed on 12 December 2003).

18 *U.S. Policy Toward Iraq*, Transcript of Hearing by the House of Representatives Committee on International Relations, Subcommittee on the Middle East and South Asia.

19 The bill, H.J. Res 75, stated that:

> (1) the United States and the United Nations (UN) Security Council should insist on a complete program of inspection and monitoring to prevent the development of weapons of mass destruction in Iraq; (2) Iraq should allow UN weapons inspectors access to areas, facilities, equipment, records, and means of transportation as required by UN Security Resolutions 707 and 1284; (3) the United States should ensure that the UN does not accept any inspection and monitoring regime that fails to guarantee such access; (4) Iraq, as a result of its refusal to comply with UN Security Council Resolution 687 and subsequent relevant resolutions, remains in breach of its international obligations; and (5) Iraq's refusal to allow UN weapons inspectors access to covered facilities and documents presents a mounting threat to the United States, its friends and allies, and international peace and security.

> The bill was passed with 392 for, 12 against, and 30 not present or not voting. See <http://thomas.loc.gov/cgi-bin/bdquery/z?d107:HJ00075:@@@L&summ2=m&#rel-bill-detail> for further details.

20 Lott, T., Lieberman, J., McCain, J., Helms, J., Brownback, S., Shelby, R., Hyde, H., Ford, H., and Gilman, B., *Congressional Letter on Iraq*, 5 December 2001. Available at <http://www.newamericancentury.org/congress-120601.htm> (accessed on 17 December 2003).

21 Brownback, S., *Iraq*, Congressional Record Online (Senate), 13 February 2002, pp. S708–9. Available at < http://frwebgate.access.gpo.gov/cgi-bin/getpage.cgi?dbname=2002_record&page=S708&position=all> (accessed on 12 August 2005).

22 Specter, A., *Impressive Steps Taken Against the War on Terrorism*, Congressional Record Online (Senate), Vol. 148, No. 13, 13 February 2002, p. S730, Available at <http://frwebgate.access.gpo.gov/cgi-bin/getpage.cgi?dbname=2002_record&page=S730&position=all> (accessed on 12 August 2005).

23 McMurray, Jeffrey, 'Sen. Shelby Warns of Iraq, al-Qaida', *Associated Press Online* (subscription only), 2 August 2002.

24 Wilson, J., *Iraq*, Congressional Record Online (House), Vol. 22, No. 8, 5 March 2002, p. H661. Available at <http://frwebgate.access.gpo.gov/cgi-bin/getpage.cgi?dbname=2002_record&page=H661&position=all> (acessed on 12 August 2005).

25 Kiely, K., 'House majority whip: Saddam must go', *USA Today*, 22 August 2002. Available at <http://www.usatoday.com/news/washington/2002-08-20-delay-saddam_x.htm> (accessed on 5 July 2005).

26 'Interview with Chuck Hagel, John Edwards', *Fox News Sunday*, 6 January 2002.

27 Strope, L., 'Tough talk against "axis"; some U.S. lawmakers want quick action at least against Iraq', *Associated Press Worldstream* (subscription only), 10 February 2002.

28 Lieberman, J., *Secretary Rumsfeld Interview with Newt Gingrich*, United States Department of Defense, 13 July 2002. Available at <http://www.defenselink.mil/transcripts/2002/t07152002_t0713ng.html> (accessed on 12 August 2005).

29 'Interview with John Kerry', *Fox News Sunday*, 28 October 2001.

30 Miga, A., 'Tough Stance as Showdown with Iraq Looms', *Boston Herald*, 14 February 2002.

31 Espo, D., 'Gephardt Backs Offensive vs. Iraq', *Associated Press Online* (subscription only), 4 June 2002.

32 See <http://www.newsmax.com/archives/articles/2002/9/19/151145.shtml> for the full text.

33 Senator Helms recalls that 'We heard 23 witnesses, including current and former Secretaries of State, former National Security Advisors, a number of experts on Iraq from academia and from prominent research institutes, an important defector from Iraq's nuclear weapons program, retired senior level military officers, and former members of U.N. inspections teams in Iraq.' Authorization of the Use of United States Armed Forces against Iraq, Congressional Record Online (Senate), vol. 148, no. 132, 9 October 2002, p. S10168. Available at <http://frwebgate.access.gpo.gov/cgi-bin/getpage.cgi?dbname=2002_record&page=S10168&position=all> (accessed on 12 August 2005).

34 See Senator Tom Daschle's statement, *Authorization of the Use of United States Armed Forces Against Iraq*, Congressional Record Online (Senate), Vol. 148, No. 133, 10 October 2002, p. S10241. Available at <http://frwebgate.access.gpo.gov/cgi-bin/getpage.cgi?dbname=2002_record&page=S10241&position=all> (accessed 26 August 2005).

35 Ibid., p. S10249.

36 McCain, J., 'Delay can be Dangerous', *USA Today*, 14 February 2003. Available at <http://www.usembassy.it/file2003_02/alia/a3021418.htm> (accessed on 19 August 2005).

37 Radelat, A., 'Mississippi lawmakers back Bush on Iraq', *Gannett News Service* (subscription only), 12 September 2002; Boyer, D., 'McCain, Lott find common ground on Iraq: Upstage Daschle with reporters', *Washington Times*, 17 September 2002.

38 *Authorization of the Use of United States Armed Forces against Iraq*, Congressional Record Online (Senate), Vol. 148, No. 133, 10 October 2002, p. S10237. Available at <http://frwebgate.access.gpo.gov/cgi-bin/getpage.cgi?dbname=2002_record&page=S10237&position=all> (accessed on 25 August 2005).

39 *Authorization of the Use of United States Armed Forces against Iraq*, Congressional Record Online (Senate), vol. 148, no. 132, 9 October 2002, pp. S10180-81. Available at <http://frwebgate.access.gpo.gov/cgi-bin/getpage.cgi?dbname=2002_record&page=S10180&position=all> (accessed on 12 August 2005).

40 During the Senate debate on the war resolution Frist stated, 'The Iraqi regime has been in contact with al-Qaida for at least a decade … Saddam Hussein has not yet struck, and we hope he doesn't. We hope he disarms his weapons of mass destruction and chooses peace over war. It is his choice. But should he force us to war, we will fight for a noble and a just cause – to prevent a future and far worse attack than that of September 11, 2001.' Ibid., p. S10187.

41 During the Senate debate McConnell argued that al-Qaida was present in Iraq and that the US had 'no choice but to fight these threats simultaneously. Our nation is at war. Given Saddam Hussein's use of chemical and biological weapons against his own people and his neighbors, it is reckless to dismiss the immediacy of the threats posed by his regime to the United States.' McConnell, M., *Authorization of the Use of United States Armed Forces against Iraq*, Congressional Record Online (Senate), Vol. 148, No. 33, 10 October 2002, p. S10328. Available at <http://frwebgate.access.gpo.gov/cgi-bin/getpage.cgi?dbname=2002_record&page=S10328&position=all> (accessed on 12 August 2005).

42 *Authorization of the Use of United States Armed Forces against Iraq*, Congressional Record Online (House), Vol. 148, No. 131, 8 October 2002, p. H7192. Available at <http://frwebgate.access.gpo.gov/cgi-bin/getpage.cgi?dbname=2002_record&page=H7192&position=all> (accessed on 26 August 2005).

43 *The Iraqi Situation*, Congressional Record Online (House), Vol. 148, No. 112, 9 September 2002, p. H6119. Available at <http://frwebgate.access.gpo.gov/cgi-bin/getpage.cgi?dbname=2002_record&page=H6119&position=all> (accessed on 2 August 2005).

44 *Iraq and the War on Terrorism*, Congressional Record Online (House), Vol. 148, No. 123, 25 September 2002, p. H6686. Available at <http://frwebgate.access.gpo.gov/cgi-bin/getpage.cgi?dbname=2002_record&page=H6686&position=all> (accessed on 2 August 2005).

45 *Authorization of the Use of United States Armed Forces against Iraq*, Congressional Record Online (House), vol. 148, no. 131, 8 October 2002, p. H7202. Available at <http://frwebgate.access.gpo.gov/cgi-bin/getpage.cgi?dbname=2002_record&page=H7202&position=all> (accessed on 26 August 2005).

46 Ibid., p. H7226.

47 *Authorization of the Use of United States Armed Forces against Iraq*, Congressional Record Online (Senate), Vol. 148, No. 132, 9 October 2002, p. S10169. Available at <http://frwebgate.access.gpo.gov/cgi-bin/getpage.cgi?dbname=2002_record&page=S10169&position=all> (accessed on 12 August 2005).

48 *Authorization of the Use of United States Armed Forces against Iraq*, Congressional Record Online (House), Vol. 148, No. 131, 8 October 2002, p. H7201. Available at <http://frwebgate.access.gpo.gov/cgi-bin/getpage.cgi?dbname=2002_record&page=H7201&position=all> (accessed on 26 August 2005).

49 *Further Consideration of H. Res. 114, Authorization for Use of Military Force against Iraq Resolution of 2002*, Congressional Record Online (House), Vol. 148, No. 131, 8 October 2002, p. H7300. Available at <http://frwebgate.access.gpo.gov/cgi-bin/getpage.cgi?dbname=2002_record&page=H7300&position=all> (accessed on 26 August 2005).

50 *Authorization of the Use of United States Armed Forces against Iraq*, Congressional Record Online (House), Vol. 148, No. 131, 8 October 2002, p. H7209.

51 *United States Policy Toward Iraq*, Hearing before the Committee on International Relations House of Representatives, 19 September 2002, p. 23. Available at <http://wwwc.house.gov/international_relations/107/81813.pdf> (accessed on 31 August 2005).

52 In February 2002 Hastert declared that, in his opinion, encouraging a revolution to topple Saddam would be better than a US invasion: 'I think that would be the best solution there. I think we probably engage in encouraging and probably help them [the Iraqi opposition] if that was possible.' Krol, E., 'Hastert: Revolt in Iraq may be "best solution"', *Daily Herald*, 26 February 2002.

53 'Cheney lobbies Armey on Iraq', *CNN.com*, 24 September 2002. Available at <http://archives.cnn.com/2002/ALLPOLITICS/09/24/cheney.armey/> (accessed on 31 August 2005).

54 Hagel agreed that 'The President cannot avoid decision on Iraq. The risks of inaction are too high.' But he cautioned that 'the stakes are so high, America must be careful with her rhetoric and mindful of how others perceive her intentions. Actions in Iraq must come in the context of an American-led, multilateral approach to disarmament, not as the first case for a new American doctrine involving the preemptive use of force.' Hagel, C., *Authorization of the Use of United States Armed Forces against Iraq*, Congressional Record Online (Senate), Vol. 148, No. 132, 9 October 2002, p. S10175. Available at <http://frwebgate.access.gpo.gov/cgi-bin/getpage.cgi?dbname=2002_record&page=S10175&position=all> (accessed on 12 August 2005).

55 *Authorization of the Use of United States Armed Forces against Iraq*, Congressional Record Online (Senate), Vol. 148, No. 116, 13 September 2002, p. S8594. Available

at <http://frwebgate.access.gpo.gov/cgi-bin/getpage.cgi?dbname=2002_record&page=S8594&position=all> (accessed on 25 August 2005).

56 White House transcript, *President, House Leadership Agree on Iraq Resolution*, The White House, 2 October 2002. Available at <http://www.whitehouse.gov/news/releases/2002/10/20021002-7.html> (accessed on 3 August 2002).

57 Ibid.

58 Sawyer, J., 'Gephardt move to make Iraq deal with Bush will have repercussions', *St. Louis Post-Dispatch*, 3 October 2002. Senator Kerry indicated that a better resolution could have been reached through Democrat pressure if Gephardt and Lieberman had not been so supportive of the White House. 'War on horizon is key Democrats hope will unlock White House', *Chicago Tribune*, 19 January 2003.

59 *Authorization of the Use of United States Armed Forces against Iraq*, Congressional Record Online (Senate), Vol. 148, No. 132, 9 October 2002, p. S10173.

60 'Veterans on Hill support Iraq hit; Two-thirds give Bush backing', *Washington Times*, 2 October 2002.

61 Edwards, J., *Iraq*, Congressional Record Online (Senate), Vol. 148, No. 115, 12 September 2002, p. S8554. Available at <http://frwebgate.access.gpo.gov/cgi-bin/getpage.cgi?dbname=2002_record&page=S8554&position=all> (accessed on 26 August 2005).

62 *Authorization of the Use of United States Armed Forces against Iraq*, Congressional Record Online (House), Vol. 148, No. 131, 8 October 2002, p. H7195.

63 Ibid., p. H7206.

64 Zuckman, J., 'Determined minority in Congress remains opposed to Iraq resolution', *Chicago Tribune*, 8 October 2002.

65 Miga, A., 'Tough Stance as Showdown with Iraq Looms,' *Boston Herald*, 14 February 2002.

66 Biden, J., *Authorization of the Use of United States Armed Forces against Iraq*, Congressional Record Online (Senate), Vol. 148, No. 133, 10 October 2002, p. S10290. Available at <http://frwebgate.access.gpo.gov/cgi-bin/getpage.cgi?dbname=2002_record&page=S10290&position=all> (accessed on 12 August 2005).

67 For example, Representative Tom DeLay continued to assert that 'Confronting Saddam Hussein is a central and defining measure of our commitment to win the war on terrorism … In the hierarchy of aggressive and military regimes, Saddam's dictatorship is a clear and present danger to the United States.' He added that 'It is not the inspectors' mission to fruitlessly scour the Iraqi countryside in a feckless search for Saddam's terror weapons.' DeLay, T., *Rejecting the Apostles of Inaction*, Congressional Record Online (House), Vol. 149, No. 15, 28 January 2003, p. H174. Available at <http://frwebgate.access.gpo.gov/cgi-bin/getpage.cgi?dbname=2003_record&page=H174&position=all> (accessed on 26 August 2005). On 27 January 2003 Senator Richard Lugar argued that Iraq had been uncooperative and its failure to declare its WMD weapons and programmes meant it was in material breach of UNSC resolution 1441. *Senator Lugar Says Weapons Reports Show Iraq Uncooperative*, 27 January 2003. Available at <http://www.usembassy.it/file2003_01/alia/a3012715.htm> (accessed on 24 August 2005).

68 *Iraq*, Congressional Record Online (Senate), Vol. 149, No. 16, 29 January 2003, p. S1716. Available at <http://frwebgate.access.gpo.gov/cgi-bin/getpage.cgi?dbname=2003_record&page=S1716&position=all> (accessed on 25 August 2005); McCain J., 'Delay can be Dangerous', *USA Today*, 14 February 2003. Available at <http://www.usembassy.it/file2003_02/alia/a3021418.htm> (accessed on 19 August 2005).

69 See, for example, Lang, W. P., 'Drinking the Kool-Aid', *Middle East Policy*, Vol. 11, No. 2, Summer 2004, p. 53.

70 Senator John Kerry, Democrat presidential candidate in 2004, said in June 2003 that Bush misled Congress. *Bush challenged over Iraq weapons*, BBC News online, 19 June 2003. Available at <http://news.bbc.co.uk/2/hi/middle_east/3002820.stm> (accessed on 18 November 2005).

9 FINDING THE EVIDENCE

1 Other organisations that comprise the intelligence community are the Office of the Director of Central Intelligence, the National Geospatial-Intelligence Agency, the intelligence components of the Army, Navy, Air Force and Marine Corps, the Energy Department's Office of Intelligence, the Federal Bureau of Investigation's Office of Intelligence and Divisions of Counter-terrorism and Counter-intelligence, the Department of Homeland Security's Directorate of Information Analysis and Infrastructure Protection, and the Treasury Department's Office of Terrorism and Financial Intelligence.

2 Bamford, *Pretext for War*, p. 278.

3 Department of Defense transcript, *Under Secretary Feith News Briefing at the Foreign Press Center*, US Department of Defense, 8 October 2002. Available at <http://www.defenselink.mil/transcripts/2002/t10082002_t1008fpc.html> (accessed on 26 July 2005).

4 Scarborough, R., 'U.S. seeks al-Qaida link to Iraq', *Washington Times*, 14 January 2002.

5 Kyl, J., *DOD's Role in Pre-War Iraq Intelligence: Setting the Record Straight*, Center for Strategic and International Studies, 3 May 2004. Available at <http://kyl.senate.gov/legis_center/iraq%20csis%20speech%206.02%20ftnote%20revised%20FINAL.pdf> (accessed on 5 September 2005).

6 Miller, G., 'Special Pentagon Unit Left CIA Out of the Loop', *Los Angeles Times*, 10 March 2004.

7 Wurmser, like Feith, had close links to Richard Perle and was part of the task force put together by Perle and Feith in the mid-1990s that produced the 'Clean Break' report for the incoming Israeli government of Benjamin Netanyahu. See Perle, R., 'A Clean Break: A New Strategy for Securing the Realm', *The Institute for Advanced Strategic and Political Studies*, 1996.

8 *Pre-war Planning for Post-war Iraq*, Office of Near East and South Asia Affairs, US Department of Defense. Available at <http://www.defenselink.mil/policy/isa/nesa/postwar_iraq.html> (accessed on 12 September 2005).

9 Kyl, *DOD's Role in Pre-War Iraq Intelligence*.

10 See Lang, 'Drinking the Kool-Aid', pp. 49–53.

11 Landay, J., 'Infighting among U.S. intelligence agencies fuels dispute over Iraq', *Knight–Ridder/Tribune News Service*, 25 October 2002.

12 Former CIA director and Defense Policy Board member James Woolsey, who fully supported the war, was reported as saying, 'A lot of what is useful with respect to what's going on in Iraq is coming from defectors, and furthermore they are defectors who have often come through an organization, namely, the INC, that neither State nor the CIA likes very much'. Dreyfuss, R., 'The Pentagon muzzles the CIA: devising bad intelligence to promote bad policy', *The American Prospect*, 16 December 2002.

13 Burrough, B., Peretz, E., Rose, D., and Wise, D., 'Special Report: The Rush to Invade Iraq – The Ultimate Inside Account', *Vanity Fair*, May 2004.

14 Landay, J. S. and Strobel, W. P., 'Former CIA Director Used Pentagon Ties to Introduce Iraqi Defector', *Knight–Ridder Tribune*, 16 July 2004. Available at <http://www.commondreams.org/headlines04/0716-04.htm> (accessed on 23 October 2005).

15 Bunscombe, A., 'US Paid $1m for "Useless Intelligence" from Chalabi', *The Independent*, 30 September 2003.

16 Ibid.

17 Borger, J., 'The spies who pushed for war', *The Guardian*, 17 July 2003.

18 *Statement of Richard Perle before the House Armed Services Committee*, 26 September 2002. Available at <http://www.house.gov/hasc/openingstatementsand pressreleases/107thcongress/02-09-26perle.html> (accessed on 1 February 2004).

19 Department of Defense transcript, *DoD Briefing on Policy and Intelligence Matters*, US Department of Defense, 4 June 2003. Available at <http://www.defenselink.mil/ transcripts/2003/tr20030604-0248.html> (accessed on 18 November 2005).

20 'Vice President Dismisses Iraq WMD Criticisms', *Global Security Newswire*, 22 November 2005. Available at <http://www.nti.org/d_newswire/issues/2005_11_22. html> (accessed on 26 November 2005).

21 Lang cites a June 2002 letter from the INC's Washington office to the Senate Appropriations Committee arguing for the transfer of the programme funding the INC from the State Department to the Pentagon. The letter said that there was already a direct flow of information from the INC into William Luti's NESA office and I. Lewis Libby's office. Lang, 'Drinking the Kool-Aid', p. 53.

22 Hersh was adamant that this group of pro-war neo-conservatives in the national security bureaucracy had undue influence and were able to 'marginalize that opposition' because they had the full support of Cheney and Rumsfeld. Dreyfuss, R., 'The Pentagon muzzles the CIA: devising bad intelligence to promote bad policy', *The American Prospect*, 16 December 2002.

23 In October 2002, Adelman, who was assistant to Defense Secretary Donald Rumsfeld from 1975 to 1977 and, under President Ronald Reagan, UN ambassador and arms-control director, argued strongly in favour of invasion, insisting 'the only realistic international inspectors for Iraq are the 101st Airborne Division'. He was equally insistent that 'Regardless of the trigger, once war's ignited, the 101st Airborne and its brethren from the Marines and other Army units will find massive arsenals of weapons of mass destruction around Iraq. Skeptics will plainly see that this war was fully justified though few, of course, will ever admit it.' Adelman, K., *The U.N. Dawdle*, Foxnews.com, 30 October 2002. Available at <http://www.foxnews.com/story/0,2933,67020,00.html> (accessed on 18 August 2005).

24 Steinberg, J., 'Arrest of Pentagon Official May Help Unravel Neo-Conservative Cabal', *Executive Intelligence Review*, 13 May 2005, Vol. 32, No. 9; see <http://www.larouchepub.com/other/2005/3219franklin-arrest.html> (accessed on 5 September 2005).

25 Lobe, J., 'Pentagon Office Home to Neo-Con Network', *Inter Press Service*, 7 August 2003. Available at <http://www.commondreams.org/headlines03/0807-02. htm> (accessed on 23 October 2005).

26 Prados, J., *Bolton the fixer*, Tompaine.com, 9 June 2005. Available at <http://www.tompain.com/print/bolton_the_fixer.php> (accessed on 2 September 2005).

27 See Lang, 'Drinking the Kool-Aid'.

28 Hersh, S., 'Donald Rumsfeld has his own special sources. Are they reliable?' *The New Yorker*, 5 May 2003.

29 Ibid.

30 Contreras, R., 'Blix says US misled itself, the world on Iraq', *Boston Globe*, 22 October 2005.

31 Clarke, R., *Against All Enemies: Inside America's War on Terror*, New York: Free Press, 2004, p. 243, p. 244.

32 'Bush Pressed for Iraq War Despite Doubtful Intelligence, Classified British Memo Indicates,' *Global Security Newswire*, 6 May 2005. Available at <http://204.71.60.36/d_newswire/issues/2005/5/6/e34efa4a-63b3-4331-a499-0e2a8f1922e1.html> (accessed on 10 May 2005); Daniszewski, J., 'Indignation Grows in U.S. Over British Prewar Documents', *Los Angeles Times*, 12 May 2005; 'Downing Street Memo', *The Times Online*, 1 May 2005. Available at <http://www.timesonline.co.uk/article/0,,2087-1593607,00.html> (accessed on 2 November 2004).

33 Prados, J., *Bolton the fixer*.

34 'U.S. Intelligence Agencies Need Reform, Resist Change, Presidential Commission Says', *Global Security Newswire*, 31 March 2005. Available at <http://www.nti.org/d_newswire/issues/2005/3/31/18854141-9742-43e5-b5ec-2c98844f614e.html> (accessed on 4 April 2005).

35 *Fact Sheet on the Commission on the Intelligence Capabilities of the United States Regarding Weapons of Mass Destruction*, The White House, 6 February 2004. Available at <http://www.state.gov/t/np/rls/fs/29153.htm> (accessed on 2 November 2005).

36 *Report on the U.S. Intelligence Community's Prewar Intelligence Assessments on Iraq*, United States Senate Select Committee on Intelligence, 7 July 2004. Available at <http://www.gpoaccess.gov/serialset/creports/iraq.html> (accessed on 2 November 2005).

37 *Intelligence and Analysis on Iraq: Issues for the Intelligence Community*: The Kerr Group, 29 July 2004, p. 11.

38 Ibid., p. 6.

39 Ibid., p. 11.

40 Levin, C., *Report of an Inquiry into the Alternative Analysis of the Issue of an Iraq–al-Qaida Relationship*, Minority Staff, Senate Armed Services Committee, 21 October 2004.

41 Pincus, W., 'Intelligence Probe Takes Shape', *Washington Post*, 10 November 2005.

42 'Pentagon to Probe Feith's Role in Iraq', *Washington Post*, 18 November 2005.

10 THE NEO-CONSERVATIVE WORLDVIEW

1 Lind, M., 'How Neoconservatives Conquered Washington – and Launched a War',

2 Isolationism still finds support on the far left and far right. Ralph Nadar and Pat Buchanan, third-party candidates in the 2000 presidential election, both supported a form of isolationism, or 'strategic disengagement' from America's overseas political and military Cold War commitments. Dueck, C., 'Ideas and American Grand Strategy', *Review of International Studies*, Vol. 30, 2004, No. 4, p. 513.

3 Ibid., p. 512. US historian Walter Russell Mead explores enduring themes of US foreign policy using a different set of labels that correlate in part to the four conventional 'grand strategies'. In his comprehensive analysis *Special Providence* he identifies four themes and associates them with four US presidents that embodied the defining characteristics of each theme: Jacksonian, Jeffersonian, Hamiltonian and Wilsonian. Hamiltonians focus on the need for international trade to be fully supported by US government and emphasise the integration of the United States into the global economy as a prerequisite for stability. Wilsonians believe the United States has a moral obligation and a vital national interest in spreading US democratic values and an international system based on the rule of law. Jeffersonians argue that US foreign policy should concentrate on safeguarding its democracy at home and are sceptical of the Hamiltonian and Wilsonian internationalist agendas. Jacksonians place US physical security ahead of economic wellbeing. They do not seek conflicts

abroad but advocate employing the full force of the US military when engaged in war. Mead, W. R., *Special Providence: American Foreign Policy and How it Changed the World*, New York: Routledge, 2002, p. xvii.

4 Daalder, I. H. and Lindsay, J. M., *America Unbound*, Washington, DC: The Brookings Institution, 2003, p. 15.
5 Clarke, J. and Halper, S., *America Alone*, Cambridge: Cambridge University Press, 2004, p. 74.
6 Kristol, I., 'The Neoconservative persuasion', *Weekly Standard*, 25 August 2003, Vol. 8, No. 47.
7 Mann, *Rise of the Vulcans*, p. 110
8 Kaplan, L. and Kristol, W., The War Over Iraq: *Saddam's Tyranny and America's Mission*, San Francisco: Encounter Books, 2003, pp. 65–67.
9 Mann, *Rise of the Vulcans*, p. 91.
10 George, J., 'Leo Strauss, Neoconservatism and US Foreign Policy: Esoteric Nihilism and the Bush Doctrine', *International Politics*, Vol. 42, 2005, No. 2, p. 184.
11 Clarke, and Halper, *America Alone*, p. 71.
12 Ehrman, J., *The Rise of the Neoconservatives*, New Haven: Yale University Press, 1995, p. 171.
13 Mann, *Rise of the Vulcans*, p. 168.
14 Kegley, C. and Wittkopf, E., *World Politics: Trend and Transformation*, Boston: Bedford/St Martins, 2001; Viotti, P. and Kauppi, M., *International Relations Theory: Realism, Pluralism, Globalism*. 2nd edition, New York: Macmillan, 1993, pp. 35–65.
15 Dueck, C., 'Ideas and American Grand Strategy', *Review of International Studies*, Vol. 30, 2004, No. 4, p. 515.
16 Ikenberry, G. J., 'Why Export Democracy?: The Hidden "Grand Strategy"', *The Wilson Quarterly*, 1999, Vol. 23, No. 2; see <http://www.mtholyoke.edu/acad/intrel/exdem.htm> (accessed on 232 August 2005).
17 Mead, *Special Providence*, p. 87.
18 Ehrman, *Rise of the Neoconservatives*, p. 174; Clarke and Halper, *America Alone*, p. 99.
19 Clarke and Halper, *America Alone*, p. 76.
20 Ibid., p. 80; Kaplan and Kristo, *War Over Iraq*, pp. 46–48
21 Ehrman, *Rise of the Neoconservatives*, p. 204.
22 Dueck, 'Ideas and American Grand Strategy'; Ikenberry, 'Why Export Democracy?'
23 Ikenberry, G. J., 'American Grand Strategy in the Age of Terror', *Survival*, Vol. 34, 2001, No. 4, p. 26; see <http://www.mtholyoke.edu/acad/intrel/exdem.html> (accessed on 23 August 2005).
24 Kegley and Wittkopf, *World Politics*; Viotti and Kauppi, *International Relations Theory*, pp. 239–248; Little, R., 'The Growing Relevance of Pluralism?' in *International Theory: Positivism and Beyond*, K. Booth, M. Zalewski and S. Smith (eds), Cambridge: Cambridge University Press, 1996, pp. 66–86.
25 Clarke and Halper, *America Alone*, p. 87.
26 Kaplan and Kristol, *The War Over Iraq*, p. 56.
27 Mann, *Rise of the Vulcans*, p. 235.
28 Clarke and Halper, *America Alone*, p. 103.
29 Ibid., p. 109.
30 Mann, *Rise of the Vulcans*, p. 233.
31 Clarke and Halper, *America Alone*. See ch. 6, 'Outreach to the Media and Evangelicals'.
32 At the time of the Iraq war these notable neo-conservatives included government officials and advisers such as Paul Wolfowitz (Deputy Secretary of Defense), I. Lewis Libby (Vice President's Chief of Staff), Douglas Feith (Under Secretary of Defense for Policy), Peter Rodman (Assistant Secretary of Defense for International

Security Affairs), John Bolton (Under Secretary of State for Arms Control and International Security), Elliot Abrams (Senior Director of Near East and North Africa Affairs at the National Security Council), Richard Perle (Chairman, Defense Policy Board), David Wurmser (Special Advisor to John Bolton), J. D. Crouch (Assistant Secretary of Defense for International Security Policy). Prominent neo-conservative journalists included Charles Krauthammer, John Podhoretz and Max Boot, and prominent pundits at neo-conservative think-tanks included William Kristol (co-director of PNAC), Robert Kagan (also co-director of PNAC), Gary Schmitt (Executive Director of PNAC), Frank Gaffney (Director of the Center for Security Policy), Joshua Muravchik (resident scholar at AEI and adviser at JINSA) Elliot Cohen (Director, Center for Strategic Studies at Johns Hopkins School of Advanced International Studies and member of the Defense Policy Board), Francis Fukuyama (also at Hopkins School of Advanced International Studies) and Reuel Marc Gerecht (senior fellow at PNAC and resident fellow at the American Enterprise Institute).

33 Clarke and Halper, *America Alone*, p. 101.
34 Monten, J., 'The Roots of the Bush Doctrine', *International Security*, Vol. 29, 2005, No. 4, p. 143.
35 Dueck, 'Ideas and American Grand Strategy', p. 515.
36 Krauthammer, C., *Democratic realism: An American Foreign Policy for a Unipolar World*, American Enterprise Institute, 10 February 2004.
37 Kristol, W. and Kagan, R., 'Toward a Neo-Reaganite Foreign Policy', *Foreign Affairs*, July/August 1996.
38 Mead, *Special Providence*, p. 93. Michael Ledeen, a neo-conservative resident scholar at the American Enterprise Institute and former adviser at the State Department, Pentagon and White House under Reagan, proclaimed America 'the one truly revolutionary country on earth which is both the reason for which we were attacked in the first place and the reason we will successfully transform the lives of hundreds of millions of people throughout the Middle East'. Ledeen, M., 'The War on Terror Won't End in Baghdad', *The Wall Street Journal*, 4 September 2002.
39 Hurst, 'Myths of neo-conservatism', p. 77.
40 Krauthammer, *Democratic realism*.
41 Dueck, 'Ideas and American Grand Strategy', p. 515.
42 Krauthammer, *Democratic realism*.
43 Kristol and Kagan, 'Toward a Neo-Reaganite Foreign Policy'; Kagan, R. and Kristol, W. (eds), *Present Dangers: Crisis and Opportunity in American Defense and Foreign Policy*, San Francisco: Encounter Books, 2000, p. 4.
44 Kristol and Kagan, 'Toward a Neo-Reaganite Foreign Policy'.
45 Krauthammer, *Democratic realism*.
46 Boot, M., 'Neocons', *Foreign Policy*, Jan/Feb 2004.
47 Ahmed, K. and Vulliamy, E., 'Hawks sit out phoney peace while war machine rolls on', *The Observer*, 2 January 2003.
48 Clarke and Halper, *America Alone*, p. 80.
49 Krauthammer, *Democratic realism*.
50 Kristol, I., 'The Neoconservative persuasion', *Weekly Standard*, 25 August 2003, Vol. 8, No. 47
51 Kristol and Kagan, 'Toward a Neo-Reaganite Foreign Policy'.
52 Monten, 'The Roots of the Bush Doctrine'.
53 Mazarr, M. J., 'George W. Bush, Idealist', *International Security*, Vol. 79, 2003, No. 3, p. 517.
54 Boot, 'Neocons'.
55 Donnelly, T., Schmitt, G. and Kagan, D., *Rebuilding America's Defenses*, Project for a New American Century, September 2000, pp. i–v.

56 George, J., 'Leo Strauss, Neoconservatism and US Foreign Policy', p. 189.
57 Kristol and Kagan, 'Toward a Neo-Reaganite Foreign Policy'.
58 Donnelly, Schmitt and Kagan, *Rebuilding America's Defenses*, p. 4.
59 Kagan and Kristol, (eds), *Present Dangers*, pp. 7, 18.
60 Barry, T. and Lobe, J., 'The Men Who Stole the Show', *Foreign Policy in Focus, Special Report #18*, October 2002.
61 Mann, *Rise of the Vulcans*, p. 199.
62 'The War Behind Closed Doors: Excerpts from 1992 Draft "Defense Planning Guidance"', PBS *Frontline*, 20 February 2003. Available at <http://www.pbs.org/wgbh/pages/frontline/shows/iraq/etc/wolf.html> (accessed on 17 October 2005).
63 Ibid; Cheney, D., 'Defense Strategy for the 1990s: The Regional Defense Strategy', United States Department of Defense, January 1993. Available at <http://www.infor mationclearinghouse.info/pdf/naarpr_Defense.pdf> (accessed on 14 October 2005).
64 Donnelly, Schmitt and Kagan, *Rebuilding America's Defenses*, p. ii.
65 Daalder and Lindsay *America Unbound*, p 15.
66 Mead, *Special Providence*, pp. 244–248. Mead argues that the conservative resurgence in the Republican Party that led to its victory in the 1994 Congressional elections had strong Jacksonian leaning.
67 Ibid., p. 307.
68 According to Mann, in August 1998 or shortly afterwards Bush decided to place Rice in charge of foreign policy during his presidential campaign. Mann, *Rise of the Vulcans*, p. 251.
69 Daalder and Lindsay, *America Unbound*, p. 31.
70 Mann, *Rise of the Vulcans*, p. xiii.
71 Bush, G. W., *A Period of Consequences*. 23 September 1999: The Citadel, South Carolina.
72 Bush, *A Distinctly American Internationalism*, 19 November 1999.
73 Bush, *A Period of Consequences*.
74 Daalder and Lindsay, *America Unbound*, p. 42
75 Ikenberry, 'American Grand Strategy in the Age of Terror', p. 25; see also Hurst, 'Myths of neo-conservatism', p. 85.
76 Nye, J., 'U.S. Power and Strategy After Iraq', *Foreign Affairs*, Vol. 82, 2003, No. 4, p. 60; Mazarr, M. J., 'George W. Bush, Idealist', p. 503
77 Clarke and Halper, *America Alone*, p. 137.
78 Bush, G. W., *Inaugural Address*, The White House, 20 January 2001. Available at <http://www.whitehouse.gov/news/inaugural-address.html> (accessed on 10 October 2005).
79 Bush, G. W., *Remarks by the President and Secretary of State Colin Powell at Swearing-In Ceremony*, The White House, 26 January 2001. Available at <http://www.whitehouse.gov/news/releases/20010126-2.html> (accessed on 10 October 2005).
80 Daalder and Lindsay *America Unbound*, p. 53; Mann, *Rise of the Vulcans*, p. xviii.
81 Hurst, 'Myths of neo-conservatism', p. 85.
82 Clarke and Halper, *America Alone*, p. 14.
83 Mann, *Rise of the Vulcans*, p. 253.
84 Ibid., p. 370.
85 Frum, D., *The Right Man: An Inside Account of the Bush White House*, New York: Random House, 2005, p. 62.
86 Mann, *Rise of the Vulcans*, p. 182; Daalder and Lindsay, *America Unbound*, p. 58.
87 Mann, *Rise of the Vulcans*, p. 273.
88 Clarke and Halper, *America Alone*, p. 14.
89 Ibid., p. 120.

90 Ikenberry 'American Grand Strategy in the Age of Terror', p. 20.

91 Daalder and Lindsay, *America Unbound*, pp. 66–67; Mann, *Rise of the Vulcans*, p. xii.

92 Kagan, R. and Kristol W., 'A National Humiliation', *The Weekly Standard*, 16 April 2001. See also Daalder and Lindsay, *America Unbound*, p. 62; Clarke and Halper, *America Alone*, pp. 129–130.

93 Kaplan and Kristol, *The War Over Iraq*, p. 68.

94 Ibid., p. 65; Guelke, 'Political Morality of the Neo-conservatives', p. 103.

95 Woodward, *Bush at War*, London: Simon & Schuster, 2002, p. 131.

96 Hurst, 'Myths of neo-conservatism', p. 82.

97 Ibid., p. 78.

98 George., 'Leo Strauss, Neoconservatism and US Foreign Policy', p. 183; Daalder and Lindsay, *America Unbound*, p. 16.

99 Clarke and Halper, *America Alone*, p. 139.

100 Daalder and Lindsay, *America Unbound*, p. 79, p. 91.

101 Ikenberry, 'American Grand Strategy in the Age of Terror,' p. 7.

102 Hurst, 'Myths of neo-conservatism', p. 86.

103 Selden, Z., 'Neoconservatives and the American Mainstream', *Policy Review*, April–May 2004, No. 124.

104 Monten, 'The Roots of the Bush Doctrine,' p. 152.

105 Daalder and Lindsay, *America Unbound*, p. 48; Suskind, *Price of Loyalty*, p. 45.

106 *The National Security Strategy of the United States of America*, The White House, September 2002, pp. 14–15; Guelke, 'Political Morality of the Neo-conservatives', p. 109.

107 Gordon, P. H., 'Bush's Middle East Vision', *Survival*, Vol. 45, 2003, No. 1, p. 156.

108 Kaplan and Kristol, *The War Over Iraq*, 2003, p. 96.

109 Mann, *Rise of the Vulcans*, p. 297.

110 Krauthammer, *Democratic realism*.

111 Gaddis. J. L., 'A Grand Strategy of Transformation', *Foreign Policy*, Nov/Dec 2002, No. 133.

112 *The National Security Strategy of the United States of America*, The White House, September 2002, pp. 1–3.

113 Rhodes, E., 'The Imperial Logic of Bush's Liberal Agenda', *Survival*, Vol. 45, 2003, No. 1, p. 135; Gaddis J. L., 'A Grand Strategy of Transformation', *Foreign Policy*, Nov/Dec 2002, No. 133.

114 Monten, 'The Roots of the Bush Doctrine', p. 140; Mazarr, 'George W. Bush, Idealist', p. 507.

115 Monten, 'The Roots of the Bush Doctrine', p. 141.

116 George, 'Leo Strauss, Neoconservatism and US Foreign Policy', p. 176, p. 183.

117 Rhodes, E., 'The Imperial Logic of Bush's Liberal Agenda', *Survival*, Vol. 45, 2003, No. 1, p. 133.

118 Clarke and Halper, *America Alone*, p. 146.

119 Meyer, K., 'America Unlimited: The Radical Sources of the Bush Doctrine', *World Policy Journal*, Vol. 21, 2004, No. 1, p. 1.

120 Bush, G. W., *President Discusses the Future of Iraq*, The White House, 26 February, 2003. Available at <http://www.whitehouse.gov/news/releases/2003/02/20030226-11.html> (accessed on 29 June 2002).

121 Cheney, D., *Remarks by the Vice President to the Veterans of Foreign Wars 103rd National Convention*, (Washington, DC: The White House, 26 August 2002). Available at <http://www.whitehouse.gov/news/releases/2002/08/20020826.html> (accessed on June 29, 2002).

122 Rice, C., *Interview Of National Security Advisor Condoleezza Rice By Al Jazeera Television*, United States Department of State, 14 March 2003. Available at

<http://www.usembassy.it/file2003_03/alia/a3031609.htm> (accessed on 12 August 2005).

123 'Bush Offers New Reason for Iraq War', *Global Security Newswire*, 29 June 2005. Available at <http://www.nti.org/d_newswire/issues/2005/6/29/2b49248e-5da4-4c54-8d9f-4a87426b94f4.html> (accessed on 4 July 2005).

124 Defense Department transcript, *Remarks by Deputy Secretary of Defense Paul Wolfowitz, Fletcher Conference, Ronald Reagan Building and International Trade Center*, Washington, US Department of Defense, 16 October 2002. Available at <http://www.defenselink.mil/speeches/2002/s20021016-depsecdef.html> (accessed on 27 January 2004). He stated in July 2002 that progress on Iraq would help progress with Israel and Palestine. 'I don't think it is an accident', he said, 'that we made so much progress in the Middle East ten years ago right after the Gulf War and after the defeat of Saddam Hussein.' Defense Department transcript, *Deputy Secretary Wolfowitz Interview with CNN Turkey*, US Department of Defense, 14 July 2002. Available at <http://www.defenselink.mil/transcripts/2002/t07172002_t0714cnn.html> (accessed on 26 July 2005).

125 Wolfowitz, P., 'Statesmanship in the New Century', in Kristol and Kagan, *Present Dangers*, p. 321.

126 Gerecht, R. M., 'Why we need a democratic Iraq', *The Weekly Standard*, 17 March 2002. Available at <http://www.aei.org/publications/pubID.16576,filter.all/pub_detail.asp> (accessed on 18 August 2005).

127 Rove, the President's most powerful aide, reportedly participates in all White House policy meetings, and has an extensive network of advisers on a variety of issues, including terrorism and foreign policy. One of these is Ledeen, who is believed to have the ear of Rove, and has regular conversations with him. Edsall, T. B. and Milbank, D., 'White House's Roving Eye for Politics', *Washington Post*, 10 March 2003; *Panorama: The War Party*, BBC, 18 May 2003. Available at <http://news.bbc.co.uk/1/hi/programmes/panorama/ 3031803.stm> (accessed on 10 September 2005).

128 Department of Defense transcript, *Secretary Rumsfeld Interview with Newt Gingrich*, US Department of Defense, 13 July 2002. Available at <http://www.defenselink.mil/transcripts/2002/t07152002_t0713ng.html> (accessed on 18 August 2005).

129 Perle, R. and Frum, D., *An End to Evil*, New York: Ballantine Books, 2004. See ch. 5, 'The War Abroad'.

130 Cheney, D., *Remarks by the Vice President to the Veterans of Foreign Wars 103rd National Convention*.

131 Defense Department transcript, *Deputy Secretary Wolfowitz Interview with Today Programme Radio Four*, US Department of Defense, 3 December 2002. Available at <http://www.defenselink.mil/transcripts/2002/t12132002_t1203dsd.html> (accessed on 26 July 2005).

132 Defense Department transcript, *Deputy Secretary Wolfowitz Interview with Greta Van Susteren, Fox News Channel*, US Department of Defense, 9 July 2002. Available at <http://www.defenselink.mil/transcripts/2002/t07102002_t0709fox.html> (accessed on 26 July 2005).

133 *Authorization of the Use of United States Armed Forces against Iraq*, Congressional Record Online (House), Vol. 148, No. 131, 8 October 2002, p. H7216. Available at <http://frwebgate.access.gpo.gov/cgi-bin/getpage.cgi?dbname=2002_record&page=H7216&position=all> (accessed on 26 August 2005).

134 Pfaff, W., *Fear, Anger and Failure*, New York: Algora Publishing, 2004, p. 74.

135 Hurst, 'Myths of neo-conservatism', p. 88.

136 Ibid., p. 91.

137 Boot, 'Neocons'.
138 Dueck, 'Ideas and American Grand Strategy', pp. 522–529.
139 Clarke and Halper, *America Alone*, p. 4.
140 Perle and Frum, *An End to Evil*, pp. 4, 6.
141 Clarke and Halper, *America Alone*, p. 139.
142 Ibid., p. 203.
143 Selden, 'Neoconservatives and the American Mainstream'.

11 CONCLUSION – AN ENDLESS ROAD?

1 Rogers, P., *Iraq: Consequences of a War*, ORG Briefing Paper, Oxford Research Group, November 2002.
2 Iraqi civilian casualties have been tracked by the Iraq Body Count group using a careful and probably conservative methodology. See www.iraqbodycount.net/
3 A detailed record of US military casualties in Iraq is available at www.icasualties.org.oif/

INDEX

Printed in the United States
92800LV00001B/15/A